THE VERSATILITY OF THE REAL ESTATE ASSET CLASS
THE SINGAPORE EXPERIENCE

Kim Hin David HO

PARTRIDGE

Copyright © 2021 by Kim Hin David HO.

Library of Congress Control Number: 2021903232
ISBN: Hardcover 978-1-5437-6360-7
Softcover 978-1-5437-6362-1
eBook 978-1-5437-6361-4

All rights reserved. No part of this book may be used or reproduced by any means, graphic, electronic, or mechanical, including photocopying, recording, taping or by any information storage retrieval system without the written permission of the author except in the case of brief quotations embodied in critical articles and reviews.

Because of the dynamic nature of the Internet, any web addresses or links contained in this book may have changed since publication and may no longer be valid. The views expressed in this work are solely those of the author and do not necessarily reflect the views of the publisher, and the publisher hereby disclaims any responsibility for them.

Print information available on the last page.

To order additional copies of this book, contact
Toll Free +65 3165 7531 (Singapore)
Toll Free +60 3 3099 4412 (Malaysia)
orders.singapore@partridgepublishing.com

www.partridgepublishing.com/singapore

CONTENTS

Foreword vii
Acknowledgements xi
About the Author xiii
Introduction xv

Chapter 1   Housing Price Dynamics in a Behavioral Context 1
Chapter 2   Strategic Behavioral Pricing of the Private Residential Development Market - A Simplified Experimental Approach 47
Chapter 3   Country Legal Origin of Direct Real Estate Risk Premiums 103
Chapter 4   The Risk-Return Behavior of Real Estate Mezzanine Investment (REMI) – The Singapore Experience 151
Chapter 5   The Conclusion 184

References 191
Endnotes 205

FOREWORD

"Over 100 years ago, this (Singapore) was a mud-
flat, swamp. Today, this is a modern city. Ten years
from now, this will be a metropolis. Never fear."
(The first Prime Minister of Singapore Lee Kuan Yew, 1965)

This book highlights and discusses the flexibility of the real estate asset class in terms of its direct real estate and indirect real estate sectors with respect to the Singapore experience. Chapter 1 looks at the heterogeneous momentum and disposition investors. Such investors form a unique difference model to interpret housing price dynamics. Three parameters are crucial, namely, auto-correlation, the rate of mean reversion and the contemporaneous adjustment towards long-term equilibrium price. Chapter 1 examines the dynamic structures that oscillate and/or diverge from equilibrium. Disposition investors predominate although the interaction between momentum and disposition investors acts as a key determinant of private housing price dynamics for a given time in a specific market. Key implication is that the 2006 boom of the Singapore private housing market does not offer as large a magnitude as that from the price gain in the 1990's boom-and-recovery over the long-term. Singapore's private housing market is low risk, offering stable returns owing to virtually no divergence even in the speculative 1990s. The best way to invest is to consider the momentum strategy and avoid the herd behaviour for profit sustainability. For policy makers, the

Singapore private housing market is over-damped in the long run. Disposition investors predominate this market, and their behaviour contributes to the market mechanism, which automatically adjusts private housing market prices. It is imperative to relax government intervention in Singapore's private housing market to enhance its efficiency.

\\

Chapter 2 then looks at game theory to examine the behaviour of "rational" residential developers for their pricing strategy under a competitive environment. A uniquely simplified experimental research design is framed within the Singapore context. The Chapter considers the private residential development oligopolistic market; the determination of residential development sale prices in an uncertain market and under incomplete information of competing developers; dynamic interaction among developers; time lags of the development project completion from project start; launching of the residential development for sale before completion and the residential development's own capacity constraints. Thus, residential developers tend to cooperate for long-term benefit, leading to a sales slowdown. Developers are motivated to deviate from cooperating at the beginning and at the end of successive periods in a sub-market. Relatively high profits, earnable in the first few periods, provide an allowance to price undercut others to sell much faster. For the last few periods, the punishment for any deviation from cooperating is insignificant or zero. First-mover advantage in a new market is evident. As uncertainty on the developer's residential prices rises, then prices decrease while price variability increases. The merits of a uniquely simplified experimental research design are discussed for the strategic behavioural pricing of the private residential development market under a game theoretic approach. Chapter 2 enhances the residential development strategy of investing-developers in the residential development market. There is limited research on pricing strategy for the private residential development market in Asia.

Chapter 3 scrutinises the institutional nature of legal origin and the total returns (TRs), derived from investing in a country's direct real estate, and via the adoption of a multi-factor arbitrage pricing theory (APT) model. Quarterly direct real estate data from the Jones Lang LaSalle Real Estate Intelligence-Asia index is used for 13 cities in Asia and across 3 sectors (office, residential and retail) are obtained. Findings confirm the existence of smoothing effects that cause a temporal bias and a seasonal lag. The 1st and 4th order autoregressive model is adopted to de-smooth the total returns (TRs). De-smoothed data is used in conjunction with 2 macroeconomic variables (real GDP growth rate and interest rate) and 1 real estate risk factor (vacancy rate) to form the multi-factor structural model. A pooled panel analysis is conducted with the law-system dummies, denoting British legal origin and French legal origin, and the factor loadings (i.e. the sensitivity of the risk factor to the TRs). Macroeconomic and real estate risk factors in equilibrium affect the TRs. Vacancy rate commands high and significant premium owing to its direct impact on the TRs, relative to GDP growth rate and interest rate. Both the British and French legal origins have a significant relationship each on the TRs.

Chapter 4 is concerned with the real estate mezzanine investment (REMI), which is a new financial instrument for Asia's real estate market, offering superior returns than those for the typical commercial bank loans. The resultant risk exposure is relatively high. With recent and robust growth of the Singapore real estate market, there is the fast-growing real estate investment trust market. Chapter 4 examines the REMI structure, the measurement and characteristics of its risks and returns via a forward-looking binomial asset tree (BAT) model. Risk neutral pricing probability is adopted to construct the BAT tree. TRs are measured by the probability weighted average returns and discussed under different scenarios. REMI bears more risk than typical commercial bank loans, resulting in higher interest rates than pure equity. Different risk issues focus on two major sources - the financial loan to value (LTV) ratio risk and the real estate and capital markets risk. Empirical analysis involves a rigorous discrete-time forecasting of the market rent and capital value expectations of Singapore's prime office sector, given the conditions and assumptions unique to this market. Chapter 4 fulfils the need to close the gap concerning the REMI structure and performance in the steady state, utilizing reliable, authoritative information and data sources.

Chapter 5 concludes this book.

Happy reading.

Yours sincerely,
Professor (Dr) HO, Kim Hin / David
Singapore
December 2020.

ACKNOWLEDGEMENTS

The Author wishes to extend his most sincere appreciation to the School of Design & Environment, under the highly able Deanship of the Provost & Chair Professor (Dr) LAM Khee Poh, of the National University of Singapore. The same wish is extended to the University of Cambridge and the University of Hertfordshire in Hatfield, UK. These three tertiary institutions of higher learning and research are globally leading Universities, inspiring and encouraging both modern and contemporary studies of large and complex physical infrastructural provision, in particularly public housing.

ABOUT THE AUTHOR

Professor (Dr) HO, Kim Hin / David

PhD (Development Economics) (Cambridge), MPhil (1st Cl Hons with Distinction) (Development Studies & Land Economy) (Cambridge); Honorary Professor (Development Economics & Land Economy) (Uni of Hertfordshire); Honorary Doctorate of Letters (International Biographical Centre) (Cambridge); Systems Engineering (US Naval Postgraduate School), MRES (UK), AM NCREIF (US), FARES (US), MAEA (US), MESS, MSIM. Retired Professor (Associate) (Tenured) (International Real Estate) (Department of Real Estate) (School of Design and Environment) (National University of Singapore, NUS). Home Address: Block 220 Ang Mo Kio Avenue 1 #02-807, Singapore 560220; email address: davidhokh1@gmail.com.

Professor HO Kim Hin / David spent 31 years across several sectors, including the military, oil refining, aerospace engineering, public housing, resettlement, land acquisition, reclamation and international real estate investing. 6 years were in Pidemco Land Ltd (now CapitaLand Ltd) and GIC Real Estate Pte Ltd. 17 years were in the NUS School of Design and Environment at the Department of Real Estate. He holds the Master of Philosophy (First Class Honors with Distinction), Doctor of Philosophy from the University of Cambridge; and the Honorary Professor from the University of Hertfordshire. He has published widely in 275 articles (inclusive of 91 articles in top peer reviewed, international journals; pertaining to real estate investment, real estate development, urban policy, consultancies, public cum private funded research projects and so also published 14 major books. He was governor of the St Gabriel's Foundation and member (District Judge equivalent) of the Valuation Review Board under the Singapore Ministry of Finance and the Singapore Courts.

INTRODUCTION

The Versatility of The Real Estate Asset Class - The Singapore Experience

Chapter 1 is concerned with two types of heterogeneous investors (momentum and disposition) form a unique difference model to interpret housing price dynamics. Three parameters are crucial, namely, auto-correlation, the rate of mean reversion and the contemporaneous adjustment towards long-term equilibrium price. For Singapore, the Chapter examines the dynamic structures that oscillate and/or diverge from equilibrium. Disposition investors predominate although the interaction between momentum and disposition investors acts as a key determinant of private housing price dynamics for a given time in a specific market. Key implication is that the 2006 boom of the Singapore private housing market does not offer as large a magnitude as that from the price gain in the 1990's boom-and-recovery over the long-term. Singapore's private housing market is low risk, offering stable returns owing to virtually no divergence even in the speculative 1990s. The best way to invest is to consider the momentum strategy and avoid the herd behaviour for profit sustainability. For policy makers, the Singapore private housing market is over-damped in the long run. Disposition investors predominate this market, and their behaviour contributes to the market mechanism, which automatically adjusts private housing market prices. It is imperative to relax government intervention in Singapore's private housing market to enhance its efficiency.

Chapter 2 adopts game theory to examine the behaviour of "rational" residential developers for their pricing strategy under a competitive environment. A uniquely simplified experimental research design is framed within the Singapore context. The Chapter considers the private residential development oligopolistic market; the determination of residential development sale prices in an uncertain market and under incomplete information of competing developers; dynamic interaction among developers; time lags of the development project completion from project start; launching of the residential development for sale before completion and the residential development's own capacity constraints. Results show that residential developers cooperate implicitly for long-term benefit, leading to a sales slowdown. Developers are motivated to deviate from cooperating at the beginning and at the end of successive periods in a sub-market. Relatively high profits, earnable in the first few periods, provide an allowance to price undercut others to sell much faster. For the last few periods, the punishment for any deviation from cooperating is insignificant or zero. First-mover advantage in a new market is evident. On the effect of uncertainty on the developer's residential prices, results show that as uncertainty increases, prices decrease while price variability increases. **The** Chapter highlights the merits of a uniquely simplified experimental research design for the strategic behavioural pricing of the private residential development market under a game theoretic approach. **Chapter 2 enhances** the residential development strategy of investing-developers in the residential development market. **T**here is limited research on pricing strategy for the private residential development market in Asia.

Chapter 3 examines the institutional nature of legal origin and the total returns (TRs), derived from investing in a country's direct real estate, and via the adoption of a multi-factor arbitrage pricing theory (APT) model. Quarterly direct real estate data from the Jones Lang LaSalle Real Estate Intelligence-Asia index is used for 13 cities in Asia and across 3 sectors (office, residential and retail) are obtained. Findings confirm the existence of smoothing effects that cause a temporal bias and a seasonal lag. The 1st and 4th order autoregressive model is adopted to de-smooth the total returns (TRs). De-smoothed data is used in conjunction with 2 macroeconomic variables (real GDP growth rate and interest rate) and 1 real estate risk factor (vacancy rate) to form the multi-factor structural model. A pooled panel analysis is conducted with the law-system dummies, denoting British legal origin and French legal origin, and the factor loadings (i.e. the sensitivity of the risk factor to the TRs). Macroeconomic and real estate risk factors in equilibrium affect the TRs. Vacancy rate commands high and significant premium owing to its direct impact on the TRs, relative to GDP growth rate and interest rate. Both the British and French legal origins have a significant relationship each on the TRs.

Chapter 4 is concerned with the real estate mezzanine investment (REMI), which is a new financial instrument for Asia's real estate market, offering superior returns than those for the typical commercial bank loans. The resultant risk exposure is relatively high. With recent and robust growth of the Singapore real estate market, there is the fast-growing real estate investment trust market. Chapter 4 examines the REMI structure, the measurement and characteristics of its risks and returns via a forward-looking binomial asset tree (BAT) model. Risk neutral pricing probability is adopted to construct the BAT tree. TRs are measured by the probability weighted average returns and discussed under different scenarios. REMI bears more risk than typical commercial bank loans, resulting in higher interest rates than pure equity. Different risk issues focus on two major sources – the financial loan to value (LTV) ratio risk and the real estate and capital markets risk. Empirical analysis involves a rigorous discrete-time forecasting of the market rent and capital value expectations of Singapore's prime office sector, given the conditions and assumptions unique to this market. Chapter 4 fulfils the need to close the gap concerning the REMI structure and performance in the steady state, utilizing reliable, authoritative information and data sources.

Chapter 5 offers this book's conclusion.

CHAPTER 1

HOUSING PRICE DYNAMICS IN A BEHAVIORAL CONTEXT

Housing prices largely affect the consumption and asset portfolios of households (Flavin and Yamashita, 2002), the financial sector[1] and the macro economy[2]. The resulting volatility and its driving forces constitute a core issue in housing economics (Mankiw and Weil, 1991) that compels researchers to seek answers in economic fundamentals. The temporary deviation of accrual prices from economic fundamentals (e.g., Clayton, 1996) and the positive autocorrelation of housing prices in the short run (e.g., Capozza and Seguin, 1996) have merely supported the belief that investors' irrational expectations and investor psychology can be held accountable. Although both explanations have been repeatedly documented in previous empirical studies (see Case and Shiller, 1989, 1990; Poterba, 1991; Cutler *et al.*, 1991; Abraham and Hendershott, 1996; Malpezzi, 1999; Meen, 2002), there has been no systematic theory explaining private housing market price dynamics features within a behavioral context[3].

Chapter 1 models the different kinds of investors' behavior (disposition and momentum) in the private housing market and derive a second-order difference equation. Disposition behavior refers to the tendency to sell winners quickly and hold onto losers. Momentum behavior refers to the tendency to buy winners and sell losers. We further translate the disposition-momentum behavioral difference equation into the standard empirical formulation of autocorrelation and mean reversion. Specifically, the autocorrelation at a one-year frequency depends on the proportion of the effect from momentum behavior in the sum effect from both disposition and momentum behaviors. The mean reversion over a longer period is determined by the proportion of the effect from disposition behavior in the sum effect from both disposition and momentum behaviors. Therefore, the interaction (trades) between the two types of investors becomes a key determinant of private housing market price dynamics. Referring to the definitions by Capozza *et al.* (2004), we further identify four types of dynamic structures, namely, convergent without oscillation, divergent without oscillation, convergent oscillation and divergent oscillation, but define them in terms of the disposition and momentum coefficients. Consequently, we provide more rigorous definitions of "cyclical dynamics" and "bubble" within the disposition-momentum behavioral theory. When the complex roots occur for the general solution to the difference equation, the dynamics is oscillatory. When the proportion of the effect from momentum behavior in the sum effect from both disposition and momentum behaviors exceeds one, it leads to divergent dynamics. These constitute one of the main differences between our study and Capozza *et al.* (2004).

Nevertheless, as more real estate funds and other institutional investors allocate capital into Asian real estate, Singapore emerged as the world's "hottest" real estate market in 2007, and is securely among the top favorites of real estate investors (the Economic Times, 2007).[4] In addition, Singapore is granted a highest real estate transparency rating and the transaction cost is generally low (Cruz, 2008). Therefore, we continue the empirical study in the context of the Singapore private housing market. Over the sample period from 1982 Q1 to 2007 Q3, the market experienced more than two boom and bust movements on different scales (Fig 1(a)). This raises some questions. Why does the upturn around 2006 differ from the 1990s' boom, i.e. a lower magnitude of price gain and a gradual recovery (Morgan Stanley report, 2007)? What are the underlying causes of such differences? Singapore's average nominal earnings per employee show a clear increasing and oscillating trend while the variable housing loan rate has remained relatively smooth, even during the 1990s (Figs 1(b) and (c)). Hence, what were the causal behavioral price dynamics during the 1990s and from 1982 to 2007? Our empirical analysis shows that the autocorrelation at a one-year frequency is around 0.7 in both periods. The market prices only converge from 0.02 to 0.03 of the total adjustment each year from 1982 to 2007, and from 0.03 to 0.04 during the 1990s. In the long run (1982 to 2007), the price dynamics are convergent to equilibrium prices without oscillations (being over-dampened). In the 1990s, the prices still fluctuated in a convergent and oscillating way, without showing divergence. Thus, the behavioral characteristics of price dynamics vary over time in the Singapore private housing market. The effect of disposition investors dominates that of their momentum counterparts in both periods. The comparative magnitude of the disposition effect to the momentum effect is larger during the 1990s than it is over the total sample period. The value of the composite autocorrelation parameter during the 1990s is larger than that over the total sample period. Both results explain the difference between the upturn around 2006 and the one in the 1990s in terms of amplitude and frequency.

Our contribution is firstly a generic and rigorous modeling of private housing market price dynamics which relaxes the homogenous investors' assumption. Second, we interpret the characteristics of private housing market price dynamics within the disposition-momentum behavioral theory and define four dynamic structures including the price bubble. Third, we relate the disposition-momentum behavioral theory to the stylized facts of private housing market price dynamics, i.e., autocorrelation and mean-reversion. Consequently, this study sheds light on the observed positive correlations between private housing market prices and trading volumes, as well as the effects of past housing price changes on housing turnover. Our fourth contribution in this Chapter is to test the bubble conjecture. All of the above contributions are meaningful for policy makers and investment managers in enhancing their in-depth understanding of the strength of policy intervention and the efficiency of real estate portfolio management.

Review of the Related Literature

Real Estate Cyclical Dynamics

Several studies emphasize the existence of the real estate cycles. Wheaton (1987) notes a recurrent cycle of office construction and vacancy while Baum (1999) cites one for office rents in four European cities. Kaiser (1997) indicates the existence of a fifty- to sixty-year cycle of real estate returns, whereas Renaud (1997) proposes the first global cycle, i.e. "the 1985 to 1994 global real estate cycle," offering a comprehensive overview and analyzing the factors that trigger it and the influence of such cyclical dynamics. Englund and Ioannides (1993, 1997) name a similar concept the "international house price cycle." They provide weak evidence of its existence by comparing the dynamics of housing prices in 15 OECD countries. As for the real estate value or price cycle, different types of real estate exhibit various cyclical patterns over time and across markets (see Wheaton, 1999; Case and Mayer, 1995). Empirical studies have tried to pin the determinants of real estate price cycles on economic fundamentals, focusing on the dynamic interrelationships between macro-economic variables and real estate prices.

For example, Poterba (1991) tests construction costs, the real after-tax user costs of homeownership and demographic factors to explain housing price movements. Muellbauer and Murphy (1997) analyze the cyclical behavior of UK housing prices by focusing on financial liberalization, the wealth effect and other economic/demographic factors. Quigley (1999) extends the factors to consider the effects of economic conditions and lagged housing prices on price variation and finds that economic fundamentals explain less than 29% of the variation. However, lagged housing prices explain most of the housing price variation. Adopting the same approach to explain the housing price dynamics of 46 prefectures in Japan, Seko (2003) obtains findings that contradict those of Quigley (1999). Another line of relevant studies concerns the estimation of housing supply elasticity and price adjustments[5] (see DiPasquale and Wheaton, 1994; Blackley, 1999; Goodman, 2005; Wigren and Wilhelmsson, 2007). These studies also include an opposite perspective from which to analyze the effects of supply constraints on housing prices (see Aura and Davidoff, 2008). Regarding estimation approaches, the prevailing examples include ordinary least-squares, structural vector auto regression (e.g., Elbourne, 2008) and the error-correction model (e.g., Hort, 1998; Malpezzi, 1999).

Several studies have adopted the artificial neural network approach (see Selim, 2008). Granger causality tests and impulse response functions investigate the interaction between housing prices and general economic conditions (see Green, 1997). All of these studies have been inspired by the strategic idea that economic fundamentals act as the underlying driving forces of real estate price cycles. Nevertheless, they present inconsistent results with respect to specific economic determinants, based on a variety of methodologies and across diverse areas, and the theoretical models of real estate cyclical dynamics have been patchy.

In addition, such theoretical models are relatively scarce. Traditionally, there are two types of theories: the representative agent model and the popular stock-flow (four-quadrant) model. Both accord due attention to economic fundamental determinants. Briefly, the representative agent model considers the new dwelling market and homeowners act as both consumers and investors. The market equilibrium condition is that homeowners obtain the same return from investing in houses in relation to other assets. As for the stock-flow model, two sub-markets are considered, with the interaction between supply and demand determining housing prices. Therefore, a similarly reduced form is derived from the two different theoretical models, but the theoretical development of housing cycles remains limited. Some recent research efforts have related to the causes or explanations of housing cyclical fluctuations.

The "honeycomb cycle" theory of Janssen *et al.* (1994) reiterates the relevance of the market conditions that trigger housing market cyclical dynamics, particularly concerning the interaction between housing price and transaction volume dynamics. More importantly, the empirical tests suggest that transaction volume dynamics are more closely related to changes in market conditions, compared with housing price dynamics. According to Chinloy (1996), the apartment rental rate is a function of the vacancy and the space absorption expectation. Rent expectations and construction lags are empirically found to be significant determinants of housing cycles. Dokko *et al.* (1999) contribute by modeling the interaction between real estate rent cycles and value cycles. Their model links economic fundamentals to real estate value and income cycles via the general relationship between real estate value and the capitalization of expected future rents. Capozza *et al.* (2004) investigate housing price dynamics by focusing on the stylized facts, i.e. autocorrelation and mean reversion. Using data from 62 metro markets, they conclude that local economic variables, construction costs, the size and the growth of a metro area can explain housing price fluctuations.

The Disposition Effect of Investors' Behavior in the Asset Market

The tendency to sell winners quickly and hold onto losers, as a prominent portfolio puzzle in the rational expectations paradigm, denotes the disposition effect established by Shefrin and Statman (1985). This tendency is found in a variety of markets with different considerations, such as the Finnish stock market (Grinblatt and Keloharju, 2001), the Taiwanese stock market (Barber *et al.*, 2006), the Australian stock market (Brown *et al.*, 2006) and in exercising company stock options (Heath *et al.*, 1999). The disposition effect has also been found in specific periods, i.e. from January to November compared with December when tax-motivated selling prevails

(Odean, 1998). Odean (1998) also finds that individual investors demonstrate a significant disposition behavior that does not seem to consider the importance of trading costs or rebalancing portfolios. In contrast, Ferris *et al.* (1988) present overwhelming evidence that the disposition behavior exists throughout the year, inclusive of the year-end. The evidence from the actual trading records of professional traders also exhibits their myopic loss aversion (Locke and Mann, 2000), although the wealthier and individual investors in professional occupations exhibit less of this disposition effect (Dhar and Zhu, 2002).

Although the existence of the disposition effect seems undisputed, there is only partial consensus on the explanation for it. Favorable behavioral explanations include prospect theory (Kahneman and Tversky, 1979), regret aversion (Loomes and Sugden, 1982), mental accounting (Thaler, 1985) and the cognitive dissonance theory (Shefrin and Statman, 1985). Muermann and Volkman (2007) show that an investor seeking pride and avoiding regret exhibits the disposition trading behavior. As for formal testing, several Chapters have recently formalized the explanations for the influence of prospect theory and loss aversion on the disposition effect. Kyle *et al.* (2006) analyze the liquidation decisions of economic agents and find evidence that the prospect theory induces agents' disposition behavior. However, Ranguelova (2001) tests the discount brokerage clients' behavior and finds that the larger the market capitalization of the firm, the more likely the disposition behavior. Such findings challenge explanations based on prospect-theory-type individual preferences. Instead, Ranguelova (2001) proclaims that individual beliefs rather than preferences lead to the disposition behavior. Hens and Vlcek (2005) query the prediction of the disposition effect based on prospect theory. Barberis and Xiong (2006) also find that prospect theory does not always produce the disposition effect. A behavioral alternative focuses on rational explanation, such as the portfolio rebalancing consideration (Lakonishok and Smidt, 1986) and the transactions cost consideration (Glosten and Harris, 1988).

The Momentum Effect of Investors' Behavior in the Asset Market

Jegadeesh and Titman (1993) popularize the asset strategies of buying winner and selling loser due to their good performance. However, the consistent profitability of such momentum strategies reveals puzzling anomalies in modern finance theory by violating the central theme of the efficient market hypothesis. Thus, the momentum effect is universally noted and appears robust to methodological tweaking. Momentum strategies have been found to be effective in twelve European countries (Rouwenhorst, 1998), and Asian markets with the exception of Japan and Korea (Chui *et al.*, 2000), because momentum profits persisted throughout the 1990s (Jegadeesh and Titman, 2001). In addition, momentum behavior is clearly identified in Michigan housing market by Piazzesi and Schneider (2009) based on the survey data. They find that a small cluster of investors believe it is time to buy a house as its price will keep increasing. Moreover, the size of such momentum cluster varies along the housing market dynamics.

Various explanations have alluded to the momentum phenomenon, a strategy denoting psychological phenomena and based on irrational behavior, such as the representative heuristic and conservatism bias in Barberis *et al.* (1998) and the self-attribution bias in Daniel *et al.* (1998). "Irrational decisions may lead to the systematic under- or over-reaction of prices relative to their fundamental value, whatever that may be" (Swinkels, 2004, p. 122). Hong and Stein (2000) argue that communication frictions cause under-reaction in the short run and over-reaction long-term, in keeping with momentum behavior.

A risk-based explanation proposed by Jegadeesh and Titman (1993) fails to provide evidence. The same is true for Fama and French's (1996) three-factor unconditional asset pricing model. Ang *et al.* (2001) provide evidence of the momentum profits as compensation for exposure to downside risk. Other explanations include the cross-sectional variation in the unconditional expected returns, instead of the predictable time-series variation in returns (Conrad and Kaul, 1998) and the industry effects (Moskowitz and

Grinblatt, 1999). However, the inconsistent results challenge both explanations (see Grundy and Martin, 2001). Recently, Antoniou *et al.* (2007) consider both risk factors and behavioral biases in a two-stage model specification to explain the momentum effect. They imply that risk factors could explain the momentum effect but behavioral factors do not matter much.

However, we do not aim to discuss the explanations for the disposition and momentum behavior. We draw on the extensive existence of disposition and momentum effects to construct a housing price dynamics model that investigates the characteristics of the housing price time path and identifies its cyclical or speculative bubble movement.

The Housing Price Dynamics Model

The housing market has long been suspected to be inefficient[6] (Case and Shiller, 1989, 1990; Tirtiroglu, 1992; Meese and Wallace, 1994). "The apparent predictability in housing prices, at least in the short run, leaves open the possibility of speculative purchases in the housing market" (Riddel, 1999, p. 272,). "Past researchers have shown that a mix of fundamental and feedback traders in a market may lead to price volatility over and above that driven by rational price forecasts" (Riddel, 1999, p. 273). Hence, housing price dynamics are deemed to be determined by investors' behavior and economic conditions. In recent years, practitioners and academic scholars have indicated that individual investors suffer from behavioral biases, such as insufficient diversification, excessive trading and some relatively simple trading strategies as reviewed by Barberis and Thaler (2002). These strategies have been divided into two major categories: the disposition strategy (effect), which relies on price reversals, and the momentum strategy (effect), which is based on price continuation (Shen *et al.*, 2005).

Among the behavioral biases, the disposition effect has gained the most attention. Although several studies use financial assets, the disposition effect has been documented in the Finnish apartment market (Einio and Puttonen 2006), individuals' behavior in the sale of housing (Genesove and Mayer, 2001) and among professional investors at an Israeli brokerage house (Shapira and Venezia, 2001). In Genesove and Mayer (2001), sellers with nominal losses require higher asking prices and have a lower hazard rate for selling. However, conditional on selling, they would receive higher prices. Given micro evidence that varies, higher pricing levels do prompt housing equity accumulation before the sale but might, during a brief spell, lower the marginal probability to sell a unit, whereas the influence on the downside is stronger. Hence, in housing market terms, the investors' disposition effect should affect their realized housing prices.

Intuitively, if only the disposition investors exist in the private housing market at any point in time, then all investors would behave as sellers or potential sellers. In reality, housing transaction prices need only require that "price and volume are simultaneously determined in equilibrium," so that "whatever process… generates price could give rise to the accompanying trading volume" (Lee and Swaminathan, 2000, p. 2065) while "past trading volume also predicts both the magnitude and persistence of price momentum" (Lee and Swaminathan, 2000, p. 2017). Thus, there must be some investors in the market engaging in contrary behavior. The literature identifies the momentum strategy as that unique, contrarian behavior (e.g., Shen *et al.*, 2005). According to Strobl (2003), the disposition effect is consistent with the price momentum. Massa and Goetzmann (2000) offer evidence that trades between the disposition investors and their counter-parties (the momentum investors) influence relative prices. It is therefore reasonable to characterize housing price dynamics by considering both types of investor behavior within the disposition and momentum behavioral theory.

Although the housing market is suspected to be an inefficient one due to the asymmetrical information and high transaction costs, similar investor's behavior in financial market, for e.g., the momentum behavior, which is observed in housing market (see Piazzesi and Schneider, 2009). Hence, we hypothesize that heterogeneous investors prevail in the housing market because it is more of an asset market, by nature, than a common commodity market. This implies that investors, even speculators, play the most important role in the housing market. In contrast, if few investors are in the housing market, then it becomes a common commodity market. No government intervention is expediently assumed. "Housing markets are inefficient and house prices, at times, deviate from fundamental or intrinsic values. A sharp run-up in housing price is partly due to irrational expectations (fads, noise traders, trend chasing) and signals a future correction, as housing prices are ultimately anchored by (i.e. cointegrated with) market fundamentals" (Clayton, 1997, p. 359-360). Because investor expectations are not rational, they are not homogeneous. Thus, there are two types of investors in the housing market: the disposition investors and the momentum investors.

Fig 2 depicts the framework for our theoretical model, in which the disposition investor seeks risk when faced with possible losses and avoids risk when a certain gain is possible (Kahneman and Tversky, 1979). Such behavior is equivalent to a utility function, which is steeper for losses than for gains (Tversky and Kahneman 1992) unless it is defined on gains and losses as opposed to levels of wealth (Odean 1998). The nature of the disposition behavior proposes an asymmetric S-shaped value function. This function is a departure from the standard, expected utility maximization framework in that an S-shaped value function for investors is centered around a profit of zero on a given trading position. According to prospect theory (Kahneman and Tversky, 1979), the disposition investors have already experienced gains or losses. Their initial state is not zero when they make decisions to hold or sell their housing units. A motivated seller's marginal probability to sell the unit is assumed to be the carrier of loss aversion (Genesove and Mayer, 2001; Engelhardt, 2003).

Fig 3 depicts the behavior of the disposition investors' value functions. Fig 3(a) displays the state of gains: from a gain point M, to increase x revenue that brings less happiness to the investors than the sorrow caused by an increasing x deficit. Fig 3(b) displays the state of losses: from a loss point N, to increase the x deficit that brings less sorrow to the investors than the happiness caused by an increasing x revenue.

However, when the market is in a good condition, the momentum investors expect the housing market to behave well, whereas when the market is in a bad condition, they expect the housing market to behave badly. The value function of the momentum investors is concave in the domain of capital gains and convex in the domain of capital losses, as depicted in Fig 4. However, their value function is different from that of the disposition investors; that is, zero becomes the reference point for the strategies of the momentum investors when the initial states of gains and losses are zero.

The Model Construction

Disposition investors sell the unit when the housing price increases. However, the price changes do not definitively lead the disposition effect because disposition investors refer to a price when making decisions. This price acts as a benchmark. In this study, we selecte the fundamental price as the reference point. The disposition investor then gains the characteristics of the "fundamental investor" as defined by Riddle (1999), "…who bases price forecasts on expected economic conditions in the area. This type of investor would be more likely to purchase a home when prices are low relative to expected fundamentals and to sell when the converse is true." In the short run, this should to be the linear relationship between the changes in disposition investors' demand and housing prices, as expressed in Eq (1)[7]:

$$D_t^D = -\alpha(P_t - P^*); \alpha > 0, \tag{1}$$

where D_t^D is the change in the disposition investors' demand in period t; P_t is the housing price in period t; P^* is the reference price in the log of the equilibrium value per unit, $P^* = P_t^* = p(X_t)$; X_t is a vector of exogenous explanatory variables that serves as a proxy for economic condition; and α indicates the sensitivity of disposition investors to housing price changes. With regard to momentum investors, the changes in their demand depend on housing price changes in every term of Eq (2). The momentum effect appears when the housing price changes exhibit inertia by increasing or decreasing continuously. We assume, for at least two periods, i.e. this period and the last period that the linear function is

$$D_t^M = \beta_1(P_t - P_{t-1}) + \beta_2(P_{t-1} - P_{t-2}); \beta_1, \beta_2 > 0$$ (2)

where D_t^M is the change in momentum investors' demand in period t; P_t, P_{t-1} and P_{t-2} are the housing price in periods t, t-1 and t-2, respectively; and β_1 and β_2 indicate the sensitivities of momentum investors to different periods' price changes. The relative magnitude between β_1 and β_2 need not be defined because although sensitivity is diminishing, i.e. the marginal value of both the gains and losses decreases with increasing changes in housing prices, as shown in Fig 4, $P_t - P_{t-1}$ and $P_{t-1} - P_{t-2}$ are only required to keep up its inertia (with the same sign), rather than be larger or smaller (comparing their absolute values).

The resulting market state can be expressed as the sum of all of the disposition and momentum investors' demand changes, plus the supply of new units in period t:

$$D_t^D + D_t^M + N = 0,$$ (3)

where N is the supply of new units.

Following the logic of Mayer and Somerville (2000), we assume that supply of new units occur only when housing market experiences transition from one equilibrium to another, a period identified by the increase of the price. Hence, all else being equal, assuming a linear supply schedule with the changes of equilibrium price, it is mathematically described as,

$$N = n\Delta P_t^*,$$ (4)

where n is constant and $n > 0$. Δ is the difference operator.

Substituting D_t^D, D_t^M and N in Eq (3) with Eq (1), Eq (2) and Eq (4), respectively, produces

$$\beta_1(P_t - P_{t-1}) + \beta_2(P_{t-1} - P_{t-2}) - \alpha(P_t - P_t^*) + n\Delta P_t^* = 0 \qquad (5)$$

Eq (5) can be rewritten as,

$$P_t + \frac{\beta_2 - \beta_1}{\beta_1 - \alpha} P_{t-1} - \frac{\beta_2}{\beta_1 - \alpha} P_{t-2} + \frac{n\Delta P_t^* + \alpha P_t^*}{\beta_1 - \alpha} = 0 \qquad (6)$$

Eq (6) is a second-order difference equation and its solution includes a particular integral and complementary functions. P_t^* is generally stochastic. In order to investigate the dynamic characteristics of the difference equation, for an illustrative example, let $P_t^* \approx P^*; \Delta P_t^* \to 0$. Let $P_t = P_{t-1} = P_{t-2} = C$, where C is a constant, then the particular integral of Eq (6) is obtained as[8]

$$C \approx \frac{\dfrac{\alpha P_t^* + n\Delta P_t^*}{\alpha - \beta_1}}{1 + \dfrac{\beta_2 - \beta_1}{\beta_1 - \alpha} - \dfrac{\beta_2}{\beta_1 - \alpha}} \approx P_t^* + \frac{n\Delta P_t^*}{\alpha} \approx P^* \qquad (7)$$

A difference equation with convergent variables tends to ultimately arrive at the particular integral. As previously mentioned, P^* is a benchmark price for the disposition investors' behavior when they take economic conditions into account to make decisions. Eq (7) shows the benchmark price for disposition investors, i.e. economic conditions, to be the determinant of the final state of the housing market. Eq (7) also provides self-proof that the equilibrium price P^* will be the final state of the housing market if no changes of equilibrium price P^* in a short run.

The complementary functions of Eq (6) are obtained by applying the "Z-transform" $\lambda^t = P_t$. A quadratic equation for the unknown λ is

$$\lambda^2 + \frac{\beta_2 - \beta_1}{\beta_1 - \alpha}\lambda - \frac{\beta_2}{\beta_1 - \alpha} = 0 \qquad (8)$$

Eq (8) is the characteristic equation from which the characteristic values (roots) can be obtained

$$\lambda_1, \lambda_2 = \frac{1}{2}(\frac{\beta_1 - \beta_2}{\beta_1 - \alpha} \pm \sqrt{\frac{(\beta_1 + \beta_2)^2 - 4\alpha\beta_2}{(\beta_1 - \alpha)^2}}) \qquad (9)$$

. When $(\beta_1 + \beta_2)^2 - 4\alpha\beta_2 > 0$, there are two real unequal characteristic roots λ_1, λ_2, hence, the solution to Eq (6) is,

$$P_t = A_1\lambda_1^t + A_2\lambda_2^t + C \quad (10)$$

A_1, A_2 are constants. When $(\beta_1 + \beta_2)^2 - 4\alpha\beta_2 = 0$, there are repeated real roots $\lambda = \frac{1}{2}(\frac{\beta_1 - \beta_2}{\beta_1 - \alpha})$, then, the solution to Eq (6) is

$$P_t = A_3\lambda^t + A_4 t\lambda^t + C \qquad (11)$$

A_3, A_4 are constants. When $(\beta_1 + \beta_2)^2 - 4\alpha\beta_2 < 0$, the roots of the characteristic equation are complex conjugates and the solution to Eq (6) is,

$$P_t = A_5 r^t \cos(\theta t) + A_6 r^t \sin(\theta t) + C \qquad (12)$$

where, $r = \sqrt{\frac{\beta_2}{\alpha - \beta_1}}$; $\theta = \arccos(\frac{\beta_2 - \beta_1}{2\sqrt{\beta_2(\alpha - \beta_1)}})$

Or $P_t = Ar^t \cos(\theta t - \phi) + C \qquad (13)$

Eq (13) is the phase-amplitude form of the general solution. $A = \sqrt{A_5^2 + A_6^2}$; phase $\phi = \arctan \frac{A_6}{A_5}$. All $A_i, i = 1,...6$, A, C and ϕ are constants that are determined by the initial conditions. The constructed model implications are subsequently discussed in terms of four key propositions and the specific derivations are provided in Appendix 1.

The Model Propositions

Proposition 1. Interaction between the disposition and momentum investors results in the time path of housing prices featured in the autocorrelation and mean reversion. The autocorrelation and mean reversion parameters are expressed by composite coefficients: the proportion of the momentum coefficient to the last period's price changes in the sum effect from disposition behavior and momentum behavior to this period's price changes; and the proportion of the disposition coefficient to this period's price changes in the sum effect from disposition behavior and momentum behavior to this period's price changes, respectively.

Specifically, with the autocorrelation parameter $\tilde{\alpha} = \frac{\beta_2}{\alpha - \beta_1}$ and the mean reversion parameter $\tilde{\beta} = \frac{\alpha}{\alpha - \beta_1}$, Eq (6) is rewritten in Eq (14)

$$P_t - (1 + \tilde{\alpha} - \tilde{\beta})P_{t-1} + \tilde{\alpha} P_{t-2} - \tilde{\beta} P_t^* - \tilde{\gamma} \Delta P_t^* = 0, \qquad (14)$$

where $\tilde{\gamma} = \frac{n}{\alpha - \beta_1}$. Substituting $P_t - P_{t-1}$ and $P_{t-1} - P_{t-2}$ in Eq (14) with ΔP_t and ΔP_{t-1}, respectively, results in the characteristics of the time path of the housing price dynamics being represented in Eq (15),

$$\Delta P_t = \tilde{\alpha} \Delta P_{t-1} + \tilde{\beta}(P_{t-1}^* - P_{t-1}) + (\tilde{\beta} + \tilde{\gamma}) \Delta P_t^* \qquad (15)$$

Eq (15) reinterprets the key stylized facts of the housing market: the positive autocorrelation of price changes at one-year frequencies (Glaeser and Gyourko, 2006), and a long-term tendency toward "fundamental reversion" with prices responding to contemporaneous economic shocks (Lamont and Stein, 1999). Distinctively, grounded in the disposition and momentum theory, Eq (15) can be duly explained. The autocorrelation parameter is determined by the proportion of the momentum coefficient β_2 to the last period price changes ΔP_{t-1} in the sum effect $(\alpha - \beta_1)$ from the disposition behavior and the momentum behavior to this period's price changes ΔP_t, i.e. $\tilde{\alpha} = \dfrac{\beta_2}{\alpha - \beta_1}$. It is the momentum effect that mainly contributes to continuous price changes, and hence it serves as a numerator in defining the autocorrelation. Following similar logic regarding the autocorrelation, the mean reversion parameter is determined by the proportion of the disposition coefficient α to this period's price changes ΔP_t in the sum effect $(\alpha - \beta_1)$ from the disposition behavior and the momentum behavior to this period's price changes ΔP_t, i.e. $\tilde{\beta} = \dfrac{\alpha}{\alpha - \beta_1}$. It is the disposition effect that mainly leads housing price changes in a reversion manner, and hence it serves as a numerator in defining the mean reversion. Both composite parameters imply that the interaction between the two types of investors affects the autocorrelation and mean-reversion.

Proposition 2. The characteristics of the housing price dynamics can be anatomized into four types based on two critical conditions: oscillating (cycling), to be determined by $(\beta_1 + \beta_2)^2 - 4\alpha\beta_2 = 0$ *or* $(1 + \tilde{\alpha} - \tilde{\beta})^2 - 4\tilde{\alpha} = 0$ *and convergent to the long-run equilibrium, to be determined by* $\beta_2 = \alpha - \beta_1$ *or* $\tilde{\alpha} = 1$.

Mathematically, a necessary condition for the housing price dynamics in oscillations (cycles) is that the complex roots occur: $(\beta_1 + \beta_2)^2 - 4\alpha\beta_2 < 0$ or $(1 + \tilde{\alpha} - \tilde{\beta})^2 - 4\tilde{\alpha} < 0$. With restrictions from the economics of the propositional problem, the absolute value of the autocorrelation $\tilde{\alpha}$ being less than one serves as a necessary condition for convergence to equilibrium (Capozza et al., 2004; Capozza and Israelsen, 2007). Subsequently, housing price dynamics can be categorized into four types under the two foregoing conditions. Here, the autocorrelation parameter $\tilde{\alpha}$ and the mean reversion parameter $\tilde{\beta}$ are composite parameters derived from α, β_1, β_2, which are the sensitivity coefficients of the disposition and momentum investors. Hence, the space of composite parameters with coefficients α, β_1, β_2 can be graphically divided into four regions, as shown in Fig 5. The various combinations of both parameter values generates dynamic patterns when the equilibrium is "shocked." Therefore, our difference model proclaims that the interaction between both types of investors is a crucial force in housing market price dynamics and determines its features.

Specifically, $(\beta_1 + \beta_2)^2 - 4\alpha\beta_2 = 0$, i.e. $\alpha = \dfrac{(\beta_1 + \beta_2)^2}{4\beta_2}$ acts as a critical condition for oscillation: if $\alpha > \dfrac{(\beta_1 + \beta_2)^2}{4\beta_2}$, then there is oscillatory behavior (overshooting); if $\alpha < \dfrac{(\beta_1 + \beta_2)^2}{4\beta_2}$, then there is damped behavior (no overshooting). $\tilde{\alpha} = \dfrac{\beta_2}{\alpha - \beta_1} = 1$, i.e. $\alpha = \beta_1 + \beta_2$ is a critical condition for convergence: if $\alpha > \beta_1 + \beta_2$, then there is convergent behavior; if $\alpha < \beta_1 + \beta_2$, then there is divergent behavior. With regard to each region, the following cases provide useful insights:

<u>Case (1).</u> When $\alpha < \beta_1$, and $\alpha < \dfrac{(\beta_1 + \beta_2)^2}{4\beta_2}$, i.e. $(1 + \tilde{\alpha} - \tilde{\beta})^2 - 4\tilde{\alpha} > 0$, then the dynamics show no oscillations. When $\alpha < \beta_1$, it also ensures that $\alpha < \beta_1 + \beta_2$, which suggests that the dynamics are divergent, as in Region III (no oscillations-divergence

dynamics). The theoretical explanation is that when the disposition investors' sensitivity to the price change is smaller than the composite sensitivity of the momentum investors, i.e. $\alpha < \frac{(\beta_1+\beta_2)^2}{4\beta_2}$, then the strength of the oscillation fluctuation contributed by disposition investors is not enough to overwhelm that of continuous rise or decline contributed by momentum investors. The total sensitivity to price change of the disposition investors is smaller than that of the momentum investors, i.e. $\alpha < \beta_1 + \beta_2$, such that if the price rises, then the demand of the disposition investors (selling) is not enough to satisfy the demand of the momentum investors (buying), leading to price divergence.

<u>Case (2) a.</u> When $\alpha > \beta_1$, and $\alpha < \frac{(\beta_1+\beta_2)^2}{4\beta_2}$, i.e., $(1+\tilde{\alpha}-\tilde{\beta})^2 - 4\tilde{\alpha} > 0$, it can be rewritten as $\beta_1 < \alpha < \frac{(\beta_1+\beta_2)^2}{4\beta_2}$.

If $\beta_1 < \beta_1 + \beta_2 < \alpha < \frac{(\beta_1+\beta_2)^2}{4\beta_2}$, then it is in Region IV (no oscillations-convergence dynamics). The theoretical explanation is that when the total sensitivity to price change of the disposition investors is larger than that of the momentum investors, then the resistance to housing price emerges from the disposition investors sufficiently enough to counteract the impetus to the housing price from the momentum investors, leading to price convergence.

If $\beta_1 < \alpha < \frac{(\beta_1+\beta_2)^2}{4\beta_2}$ and $\alpha < \beta_1 + \beta_2$, it suggests Region III (no oscillations-divergence dynamics). The theoretical reasons are the same as those in Case (1).

<u>Case (2) b.</u> When $\alpha > \beta_1$, and $\alpha > \frac{(\beta_1+\beta_2)^2}{4\beta_2}$, i.e. $(1+\tilde{\alpha}-\tilde{\beta})^2 - 4\tilde{\alpha} < 0$,

if $\dfrac{(\beta_1+\beta_2)^2}{4\beta_2} < \alpha < \beta_1+\beta_2$, it suggests Region II (oscillations-divergence dynamics);

if $\alpha > \dfrac{(\beta_1+\beta_2)^2}{4\beta_2}$ and $\alpha > \beta_1+\beta_2$, it suggests Region I (oscillations-convergence dynamics). The abovementioned logic provides the corresponding explanation.

Proposition 3. On housing price dynamics in oscillations, the amplitude increases sharply and concussively with the increase of $\dfrac{\beta_2}{\alpha-\beta_1}$ or the autocorrelation parameter $\tilde{\alpha}$, but becomes ambiguous in $\dfrac{\alpha}{\alpha-\beta_1}$ or the mean reversion parameter $\tilde{\beta}$; the frequency decreases steeply with the increase of $\dfrac{\beta_2}{\alpha-\beta_1}$ or the autocorrelation parameter $\tilde{\alpha}$, but is also ambiguous in $\dfrac{\alpha}{\alpha-\beta_1}$ or the mean reversion parameter $\tilde{\beta}$.

As for the oscillations, the amplitude and frequency are expressed as,

$$\text{Amplitude} = 2|P_0 - P^*| \cdot \sqrt{\dfrac{\alpha(\alpha-\beta_1)}{4\alpha\beta_2-(\beta_1+\beta_2)^2}} \cdot \left(\sqrt{\dfrac{\beta_2}{\alpha-\beta_1}}\right)^t \quad (16a)$$

$$= 2|P_0 - P^*| \cdot \sqrt{\dfrac{\tilde{\beta}}{4\tilde{\alpha}\tilde{\beta}-(\tilde{\alpha}+\tilde{\beta}-1)^2}} \cdot \left(\sqrt{\tilde{\alpha}}\right)^t \quad (16b)$$

where P_0 is a constant from initial conditions

$P(0) = P(1) = P_0, P_0 \neq 0 \text{ and } P_0 \neq P^*$,

$$\text{Frequency} = \dfrac{1}{2\pi} \cdot \arccos\left[\dfrac{\beta_2-\beta_1}{2\sqrt{\beta_2(\alpha-\beta_1)}}\right] = \dfrac{1}{2\pi} \cdot \arccos(\dfrac{\tilde{\alpha}-\tilde{\beta}+1}{2\sqrt{\tilde{\alpha}}}) \quad (17)$$

Eq (16a) states that the amplitude of oscillations depends on the distance of the system, at the initial point, from equilibrium as well as the sensitivity coefficients of both the disposition and momentum investors. In Eq (17), the frequency is determined by the sensitivity coefficients of both investors. According to Eq (16b) and Eq (17), the relationships connecting frequency and amplitude with the two composite parameters, $\tilde{\alpha}, \tilde{\beta}$, are graphed in Fig 6.

The graphs in Fig 6 clearly depict proposition 3. Intuitively, if the momentum coefficient β_2 to the last period's price changes is a large proportion of the sum effect $(\alpha - \beta_1)$ from the disposition behavior and the momentum behavior to this period's price changes, it implies that the momentum behavior greatly affects the housing market.

Because the momentum effect continuously leads housing prices to keep increasing or decreasing, the larger the proportion of $\dfrac{\beta_2}{\alpha - \beta_1}$, the larger scale (amplitude) of housing prices increase or decrease at the same time; and the longer period (1/frequency) for which housing prices continue to increase or decrease. As for the proportion of $\dfrac{\alpha}{\alpha - \beta_1}$, it does not capture the sum of the competing effects from the disposition and momentum behavior in the housing market, so the trend of amplitude and frequency changes is ambiguous with this parameter.

Proposition 4. Other relevant parameters remaining invariant, the speed at which the amplitude decreases increases while the duration of convergence to the equilibrium is shorter, in line with the increase in the disposition coefficient α or the mean reversion parameter $\tilde{\beta}$.

Based on Eq (8), the damped ratio ς in our model is given in Eq (18).

$$\varsigma = \frac{\beta_2 - \beta_1}{2\sqrt{\beta_2(\alpha - \beta_1)}} = \frac{\tilde{\alpha} - \tilde{\beta} + 1}{2\sqrt{\tilde{\alpha}}} \qquad (18)$$

It is reversed from the disposition coefficient α and mean reversion parameter $\tilde{\beta}$, whereas if other parameters are kept invariant, then the damped ratio ς decreases with the increase in α or $\tilde{\beta}$. Specifically, the damped ratio characterizes the time length of price that is converging to its long-term equilibrium level. If housing prices increase, then the disposition investors tend to sell their housing units, which increases the market supply and increasing prices are restrained. The larger the disposition coefficient α, the greater the strength of its counteraction to the housing price fluctuations, i.e. the less time that housing prices need to be back at the long-term equilibrium level. More intuitively, in the autocorrelation and mean reversion domain, the larger the mean reversion parameter $\tilde{\beta}$, the faster prices must return to equilibrium, i.e. the smaller the damped ratio ς.

3.3 Model of Reference Price

In model estimation, our aim is to investigate the characteristics of Singapore private housing market price dynamics within the disposition-momentum behavioral theory, and to test the differences in different periods of shock to the local economy. These differences are captured by examining those points, determined by various values of $\tilde{\alpha}, \tilde{\beta}$ from the studied periods, which appear in different Regions as illustrated in Fig 5.

P^* is important in estimating the parameters $\tilde{\alpha}, \tilde{\beta}$ in Eq (15). $P^* = f(X)$, where X is a vector of independent variables that considers economic conditions. Hence, the key consideration lies in the selection of $P^* = f(X)$. Relevant studies have adopted a reduced form price equation, which they estimate based on some underlying notion of the determinants in the context of supply and demand. Generally, the fitted regression of housing price on a set of the potential determinants is interpreted as the price level justified by fundamental factors (forces) within the economy. The priori and important factors are sometimes insignificant, have opposite signs or are significant. The finance-based approach features an underlying notion of arbitrage, typifying the ratio of rental income to house prices as a standard metric.

However, the underlying supply and demand factors, such as income, are not modeled. In addition, the adjustment path of housing prices compared to their fundamental level is beyond this approach. Recent theoretical models even highlight that borrowing can make asset prices more sensitive to fundamental shocks (see Lamont and Stein, 1999). Housing loans and housing prices are interdependent in the long run and they have a positive contemporaneous effect on each other in the short run, according to Gimeno and Martínez-Carrascal (2006). Moreover, the variable mortgage rate influences the growth rate of housing prices (Otto, 2007). Income and interest rates can explain housing price movements through time (Case and Shiller, 2003). Therefore, we select the hybrid method from McQuinn and O'Reilly (2008) because their model captures the significant roles of credit, income and interest rate as drivers of housing demand in Eq (19).

$$HL_t = kY_t \left(\frac{1-(1+R_t)^{-\tau}}{R_t} \right), \tag{19}$$

, where HL_t is the housing loan amount that can be borrowed in period t; k is the proportion of household income that goes into mortgage repayments; Y_t is the disposable income per household; R_t is the mortgage interest rate; and τ is the duration of the mortgage. After nesting Eq (19) for the purpose of a general housing market model, the resulting expression is simplified in Eq (20).[9]

$$P_t^* = \zeta + \psi X_t, \tag{20}$$

, where X_t is defined as the time-varying component of HL_t.

Two advanced regression models are adopted to estimate long-term equilibrium prices in Eq (20): the dynamic ordinary least squares

(DOLS) model of Stock and Watson (1993) and the fully-modified OLS (FM-OLS) of Phillips and Hansen (1990). Recently, the single equation DOLS approach has been popular in different models in the housing market studies, such as those by Muellbauer and Murphy (1997), Fitzpatrick and McQuinn (2007) and McQuinn and O'Reilly (2008). The potential correlation between the explanatory variables (factors) and the error process are explicitly permitted in the DOLS model. The expression is

$$y_t = a_0 + a_1 x_{it} + \sum_{j=-k}^{k} \varphi_{ij} \Delta x_{i,t+j} + \varepsilon_t, \qquad (21)$$

, where x_{it} is endogenous. As Eq (21) reveals, and to correct for correlations, the DOLS involves the leads and lags of the differenced regressors in the specification. The FM-OLS is more complex and its advances lie in correcting the OLS for possible autocorrelation and endogenity in the regressors caused by the existence of a cointegrating relationship.

Results and Analysis

The Data

Our data set includes three time series: the nominal private housing price index, the average monthly nominal earnings per employee and the variable housing loan rate for 15 years, a long enough period to enable meaningful analysis. The data are quarterly span 1982 Q1 to 2007 Q3. The quarterly disposable incomes of households are not available for Singapore and the average monthly nominal earnings per employee from all of the industries are selected as a proxy (Fig 1(b)). The percentage of housing in the household expenditure is 22% (SingStat, 2005, p. 6), which is well below the widely accepted and cautious notion that the average monthly nominal earnings per employee for Singaporeans should exclude the CPF (the central provident fund form of social security), and that the average proportion of earnings going into housing loan repayments should not exceed 30%.[10] The variable housing loan rate is selected because it captures the economy changes better than its fixed counterpart. The amount of the housing loan is obtained from Eq (19).

Preliminary Tests and Long-term Equilibrium Estimation

To prepare for the DOLS and FM-OLS regressions, the unit roots in both the logarithmic levels and the logarithmic levels of the first differences for each variable are tested. The ADF, DF-GLS (Generalized Least Squares) and PP (Phillips-Perron) tests are conducted, and the results for the log level of the private housing price index and the housing loan are reported in Table 1. All of the cases fail to reject the unit root hypothesis at the 1% level of significance, and at the log level of the first differences, almost all of tests reject the unit root hypothesis at the 1% level of significance.

The correlation between the private housing market price index and the housing loan is 0.704181 (0.812251 in the logarithm form), which implies a long-term relationship between both series. The cointegration tests are presented in Table 2, and to avoid spurious results from a single test, the Johansen and the Engle-Granger (1987) cointegration tests are conducted for a robust conclusion. As Table 2 shows, the results from the Johansen tests provide evidence of one cointegrating vector at the 5% significance level, while the Engle and Granger test rejects the null hypothesis of no cointegration at the 5% level.

Because "the DOLS estimator falls under the single-equation Engle Granger (1987) approach to cointegration while allowing for endogeneity within the specified long-run relationships" (McQuinn and O'Reilly, 2008, p. 384), the above cointegration results enable us to proceed to the DOLS regression. Table 3 reports the results from the DOLS, FM-OLS and OLS for the housing price index and housing loan in the long run. As expected, the estimators from each method correspond closely. The coefficient of the housing loan shows the expected sign. In particular, the housing loan calculated from the housing loan rate and average earnings as a proxy for the determinants of housing demand under certain economy conditions is positively and significantly related to private housing price.

Furthermore, the parameter stability for equations containing the I(1) processes is investigated under Hansen's (1992) method.[11] The results of the FM-OLS estimators are presented in Table 4. All of the test statistics fail to reject the null hypothesis of parameters' stability at the 5% significance level, as Fig 7 reveals.

4.3 Dynamic Responses Estimation

We investigate the characteristics of Singapore private housing market price dynamics during two periods: the whole sample period from 1982 Q2 to 2007 Q3, and the sub-period from 1990 Q1 to 2001 Q1. Using the results from the equilibrium estimation from DOLS for both period samples, we estimate Eq (15) together with the form proposed by Capozza et al. (2004) in Eq (22) adopting the OLS.

$$\Delta P_t = \sum_i \tilde{\alpha}_i (X_{it} - \overline{X}_i)\Delta P_{t-1} + \sum_i \tilde{\beta}_i (X_{it} - \overline{X}_i)(P^*_{t-1} - P_{t-1}) + \tilde{\eta}\Delta P^*_t \quad (22)$$

In this Chapter, $X_t = HL_t$ and $\tilde{\eta} = \tilde{\beta} + \tilde{\gamma}$.

The results are reported in Table 5. First, for both periods, $\tilde{\eta}$ denotes the contemporaneous adjustment of prices to current shocks and $\tilde{\alpha}$ represents the autocorrelation. According to efficient market theory, $\tilde{\eta}$ should be 1 and $\tilde{\alpha}$ would be zero. However, several studies obtain the autocorrelation of housing price dynamics to be more than zero, such as the range from 0.25 to 0.5 suggested by Case and Shiller (1989) for four cities; 0.4 for a panel of 29 cities with 0.2 for the inland cities and 0.5 for the coastal cities by Abraham and Hendershott (1993); around 0.45 for 15 OECD countries in Englund and Ioannides (1997); and a range from -0.2 to 1.7 for 992 metro areas in Capozza et al. (2004). Here, $\tilde{\alpha}$ is significant at around 0.7, which is consistent with existing studies. $\tilde{\eta}$ is almost zero with a large p-value, suggesting that during both periods, almost 100% of housing price adjustments occur gradually over time. Both values of $\tilde{\alpha}$ and $\tilde{\eta}$ imply that the Singapore private housing market was inefficient from 1982 to 2007. With regard to the mean reversion parameter $\tilde{\beta}$ [12], no theory predicts its estimated value (Capozza et al., 2004). However, if housing prices converge to their equilibrium values in the long run, $\tilde{\alpha} > 0$ implies $\tilde{\beta} > 0$ [13] (Capozza et al., 2004).

In this Chapter, the pairs of $\tilde{\alpha}$ and $\tilde{\beta}$ in Table 5 are significant and consistent with previous observations. Owing to the zero value of $\tilde{\eta}$, market prices converge 2% (0.02) to 3% (0.03) of the total adjustment each year from 1982 to 2007, according to the value of $\tilde{\beta}$; and 3% (0.03) to 4% (0.04) from 1990 to 2001. Our findings are consistent with those of Abraham and Hendershott (1996), who report a value of zero for Midwestern cities in the U.S.

The results of Eq (22) in Table 5 shed light on the endogenous adjustments of housing price dynamics. The changes in housing loans[14] consider the loans' influence on the autocorrelation and mean reversion parameters, denoted as $\tilde{\alpha}_1, \tilde{\beta}_1$. However, for the whole and sub-periods, $\tilde{\alpha}_1$ and $\tilde{\beta}_1$ are statistically insignificant with high probability values (see Table 5). Thus, the changes in housing loans do not lead to statistically significant differences in autocorrelation and mean reversion in Singapore private housing market price dynamics. This implies that housing loans, which represent economic conditions, affect housing market price dynamics by comprehensively entering the equilibrium price P_t^* for the Singapore private housing market. Our model offers a stylized investment market in which the fundamental housing value changes exogenously. This means that housing market price dynamics should be explained beyond general economic conditions, providing support for our Eq (15) on the basis of the disposition and momentum behavioral theory.

Given the locations of the points determined by $\tilde{\alpha}$ and $\tilde{\beta}$, as plotted in the 'Region' map (see Fig 8), it is clear that for the whole sample period, housing market price dynamics lie in Region IV (convergent but no oscillations). However, for the shorter sub-period, both of the models point toward Region I (convergent with oscillations). It can be concluded that from 1982 to 2007, Singapore private housing market price dynamics are convergent with equilibrium prices without oscillations (being over-damped). From 1990 to 2001 when the Singapore private housing market is deemed speculative, the housing market prices fluctuating is in a convergent and oscillating manner without showing divergence. This implies that Singapore private housing market price dynamics are far from a speculative price bubble.

According to Proposition 1 and within our disposition and momentum framework, every pair of significant $\tilde{\alpha}$ and $\tilde{\beta}$ shows the positive sign, suggesting $\alpha > \beta_1$. Our results show that the housing market price dynamics lie in Region IV for the whole sample period, and it should be in Proposition 2, Case (2)a, i.e. $\beta_1 < \beta_1 + \beta_2 < \alpha < \frac{(\beta_1 + \beta_2)^2}{4\beta_2}$. Thus, the Singapore private housing market is strikingly dominated by the disposition investors, compared with the momentum investors, from 1982 to 2007. In the long run, the housing price dynamics converge to equilibrium. In terms of the shorter sub-period, the housing price dynamics lie in Region I, which corresponds to the situation in Case (2)b, i.e. $\alpha > \frac{(\beta_1 + \beta_2)^2}{4\beta_2}$ and $\alpha > \beta_1 + \beta_2$. Once again, the disposition investors dominate and the housing market price dynamics do not show divergence even in the so-called speculative period (1993-1996, 2000-2001). Our results here are consistent with those of extensive domestic sources, such as financial advisory firms, online comments and academicians. For example, at the IPAC (2007) panel, three presentations reiterate that the housing price bubble is not in the offing.[15] Abeysinghe (2007) mentions that the rise in housing prices is below the long-term equilibrium level, i.e. the pace of housing price rises is still below the expected level based on market fundamentals. Because α is larger than $\frac{(\beta_1 + \beta_2)^2}{4\beta_2}$ in the sub-period and smaller in the whole period, the comparative magnitude of α to β_1, β_2 for the sub-period is larger than it is for the whole period. In Table 5, the value of $\tilde{\beta}$ in the sub-period is slightly larger than that in the whole period.

According to Proposition 4, a larger α or $\tilde{\beta}$ contributes to faster recovery, which explains the fast recovery from the 1990s' boom and bust. The value of $\tilde{\alpha}$ in the sub-period is larger than that in the whole period, according to Proposition 3, for which the amplitude of the 1990s' upturn is higher. Thus, combining the estimates of α and $\tilde{\alpha}$ from Propositions 4 and 3, respectively, explains the 1990s' boom and bust in terms of the autocorrelation-mean reversion and investors' behavior. In short, Singapore private housing market boom in the 1990s' differs from the other upturns observed from 1982 to 2007: the recovery from the 1990s' bust was faster and the magnitude of the price gain was significantly higher. These characteristics are consistent with Morgan Stanley's (2007) analysis of Singapore private housing market. The patterns of housing market price dynamics can vary over periods. According to Cappozza *et al.* (2004), 26% of the observed housing price dynamics exhibit convergence with no oscillation (i.e. in Region IV) while 67% exhibit convergence with oscillations (i.e. in Region I), whereas zero% lie in Region III.

Hence, Singapore private housing market price dynamics, while consistent, exhibits a uniqueness that can be attributed to a variety of price dynamics corresponding with various periods. From 1982 to 2007 in Singapore, the damped convergence was a reaction to price shocks (in Region IV) while in the sub-period and inclusive of the "speculative" period (1990 to 2001), the convergent oscillation was the reaction to price shocks (in Region I). Finally, although we have not included the influence of the public policy effect, it is deemed to be part of investors' behavior, i.e. policy acts as an exogenous variable and does not affect the model structure. This is primarily because the Singapore government has regularly and strongly intervened in the housing market with the overall aim of housing price stabilization. [16] Thus, the over-damped convergence of the Singapore private housing price dynamics is caused by the aggregate effects of the disposition and momentum investors' behavior and long-term government policy.

The Robustness Checks

To enable the robustness of our results, a number of alternative specifications were attempted for the six specific cases. The first case addresses the price dynamic response regressions for the shorter (relative to the equilibrium) results from the DOLS for the same period. Although R^2 increases, the values of $\tilde{\alpha}$, $\tilde{\beta}$ are consistent with the earlier results. The second case arises because new private housing supply in the whole sample period is limited,[17] N in Eq (3) is set to zero. The third case concerns the proportion of income to mortgage payment, which is adjusted to a lower proportion of 26%. For the fourth case, the data is seasonally adjusted, adopting the Census X12 statistical mode. The fifth case notes certain variables in real terms to explain economic phenomena. The sixth case adjusts the data set in real terms. All the results of the long-term equilibrium that are not reported in the tables are very similar to Table 3.

All the results of the dynamic response regressions for the six different cases are provided in Table 6. It is clear that the variables in seasonally adjusted real terms exhibit less autocorrelation and similar mean reversion compared with their 'un-seasonally' adjusted data. However, for the whole period, the points determined by $\tilde{\alpha}$, $\tilde{\beta}$ from Eq (22) are associated with a higher R^2, compared to Eq (15), and all are located in Region IV (convergence with no oscillations). Interestingly, all the points determined by $\tilde{\alpha}$, $\tilde{\beta}$ from Eq (15) lie close to the oscillations' critical line. Regarding the sub-period, both equations exhibit similar results and all the points are located in Region I (convergence with oscillations). Overall, our results are robust with respect to the main features of the Singapore private housing market price dynamics.

Concluding Remarks

This Chapter develops a rigorous model of private housing market price dynamics within behavioral theory. A key assumption is that the investors are a heterogeneous mix of the disposition and momentum types. The decision-making of the two types' investors shows different sensitivities to housing market price changes. This Chapter sheds light on the behavioral explanation of empirical estimates for housing market price's autocorrelation and mean reversion time path, as in the recent study by Gao, Lin and Na (2009) and Titman, Wang and Yang (2014). The interaction between the two types of investors and the aggregate effect of their behavior are important determinants of the private housing market price dynamics.

This Chapter highlights the definition and interpretation of the patterns (features) of the private housing market price dynamics, in accordance with the disposition-momentum behavioral theory. The Chapter categorizes the private housing market price dynamics into four patterns, including the price bubble via the composite autocorrelation and mean-reversion parameters, within the disposition-momentum domain, i.e. convergent or divergent and oscillatory or not oscillatory, as established by Capozza *et al.* (2004).

The Chapter empirically investigates the features of the Singapore private housing market price dynamics and interprets them within both the autocorrelation-mean reversion and the disposition-momentum domains. The private housing market price dynamics exhibit a variety of features over different periods with variant autocorrelation and mean reversion parameters: during the longer period (1982 to 2007). Then there is the convergence without oscillation, which in effect is the reaction to price shocks while in the shorter, so-called "speculative" period (from 1990 to 2001). The private housing market price dynamics display convergent oscillation rather than divergence. It is found that the characteristics of the private housing market upturn around 2006 differ from those of the 1990s' boom-and-recovery, which had been slower and that the magnitude of the price gain tend to be lower. In both periods (around 2006 and the 1990s' boom-and-recovery), the disposition investors prevail, as compared to the momentum investors of the Singapore private housing market.

Furthermore, this Chapter's model offers a stylized investment market, in which the fundamental value changes exogenously. Such a stylized investment market provides potential evidence that investor behavior is endogenously crucial in explaining the private housing market price dynamics. The average autocorrelation parameter in this Chapter is approximately 0.7. The instantaneous adjustment parameter is almost zero with a large p-value, suggesting that during both periods, i.e. around 2006 and the 1990s' boom-and-recovery, almost 100% of housing price adjustments occur gradually over time. The housing market prices merely converge to the 2-3% range of the total adjustment each year, from 1982 to 2007; to the 3-4% range from 1990 to 2001. A key implication for investors is that the boom around 2006 of the Singapore private housing market does not provide as large a magnitude as that from the price gain in the 1990's boom-and-recovery, viewed from a long-term perspective. However, the Singapore private housing market seems to be low risk, offering stable returns, thanks to virtually no divergence, even in the speculative 1990s.

Given that the disposition investors prevail in the private housing market, the best way to invest is to consider the momentum strategy and to avoid the herd behavior for profit sustainability. For policy-makers, the Singapore private housing market is over-damped in the long run. Moreover, the disposition investors predominate this private housing market, and that their behavior contributes to the market mechanism, which automatically adjusts the private housing market prices. The implication is to consider the appropriateness of relaxing government intervention in the Singapore private housing market, in order to make it more efficient.

Acknowledgement: *The Author wishes to gratefully acknowledge the initial work carried out for Chapter 1 by Dr SUN Jingbo, a doctoral graduate of the NUS Department of Real Estate, and in consultation with Honorary Professor (University of Hertfordshire, Hatfield, UK), Dr HO Kim Hin / David; during their meaningful brain storming sessions before Professor HO retired from the NUS SDE Departments of Real Estate and Building in May 2019.*

Tables and Figures for Chapter, entitled "Private Housing Market Cyclical Price Dynamics"

Table 1. Unit Root Tests

	Private Residential Price Index	Housing Loan	1%	5%	Stationary
Level & Intercept					
ADF t-test	-0.962	-3.452	-3.496	-2.890	no
DF-GLS	-0.105	0.577	-2.588	-1.944	no
PP-GLS	-1.311	-2.237	-3.496	-2.890	no
1st Difference & Intercept					
ADF t-test	-4.055	-3.655	-3.497	-2.891	yes
DF GLS	-3.969	-1.782★	-2.588	-1.944	yes
PP GLS	-4.067	-41.905	-3.496	-2.890	yes

Notes: For the ADF, DF tests, the lag length for the test regressions is chosen using Ng and Perron's Modified AIC procedure; the maximum lags are eight; keeping all of these settings consistent, we also conduct the tests based on Trend and Intercept and all of the results report the I(1) process. ★ shows the I(1) process at the 10% level of significance with critical value (-1.614487).

Table 2. Cointegration Tests for Private Residential Price Index and Housing Loan

Johansen tests	Hypothesized no. of cointegration equation		5% critical values	
	None	At most 1	None	At most 1
No intercept or trend				
Trace Stat.	19.631	3.548	12.321	4.130
Max-Eig. Stat.	16.083	3.548	11.225	4.130
Intercept and no trend				
Trace	27.899	4.561	20.262	9.165
Max-Eig. Stat.	23.338	4.561	15.892	9.165
Intercept and trend				
Trace	23.858	3.627	25.872	12.518
Max-Eig. Stat.	20.231	3.627	19.387	12.518

Summary of Johansen tests	Selected (0.05 level) number of cointegrating relations by model		
Data trend	None	None	Linear
Test type	No Intercept, No Trend	Intercept, No Trend	Intercept, Trend
Trace	1	1	0
Maximum Eigenvalue	1	1	1
Engle-Granger Cointegration Test		5% Critical Values	10% Critical Values
Stat.	-3.503	-3.40	-3.09

Table 3. Long-Run Model DOLS, FM-OLS and OLS Estimates

Variable	DOLS estimate	FM-OLS estimate	OLS estimate
Constant	0.76★★★	0.78★★★	0.75★
	(1.4)	(1.6)	(8.3)
Log of Housing loan	0.62★★	0.63★★	0.62★
	(2.3)	(2.4)	(15.5)
R^2	0.67	n.a.	0.66

Notes: Values in parenthesis are t-statistics of each estimate; R^2 is centered R^2 for both DOLS and OLS; the R^2 of FM-OLS is not calculated because to do so would not make sense in a cointegrating regression; the results of DOLS, OLS are obtained from the RATs 7.0 program; the FM-OLS results are obtained from the Matlab program. ★ denotes significance at the 0.001 level; ★★ denotes significance at the 0.05 level; ★★★ denotes significance at the 0.2 level.

Table 4. Applying Hansen (1992) Test of Parameter Stability in Regression with I(1) Series

	Stability Test Stat.	P value of rejecting stability null★
LC	0.132	0.200000
MeanF	1.588	0.200000
SupF	4.917	0.200000

Notes: ★ $p >= 0.200000$ is restricted to $p = 0.200000$; the estimations in Table 4 and Fig 7 are obtained using the Matlab code programmed by Professor Bruce Hansen; the pre-whitened and Bartlett kernel are adopted for each test.

Table 5. Price Dynamic Responses Regressions

	Total sample period: 1982 Q2 to 2007 Q3					
	Equation (15)			Equation (22)		
Coefficient	Estimator	T-Statistic	Prob.	Estimator	T-Statistic	Prob.
$\tilde{\alpha}$	0.72★	10.4	0.000	0.66★	7.4	0.000
$\tilde{\alpha}_1$				0.31	0.9	0.350
$\tilde{\beta}$	0.03★★	2.5	0.015	0.02★★★	1.7	0.0997
$\tilde{\beta}_1$				0.04	0.7	0.487
$\tilde{\eta}$	-0.01	-0.18	0.858	-0.01	-0.1	0.891
R^2	0.51			0.52		
	Sub-period: 1990 Q1 to 2001 Q1					
	Equation (15)			Equation (22)		
Coefficient	Estimator	T-Statistic	Prob.	Estimator	T-Statistic	Prob.
$\tilde{\alpha}$	0.77★	8.0	0.000	0.77★	7.8	0.000
$\tilde{\alpha}_1$				-0.63	-0.6	0.564
$\tilde{\beta}$	0.04★★★	1.9	0.069	0.03★★★★	1.7	0.103
$\tilde{\beta}_1$				-0.01	-0.03	0.976
$\tilde{\eta}$	-0.05	-0.6	0.534	-0.05	-0.61	0.544
R^2	0.58			0.58		

Notes: $\tilde{\alpha}_1, \tilde{\beta}_1$ are the changes in housing loans plus autocorrelation and mean reversion, respectively. ★ denotes significance at the 0.001 level; ★★ denotes significance at the 0.05 level; ★★★ denotes significance at the 0.1 level; ★★★★ denotes significance at the 0.2 level.

Table 6. Robust Checks of Price Dynamic Response Regressions

Total sample period: 1982 Q1 to 2007 Q3

	Based on sub-period sample		N=0		k=26%		k=30%, Nominal, SA		k=30%, Real		k=30%, Real, SA	
	Equation (15)	Equation (22)	Equation (15')	Equation (22')	Equation (15)	Equation (22)	Equation (15)	Equation (22)	Equation (15)	Equation (22)	Equation (15)	Equation (22)
$\tilde{\alpha}$	0.75	0.73	0.72	0.66	0.72	0.66	0.69	0.59	0.70	0.65	0.67	0.58
$\tilde{\beta}$	0.03	0.06	0.03	0.02	0.03	0.02	0.03	0.03	0.03	0.02	0.03	0.03

The selected sub-period: 1990 Q1 to 2001 Q1

	Based on sub-period sample		N=0		k=26		k=30, Nominal, SA		k=30, Real		k=30, Real, SA	
	Equation (15)	Equation (22)	Equation (15')	Equation (22')	Equation (15)	Equation (22)	Equation (15)	Equation (22)	Equation (15)	Equation (22)	Equation (15)	Equation (22)
$\tilde{\alpha}$	0.75	0.73	0.75	0.75	0.77	0.77	0.75	0.72	0.75	0.75	0.73	0.74
$\tilde{\beta}$	0.03	0.06	0.02	0.02	0.04	0.03	0.03	0.06	0.04	0.03	0.03	0.04

Notes: Equation (15') is from Equation (15) when N=0: $\Delta P_t = \tilde{\alpha} \Delta P_{t-1} + \tilde{\beta}(P^*_t - P_{t-1})$; Equation (22') is from Equation (22) when N=0:

$$\Delta P_t = \sum_i \tilde{\alpha}_i (X_{it} - \bar{X}_i) \Delta P_{t-1} + \sum_i \tilde{\beta}_i (X_{it} - \bar{X}_i)(P^*_t - P_{t-1})$$

THE VERSATILITY OF THE REAL ESTATE ASSET CLASS - THE SINGAPORE EXPERIENCE

Fig 1. Housing Prices, Earnings and Housing Loan Rates

a. **Price Index of Singapore Private Housing Properties**

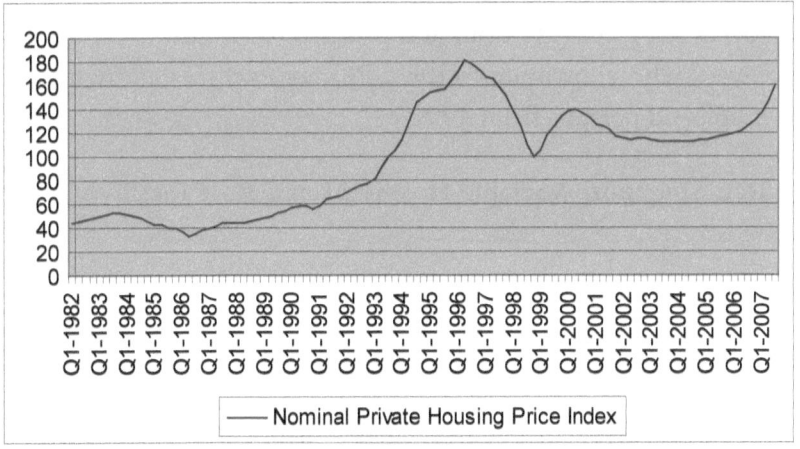

(*Source:* Singapore Urban Redevelopment Authority (URA), 2018)

Notes: 1998 Q4 = 100; the nominal price index is computed based on fixed weights before 1998 Q4; the weights used to compute the index are updated every quarter from 1998 Q4. The URA publishes the data named the residential price index, which refers to the nominal private housing price index in the text.

Fig 1(b). Singapore Average Nominal Earnings per Employee

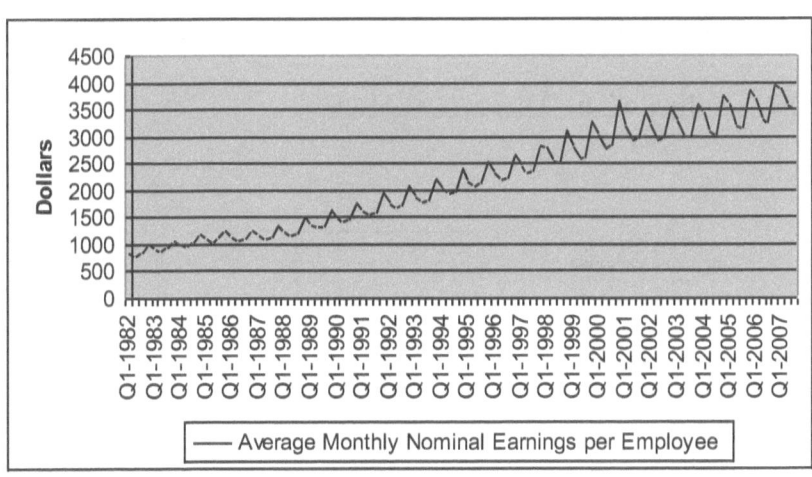

(*Source:* Singapore Ministry of Manpower, 2018)

Notes: The series is computed using data from the Central Provident Fund (CPF) Board and complied using 5-digit fields instead of the 4-digit fields from 1998; it includes bonuses, if any, but excludes employers' CPF contributions and pertains to all full- and part-time employees who contribute to the CPF, but excludes all identifiable self-employed persons from 1992.

Fig 1(c). Singapore Variable Housing Loan Rate for 15-year

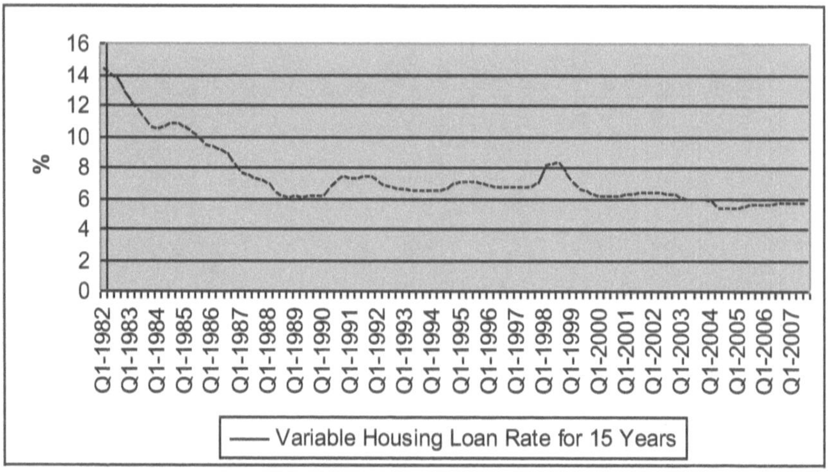

(*Source:* Monetary Authority of Singapore, 2008)

Notes: The housing loan rate refers to the average rates compiled from those quoted by 10 leading finance companies.

Fig 2. Outline of the Theoretical Model

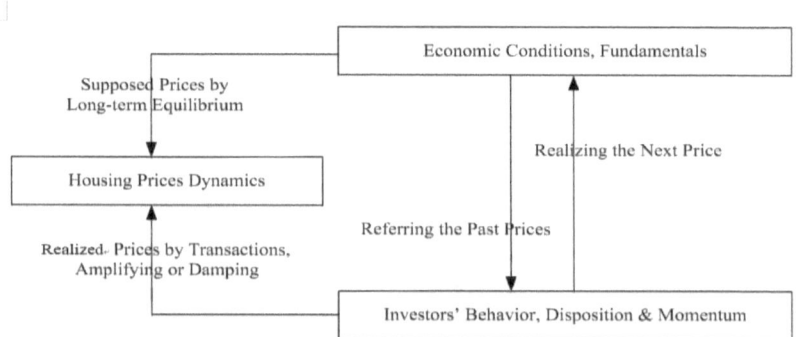

(*Source*: Authors, 20016)

Fig 3. Value Function of Disposition Investors in Gains and Losses Condition

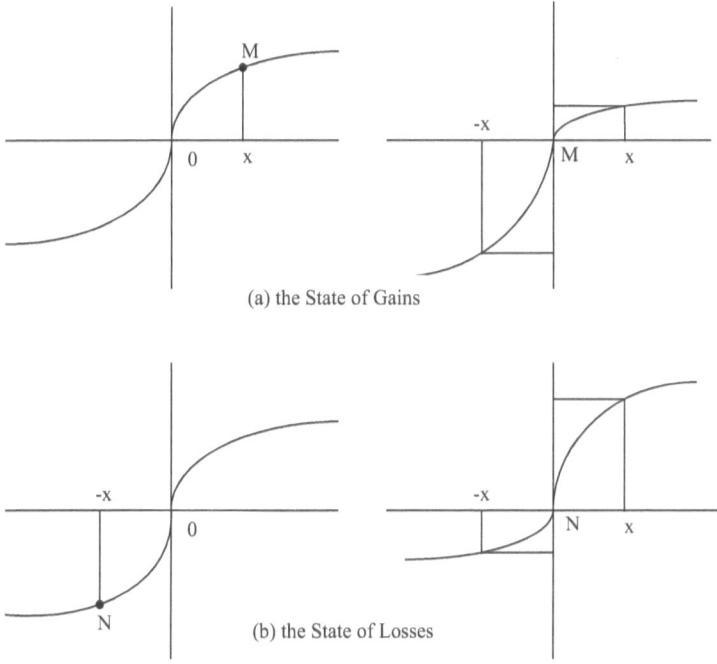

(a) the State of Gains

(b) the State of Losses

(*Source:* Tao Guan, 2007 (unpublished); Authors, 20016)

Fig 4. Value Function of Momentum Investors in Gains and Losses Condition

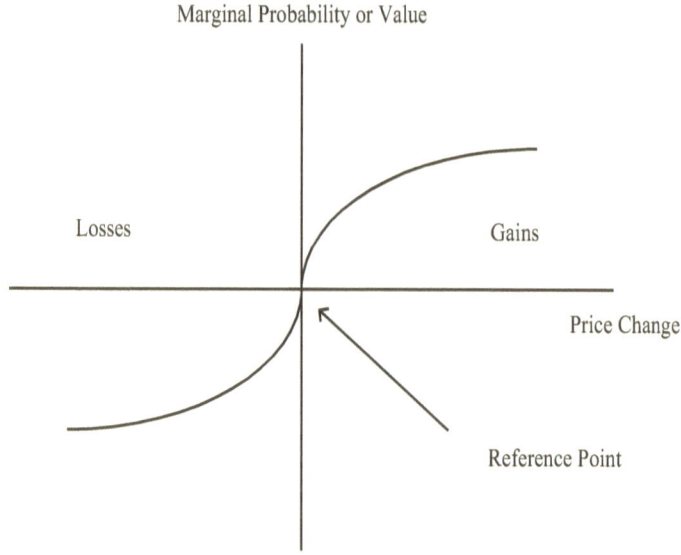

(*Source:* Tu *et al.*, 2007; Authors, 2018)

Fig 5. Housing Price Dynamic Features from the Difference Equation

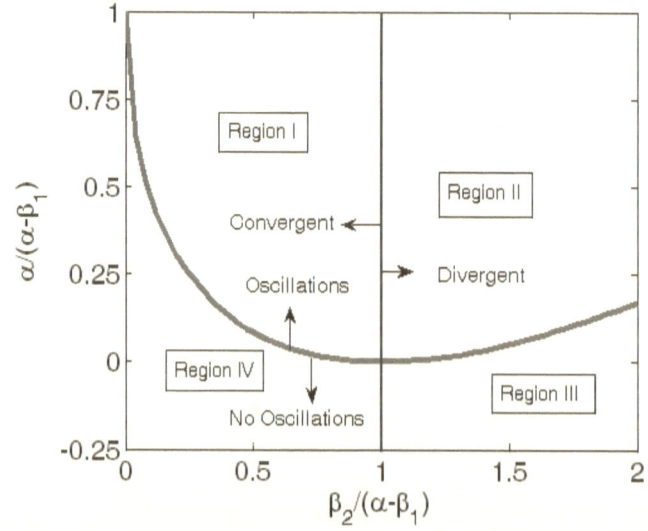

(*Source:* Capozza *et al.*, 2004; Authors, 20016)

Fig 6. Amplitude and Frequency of the Oscillations with the Composite Parameters

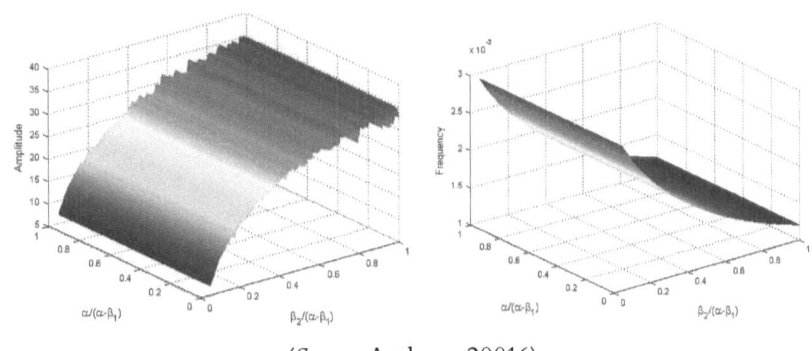

(*Source:* Authors, 20016)

Notes: The Amplitude is portrayed at t=2.

Fig 7. Hansen's Stability Tests for Private Housing Price upon Housing Loan, 1982 Q1 - 2007 Q3

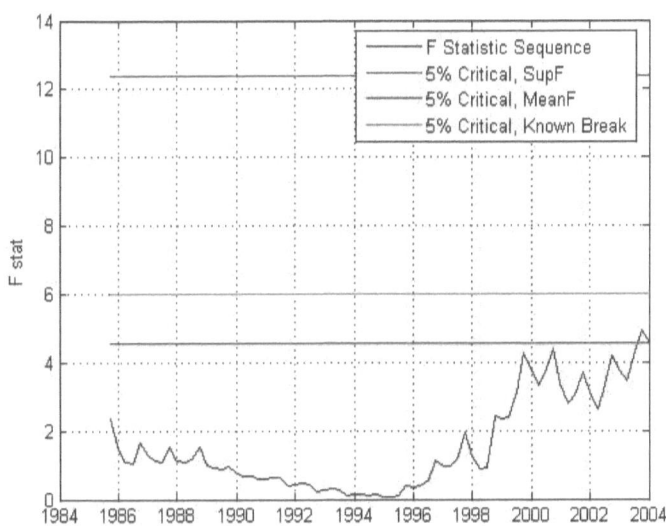

(*Source:* Authors, 20016)

Fig 8. Parameters Allocation in the Region Map

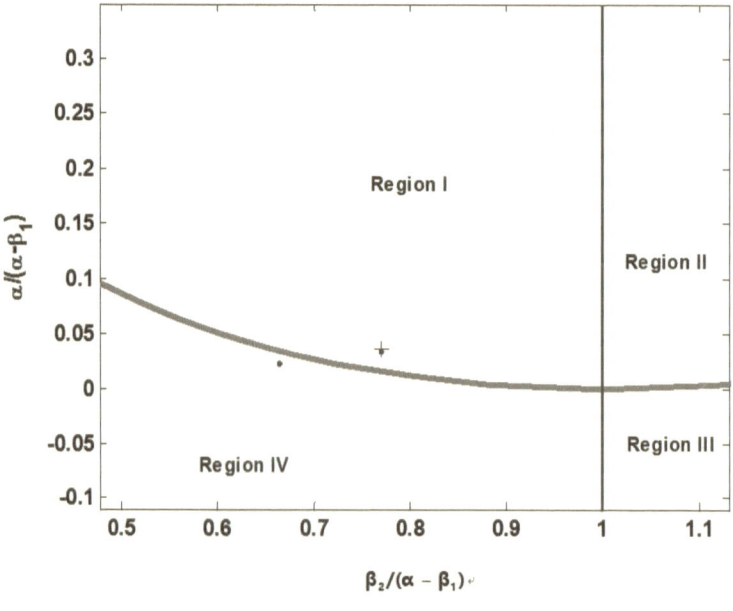

(Source: Authors, 2018)

Notes: The dot below the line is obtained from the regression based on Eq (22) for the whole sample period, because the model of Eq (22) has a higher R^2 than that of Eq (15); two dots above the line are obtained from the regression based on Eq (15) and Eq (22) for the sub-period.

Appendix 1: Features Derivation of the Second-Order Difference Equation

Solutions of the Second-Order Difference Equation

Let $P_t^* \approx P^*; \Delta P_t^* \to 0$, then Eq (6) can be rewritten as,

$$P_t + \frac{\beta_2 - \beta_1}{\beta_1 - \alpha} P_{t-1} - \frac{\beta_2}{\beta_1 - \alpha} P_{t-2} = \frac{-\alpha P^*}{\beta_1 - \alpha}$$

Initial Conditions,
Let $P(0) = P(1) = P_0$, where P_0 is a constant, but $P_0 \neq 0$ and $P_0 \neq P^*$.

The roots of the characteristic equation based on the Eq (6) are,

$$\lambda_1, \lambda_2 = \frac{1}{2}\left[\frac{\beta_1 - \beta_2}{\beta_1 - \alpha} \pm \sqrt{\frac{(\beta_1 + \beta_2)^2 - 4\alpha\beta_2}{(\beta_1 - \alpha)^2}}\right]$$

When there are complex roots, i.e. $(\beta_1 + \beta_2)^2 - 4\alpha\beta_2 < 0$, the solution of the Eq (6) is,

$$P_t = A_5 r^t \cos(\theta t) + A_6 r^t \sin(\theta t) + C, \text{ where, } C = P^*,$$

$$A_5 = P_0 - P^*;$$

$$A_6 = (P_0 - P^*)\left[\frac{2\alpha - \beta_1 - \beta_2}{\sqrt{4\alpha\beta_2 - (\beta_1 + \beta_2)^2}}\right]$$

$$r = \sqrt{\frac{\beta_2}{\alpha - \beta_1}},$$

$$\cos\theta = \frac{\frac{\beta_2 - \beta_1}{2(\alpha - \beta_1)}}{\sqrt{\frac{\beta_2}{\alpha - \beta_1}}} = \frac{\beta_2 - \beta_1}{2\sqrt{\beta_2(\alpha - \beta_1)}}, \text{ so,}$$

$$\theta = \arccos\left[\frac{\beta_2 - \beta_1}{2\sqrt{\beta_2(\alpha - \beta_1)}}\right],$$

$$\text{Amplitude} = \sqrt{A_5^2 + A_6^2} \cdot r^t$$

$$\text{Frequency} = \frac{\theta}{2\pi}$$

Rewriting the Features of the Difference Equation

Let $\tilde{\alpha} = \frac{\beta_2}{\alpha - \beta_1}$, $\tilde{\beta} = \frac{\alpha}{\alpha - \beta_1}$, all the solutions can be expressed in terms of $\tilde{\alpha}, \tilde{\beta}$. For example,

The roots of the characteristic equation based on Eq (6) are,

$$\lambda_1, \lambda_2 = \frac{1}{2}\left[\frac{\beta_1 - \beta_2}{\beta_1 - \alpha} \pm \sqrt{\frac{(\beta_1 + \beta_2)^2 - 4\alpha\beta_2}{(\beta_1 - \alpha)^2}}\right]$$

$$= \frac{1}{2}\left[(\tilde{\alpha} - \tilde{\beta} + 1) \pm \sqrt{(\tilde{\alpha} + \tilde{\beta} - 1)^2 - 4\tilde{\alpha}\tilde{\beta}}\right],$$

When there are complex roots, i.e. $(\beta_1 + \beta_2)^2 - 4\alpha\beta_2 < 0$, i.e. $(1 + \tilde{\alpha} - \tilde{\beta})^2 - 4\tilde{\alpha} < 0$, the solution of Eq (6) is,

$$P_t = A_5 r^t \cos(\theta t) + A_6 r^t \sin(\theta t) + C, \text{ where, } C = P^*,$$

$$A_5 = P_0 - P^*;$$

$$A_6 = (P_0 - P^*)\left[\frac{2\alpha - \beta_1 - \beta_2}{\sqrt{4\alpha\beta_2 - (\beta_1 + \beta_2)^2}}\right];$$

$$= (P_0 - P^*) \left[\frac{1 - \tilde{\alpha} + \tilde{\beta}}{\sqrt{4\tilde{\alpha}\tilde{\beta} - (\tilde{\alpha} + \tilde{\beta} - 1)^2}} \right],$$

$$r = \sqrt{\frac{\beta_2}{\alpha - \beta_1}} = \sqrt{\tilde{\alpha}},$$

$$\theta = \arccos \left[\frac{\beta_2 - \beta_1}{2\sqrt{\beta_2(\alpha - \beta_1)}} \right] = \arccos \left[\frac{\tilde{\alpha} - \tilde{\beta} + 1}{2\sqrt{\tilde{\alpha}}} \right],$$

$$\text{Amplitude} = |P_0 - P^*| \cdot \sqrt{\frac{4\alpha(\alpha - \beta_1)}{4\alpha\beta_2 - (\beta_1 + \beta_2)^2}} \cdot \left(\sqrt{\frac{\beta_2}{\alpha - \beta_1}} \right)^t$$

$$= |P_0 - P^*| \cdot \sqrt{\frac{4\tilde{\beta}}{4\tilde{\alpha}\tilde{\beta} - (\tilde{\alpha} + \tilde{\beta} - 1)^2}} \cdot \left(\sqrt{\tilde{\alpha}} \right)^t$$

$$\text{Frequency} = \frac{1}{2\pi} \cdot \arccos \left[\frac{\beta_2 - \beta_1}{2\sqrt{\beta_2(\alpha - \beta_1)}} \right]$$

$$= \frac{1}{2\pi} \cdot \arccos(\frac{\tilde{\alpha} - \tilde{\beta} + 1}{2\sqrt{\tilde{\alpha}}})$$

Appendix 2: The Singapore Housing Property Demand and Supply Dynamics

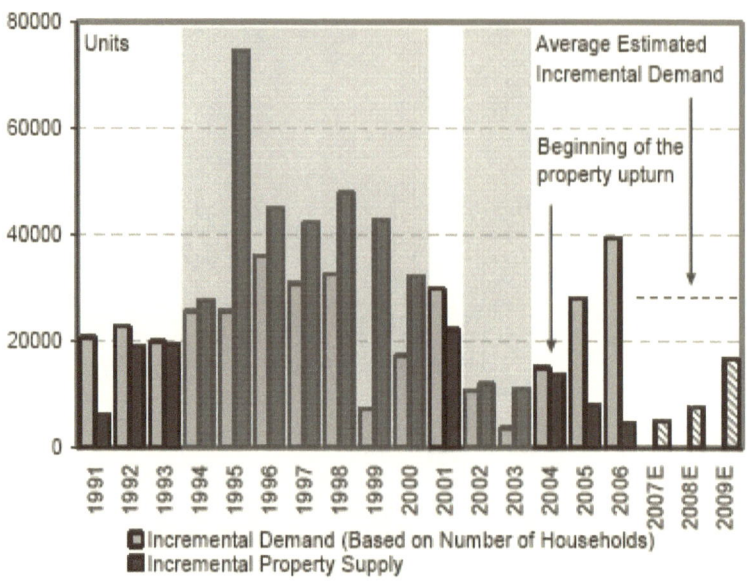

(*Source*: CEIC, Morgan Stanley Research, 2007)

Notes: Area shaded in grey are for periods when there is oversupply; incremental demand is calculated based on the increase in the number of households; incremental property supply includes both private housing property and public housing property. Supply data up till 2006 refers to additional supply net of demolishment. Supply data after 2006 refers only to the gross private housing property supply.

CHAPTER 2

STRATEGIC BEHAVIORAL PRICING OF THE PRIVATE RESIDENTIAL DEVELOPMENT MARKET - A SIMPLIFIED EXPERIMENTAL APPROACH

Residential developers are increasingly aware of inter-firm competitive effects in formulating pricing strategies that impact sales, profitability and return on investment. It is common practice in Asia for the residential developer to be the investor in its residential development project at the same time. The developer is responsible for owning and raising the required capital structure, and for seeing through the entire development process from start to completion. Marketing researchers observe that a market player's pricing strategies and their tactics are diverse (Fader & Lodish, 1990). Nevertheless, there is limited research on pricing strategy for the private residential development market in Asia. Chapter 2 adopts game theory to examine the behavior of "rational" residential developers for their pricing strategy under a competitive environment. A uniquely simplified experimental research design is framed under such a game theoretic approach, within the context of Singapore. On the whole, it considers competitors' actions and leading indicators as imperative to pricing pre-completed units (Ong, Cheng, Boon, & Sing, 2003; Shankar & Bolton, 2004). In particular, it incorporates several interesting features of the private residential development market like its oligopolistic market structure; the determination of residential development sale prices in an uncertain market and under incomplete information of competing developers; dynamic interaction among the developers; time lags of the development project completion from project start; launching of the residential development for sale before completion and the residential development's own capacity constraints.

Chapter 2 adopts game theory to better understand Singapore's private residential development process by highlighting essential features of its private residential market. Singapore's residential sector can be broadly categorized into two major components, the public housing sector and the private residential market. The public housing sector comprises high-rise and high density apartments constructed by the public housing authority, the Housing Development Board of Singapore (HDB), under the purview of the Ministry of National Development.

Fig 1. Historical index of private residential price index and housing stock in Singapore

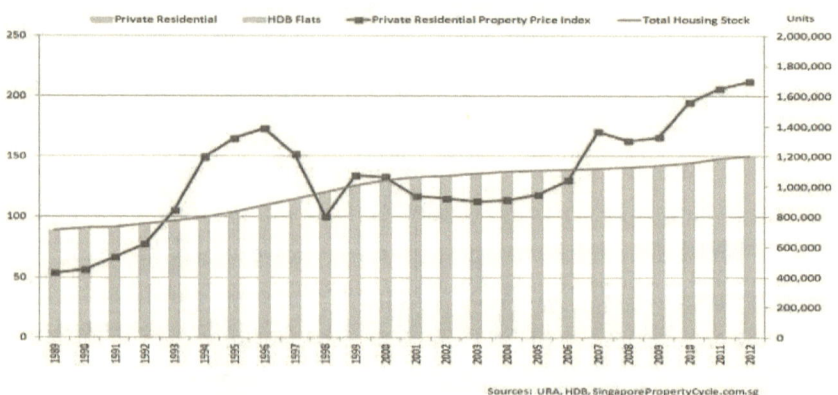

THE VERSATILITY OF THE REAL ESTATE ASSET CLASS - THE SINGAPORE EXPERIENCE

Total housing stock, Singapore (end 2012) = 1,200,113 units (+1.5% from 2011)
Public housing stock (end 2012) = 922,493 units (+0.9% from 2011)
Private residential stock (end 2012) = 277,620 units (+3.3% from 2011)
Source: URA, HDB and Global Property Guide.Com, 2011, 2020.

In Fig 1, the public housing stock makes up the majority of Singapore's housing stock (~80)[1] while the private market represents a sizable percentage (~20). The private residential market in turn is stratified into landed housing (~1-3 %) while the rest are high-rise condominiums and apartments (~18 %). The private residential market is dominated by several large public listed and private developers, who obtain land from the government via bidding under the Government Land Sales (GLS) program. Private residential units supply is dominated by such large enterprises that are able to afford high land prices through quality residential product, design, marketing, cost and project management differentiation. As the Government controls and develops a major portion of the housing stock, i.e. public housing, there is all but limited room for the private market to develop. Singapore's private residential developers inevitably compete for the same target group of the middle working class, dual income-earning households with the husband and wife earning at least a $5,000 gross monthly salary each, and with the household affordability to purchase the mid-range, private condominiums within the wide enough price range of S$400 per sq ft to S$1,200 per sq ft. Within the private market, high-rise condominiums dominate the market, leaving little room for product diversity in Singapore's private residential market.

Three pertinent research questions can be posed. First, what would be the private residential development sale price of its units and its intrinsic pricing pattern? In a competitive market, Singapore private residential developers often engage in price cuts to maximize their development profit. The Bertrand equilibrium suggests that the profit margin would be zero but factors like capacity constraints, repeated interactions and incomplete information that are inherent

---

[1] (Phang, 2004)

to the private residential development market, may well alter the outcomes. Secondly, would the first mover or the second mover more advantageous for the dynamic private residential development market? Choi and Jagpal (2004) find that the second-mover is more advantageous when private residential demand is uncertain, while Amir and Stepanova (2006) show that when two firms do not have the cost-advantage, i.e. the unit costs of the two firms are close enough, there is always a second-mover advantage. Given that the private residential development market is uncertain, developers do not normally have the cost advantage. Chapter 2 is thus concerned with behavioral pricing affected by private residential development market uncertainty. Thirdly, do residential developers change their pricing strategy, i.e. change equilibrium prices, given different market volatilities? These research questions are addressed within a uniquely simplified experimental research design primarily because empirical data pertaining to developers' behavioral pricing is not publicly available. The research design readily helps to reveal the regularities in pricing private residential development sale units, given the correct incentive structure for a simulated environment that accords well with the real world setting (Brookshire, Coursey, & Schulze, 1987). On the one hand, the experimental design permits several to many constraints either endogenously or exogenously to be incorporated into the game setting so as to well simulate the real world. On the other hand, the experimental design simplifies the essence of reality. Shugan (2004) reiterates the need to allow different types of exogenous constraints rather than to make all variables endogenous to enable the realistic setting.

As a result, Chapter 2's simplified experimental research design comprises two games. In game 1, there is a game setting that consists of twelve sub-games. Each sub-game represents a sub-market of the simulated private residential development market. Participating actors (i.e. private residential developers) compete with other developers in the game by pricing their units at each sub-market. Game 1 addresses the first and second research questions above where market volatility is held constant across periods. Equilibrium price is defined to be a stable or optimal outcome in which none of the developers has the incentive to deviate. Thus, the first research question is examined through modeling the strategic pricing pattern, and to see whether or not there are stable outcomes. Qualitatively, it would be constructive to know the reasons behind the strategic pricing. Developers who participant in the simplified experimental research design experiment are consulted for their reasons after the experiment. The second research question is examined by scrutinizing the profits gained by the price leader and by the followers in every sub-game each period. It can be postulated that the profit by any of the followers is equal or greater than the leader. This postulation is tested via the non-parametric Wilcoxon matched-pairs, signed-rank test. The participating residential developers would be asked whether they prefer to be the first mover or the second mover and for their reasons.

In game 2, market volatility would be increased and the reactions of the participating residential developers scrutinized. It can be postulated that private residential development sale prices would drop on the whole as volatility increases, and the non-parametric Mann-Whitney test is adopted to test whether or not there is a significant change in prices between game 1 and game 2. Lastly and in order to examine the behavior of the experienced developers, all the participating residential developers would play the game several times, and only the results of the last few games would be selected for subsequent analysis. Hence, Chapter 2 is organized along several sections. The first section provides the introduction while the next section reviews the related literature. The third section discusses the uniquely simplified experimental research design while the fourth section discusses the results and findings. The fifth section concludes Chapter 2.

The Related Literature

On the whole, two research areas are closely related for Chapter 2, namely game theory and pricing strategy. Economists are interested to examine decision behavior while Von Neumann and Morgenstern (2007) allude to game theory as being a collection of mathematical models, formulated to examine decision-making for situations involving conflict and cooperation. Optimal solutions or stable outcomes can be found when various decisions makers hold conflicting objectives (Lucas, 1972). Several studies reiterate that competitor factors are the key determinants in the pricing strategy for a highly competitive environment (Shankar and Bolton, 2004). Other studies adopt game theory to advise decision makers in their pricing judgment, but none develop pricing models to reveal the structural pricing model for the private residential development market. Rao and Shakun (1972) and Di Benedetto (1986) develop a "quasi-game-theoretic" pricing model that offers a conceptual understanding of decision-making in a classical Bertrand duopoly game, in which two oligopolistic players play the game. Decisions are made simultaneously with perfect information. This classical price competition model has been criticized for a while. It is argued that certain underlying assumptions are not realistic. (Edgeworth, 1925); Hotelling (1990) Kreps and Scheinkman (1983) and Friedman (1977) highlight that the Bertrand model becomes more realistic if the assumption of the constant return to scale is relaxed; if the goods are not homogeneous; if capacity constraints are introduced or if firms compete repeatedly.

The model becomes more relevant in structurally pricing private residential developments when all the said assumptions are relaxed. Nevertheless, there are limited empirical studies that address the pricing structure in such a complex setting. Besides, the pricing decisions are made in a dynamic environment and under incomplete information concerning the market and competitors. Choi and Jagpal (2004) incorporate these factors into the duopoly-pricing model. They find that when the market becomes more uncertain, then equilibrium prices are lower. Their findings show that it is better to act as a price follower in a Stackelberg game when the demand is uncertain; and that when two firms do not have the cost advantage each, i.e. the unit costs of the two firms are close, then the second-mover would always be advantageous.

The second area of research concerns the development of pricing theories on the private residential development market, with past studies focusing on demand aspects. Read (1988), Kang and Gardner (1989) and Ben-Shahar (2002) examine the interaction between sellers and buyers, and between pricing pattern and the time on the market. They develop a theory that addresses how the prices of heterogeneous goods are set, and how sellers may optimally adjust them. Initial price is a function of the information the seller has about potential buyers; and that the frequency and size of subsequent price cuts are functions of learning, which takes place during the marketing period. In most cases, the private residential development market has an oligopolistic market structure, and the oligopolistic residential developers' pricing decisions have significant impacts on one another. Thus, an interactive game theoretic approach can be appropriate to advise residential developers on their pricing strategies. However, the extension of game theory to pricing strategy in the private residential development market is limited but it can offer some useful insights, where developers rely on the forecasted market price and on the actions of their rival residential developers. Perhaps, the actions of buyers would not be much of a concern unless the buyers are few and influential. Pricing strategies may well even differ across developers and market conditions. When the private residential development market is on an up-trend, the variation in prices is greater. In the downtrend market, the variation of prices declines, as residential developers have to price more competitively. Perhaps, the best strategy is to price competitively but not aggressively. In a simplified experimental research design, the players can be deemed to act simultaneously but in reality, residential developers price their residential sale units in different time periods. There ought to be a residential developer who sets (or changes) the price of its newly launched units first. Then, fellow developers can observe the price that is set (changed) and react to it. In short, pricing should be in a dynamic setting.

On the pricing concept, private residential developers often face difficulties in setting a right price for their residential development sale units that impact profitability and demand significantly. In the oligopolistic private residential development market, each developer's actions significantly affect the decisions of its relatively few competitors. This leads to a question of high interest: how are prices formed when there are only a few competitors in the market? The pricing concept can therefore be examined from the perspective of game theoretic solutions. Game theory seeks to provide a formal language for the description of conscious goal-oriented decision-making processes, involving one or more than one individual (Shubik, 1972). The resulting interactions are formalized into games where the playing residential developers are decision makers, and they make their decisions on the basis of other developers' chosen strategies and their anticipated reactions in response.

Hence, two types of games can be generally conceptualized - the cooperative game and the non-cooperative game. A game is cooperative if negotiation and binding contracts are possible. Otherwise, it is a non-cooperative game. Chapter 2 concentrates on the non-cooperative game where the game can be classified by the nature of the information set. Chapter 2 is also concerned with the repeated dynamic game under incomplete, symmetric, certain and imperfect information:

1. A game is deemed to have incomplete information if each player's identity, i.e. the payoff/cost function and the strategies available, is not common knowledge among all the playing residential developers.
2. In a game of symmetric information, no playing residential developer has information different from other residential developers when and after he moves.
3. A game is deemed to have uncertain information if demand does move after any playing residential developer moves.
4. A game is deemed to have imperfect information if the playing residential developers move one or more at a time,

and the residential developer with each move does not know what earlier moves have occurred (i.e. profit gained) thus far in the game.

The Dynamic Pricing Game

The classic Bertrand model advocates that firms compete on price-setting strategies but such a static Bertrand game can be modified to the dynamic form (Von Stackelberg, 1934). The Stackelberg game specifies possible orders of events where players make decisions in sequence. This game provides an opportunity for the playing residential developers to observe the others' actions before making decisions. It is crucial to anticipate what the playing residential developers would do tomorrow in response to one developer's actions today. A natural question for the dynamic game is which position is more advantageous? Chapter 2 accordingly focuses on the first- and second-mover advantage. Under market uncertainty and incomplete information about the playing residential developers, the first mover determines its own pricing strategies (with higher risks) and the unpredictable followers' reaction function. In contrast, the second mover determines its pricing strategy after the first mover has made its pricing decision, and the second mover's position is more certain and would have less risk.

However, there are several reasons that the first-mover advantage prevails. There must be a period for the first mover to monopolize the private residential development market. This enables the residential developer to 'grab' sales quickly, and it is able to reduce the average cost of the product over its rival residential developers. With such a cost advantage, the residential developer is more flexible on its pricing. It can reduce the price to make the private residential development market less attractive for new entrants. Therefore, which position is better would depend on the strength of the foregoing reasons.

Repeated Games

Repeated Games denote another form of the game pioneered by Friedman (1971) and they occur over multiple periods. The group of residential developers repeatedly plays the game in a finite or infinite horizon. Under such a framework, the ongoing relationship among the playing residential developers exists, and they would choose an action today depending on past interactions. In another words, your current action would affect future interactions. Repeated interaction is at the heart of a key issue in oligopoly theory, i.e. collusion. The nature of repeated interaction motivates the residential developer to sustain collusive pricing strategies. This is because the relatively "small-group" of oligopolists would come to realize their interdependence, and they act to maximize joint profits, according to Chamberlin (1929) and Friedman (1971). Fig 2.2 depicts the nature of the interaction examined in Chapter 2. Consider a duopoly game where firm 1 and firm 2 are interacting repeatedly. Firm 1 sets the price first. Firm 2 can either fight (follow the price) or accommodate (undercut the price). Then, firm 1 acts again, and it can fight against or accommodate firm 2's strategy. The game repeats as such. Adopting backward induction, the sub-game-perfect equilibrium (SPE) would be firm 1 choosing the highest possible price in period 1, with the two firms choosing to fight in the subsequent periods until one of the firms' profit becomes zero (or less than ε). The zero-profit firm then chooses to accommodate.

THE VERSATILITY OF THE REAL ESTATE ASSET CLASS - THE SINGAPORE EXPERIENCE

Fig 2. Diagrammatic Representation of a Repeated Game between Firm 1 & Firm 2

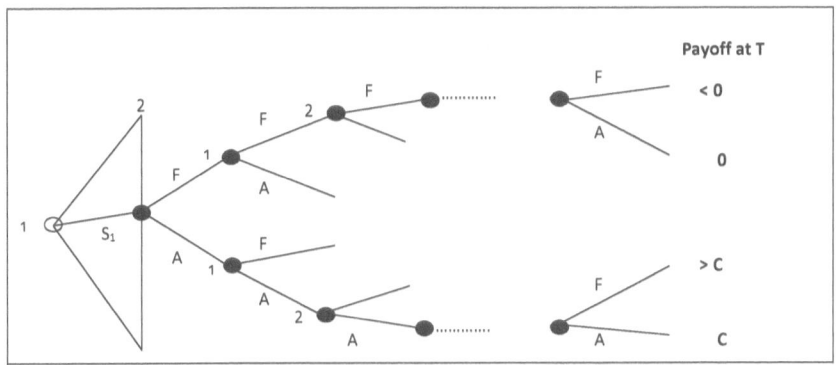

(Source: Authors, 2009, 2020)

However, a rational playing residential developer would choose to cooperate in the beginning rather than to follow the SPE in each sub-game, because he knows that the overall payoff of the cooperative game is better than that of the non-cooperative game. Fig 2 can be simplified to Fig 3. Collusive strategy profiles are efficient and not stable but what if there are deviations occurring in the middle of the cooperation? Therefore, trigger strategies are prominently used in repeated games. The firm would begin by cooperating. It would continue to cooperate as long as rival residential developers do so. Once deviation occurs, it would play non-cooperatively. There are two types of trigger strategies - the grim trigger strategy and the tit-for-tat strategy. For the grim trigger strategy, one would play cooperatively until a rival deviates, after which he would play non-cooperatively for the rest of the game. For the tit-for-tat strategy, one would cooperate as long as the rival cooperates in the most recent period. He would cheat if the rival cheats in the most recent period. Given the punishments under the trigger strategies, a rational player would choose to cooperate. In finite games, there exists an end-game effect. Players have no incentive to cooperate in the last period, say the Nth period, for the deviation would not incur any loss in future. If we adopt backward induction then we find that cooperation is impossible. This is because in the N-1th period, the playing residential developers know that their rivals would not cooperate in Nth period, and there is no opportunity cost to cheat in N-1th period. The same logic continues backwards and towards period 1. However, if the Nth period is long enough that the incentive to deviate is less than ε, owing to discount factors, or if it is an infinite game, then the end effect would not occur.

Fig 3. Simplified Representation of Repeated Game between Firm 1 and Firm 2

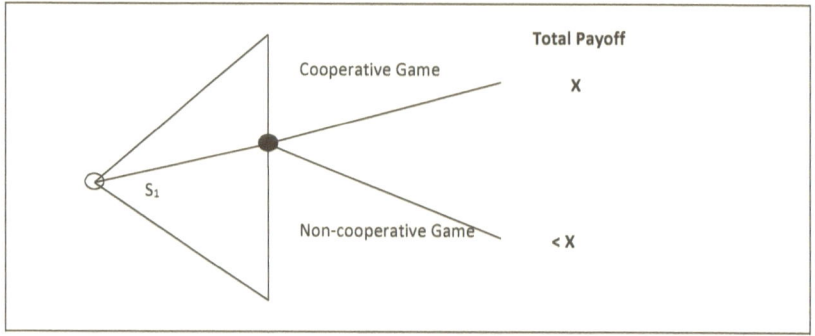

(Source: Authors, 2009, 2020)

Real Option Theory

In a dynamic environment like the private residential development market, real options can exist in various forms. Chapter 2 evaluates the option value for entering a new market. The aim is to find out whether to invest earlier or later is better, and to find out the decision boundaries from the perspective of real option theory. Residential development projects take significant time to complete. Today's decision for each residential developer player to enter a new private residential development market is much influenced by today's assumption and information about the private residential market outlook. The demand for the new market is uncertain. The investment is very risky as it is capital intensive. By deferring the decision, the rival residential developers may enter the market first for a similar residential product. Then, that developer is able to observe the response for the market, making the investment decision a little less uncertain. The following experimental example depicts the case in Fig 3. For instance, firm 1 has options to invest now or 2 periods later in a new private residential development market. Invest now because the market condition is uncertain and firm 1 may enter a 'below-average', the 'average', or an 'above-average' market with equal probabilities (i.e. 1/3). By entering a 'below-average' market, the constant demand, q_t for each period is 1. If the market appears to be 'average' or 'above-average' then q_t is 2 and 3 respectively. However, Firm 1 monopolizes the market for the first 2 periods, after which there would be n firms coming into the market and sharing the demand. Given the profit per unit, π, then firm 1's option value of investing now is estimated by eq 1, and the option value for node 1 in the different scenarios would be obtained as depicted in Fig 3.

$$V0 = \pi \{1/3 [2(1) + (T-2)(1)/n] + 1/3 [2(2) + (T-2)(2)/n] + 1/3 [2(3) + (T-2)(3)/n]\} \quad (1)$$

If firm 1 defers the real estate development after observing the market condition, then it must take at least another 2 periods to enter the market, owing to construction and other preparation works before the potential real estate development can be launched. By that time n firms play the market. Thus the option values for investing 2-periods later can be estimated by eq 2, and the option value for nodes 5, 6, and 7 in different scenarios can be estimated as depicted in Fig 3. Details of the equation calculus are provided in the Appendices for information.

$$V2 = \pi (T-2) qt/n \quad (2)$$

The values for deferring the real estate development decision would result from the difference between the two option values, V_0 and V_2. These values are presented in Table 1.

Table 1. The Value Of Deferring The Real Estate Development Decision

	10			20			40		
q_t	2	3	4	2	3	4	2	3	4
1	-40	-33.4	-30	-65	-50	-42.5	-115	-83.4	-67.5
2	-20	-20	-20	-20	-20	-20	-20	-20	-20
3	0	-6.7	-10	25	10	2.5	75	43.3	27.5

(Source: Authors, 2009 and 2020)

Fig 3. The Trinomial Option Tree To Defer

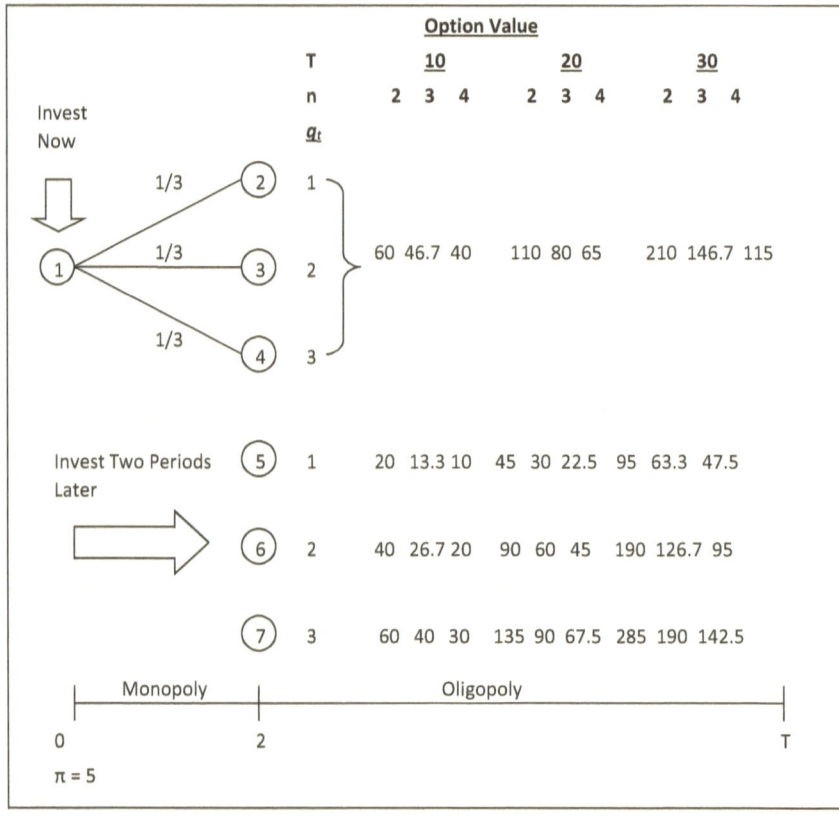

(Source: Authors, 2009 and 2020)

We can see that the real option to defer is only of value when the market is favorable when the q_t is 3, and that T must be greater than 10. This implies that the second movers are better off when the market appears to be 'above-average'. We can observe that the real option value decreases as the number of players increase, and as the number of periods in the market decrease. There can be more scenarios available. Thus, to pick the right option, the developers must find the most likely scenario in order to make their development decisions accordingly.

Specification of 'The Simplified and Unique Experimental Research Design'

A simplified experimental research design is uniquely configured for Chapter 2 to capture the setting of Singapore's private residential development market. It incorporates as many key features as possible to reflect the real world setting. Certain aspects need to be simplified because it is impossible to capture all possible states of this market in the real world. Furthermore, the participating real estate developers may be confused if the experiment is too complex. They are not fully experienced private residential developers, as we use undergraduate students in the Department of Real Estate, National University of Singapore to be the participating residential developers as the players under guided instructions. The game theoretic approach is adopted to conduct the simplified experimental research design. The players are deemed to be oligopolistic ones that are engaged in an interactive "game", as their actions are highly influential on other players. The "game" in turn is highly specified in terms of its several unique features, the nature of interaction and assumptions as outlined below.

Feature 1 – The private real estate development market is oligopolistic. The game models an oligopolistic private residential development market in Singapore, where participating residential developer's actions highly influence one another, and that the combination of their strategies determines the payoffs for each player. There are 12 players acting as the oligopolistic developers, with each developer being given a set of instructions before a game starts. Calculation sheets are issued to enable them to record their pricing details (see Appendices). After their games, they are asked to answer some qualitative questions (see Appendices). Consistent with game theory, their strategies should be exhaustive through each of the 12 developers stating all the strategy possibilities that a player would adopt. Owing to practical constraints of the experimental research, the strategies also conform to the following features 2 to 9 below.

Feature 2 – Residential developers hold conflicting interests and compete with one other through pricing strategies. Each of the 12 residential developer aims at maximizing its profits through pricing strategies. The first player who first sets the price in a new sub-market, i.e. the price leader, resort to the following strategies:

i) Setting a high price to get high profit.
ii) Setting a low price to depress the market price.
iii) Revising the initial or previous price in response to the rivals' actions. The strategies available are the same for the price followers.

Subsequent developers, i.e. the price followers, resort to the strategies:

i) Following the prevailing price set by the previous player.
ii) Pricing the units higher than the prevailing price.
iii) Pricing the units lower than the prevailing price.

Feature 3 - Developers have the opportunities to enter a new sub-market. When the residential developers have sufficient funds, they resort to the following strategies:

i) Entering a new sub-market and being the first mover of a new residential development product.
ii) Entering into another and old sub-market.
iii) Do nothing.

Feature 4 - Payoffs to the residential developer are a function of the actions by all developers. The playing residential developers' payoffs are determined by the combined strategies by all developers in a sub-game. The price of developer i in a sub-game (SGx) is a function of several related factors as defined by eq 3.

$$p_i = f(p_{-i}, c_i, n, \mu_d, \sigma_d^2, OMV\hat{}, K) \quad (3)$$
, where $p_{-i} = (p_1, \ldots, p_{i-1}, p_{i+1}, \ldots, p_n)$

The demand function for player i is expressed in eq 4:

$$\text{If} \begin{cases} p_i = p\star, & q_i = q_t / n\star, \text{ where } q_i, q_t \in N^+ \\ p_i > p\star, & q_i = 0 \\ p_i < p\star, & q_i = q_t \end{cases} \quad (4)$$

The payoff function is $\Pi_i = (p_i - c_i) q_i$ \quad (5)

, where p_i and c_i denote respectively the product price per unit and cost per unit of developer i and $p\star$ is the lowest unit price offered by all developers in sub-game SGx up to period t. The "n" denotes the number of players in SGx. The μ_d and σ_d^2 are the mean and variance of a normally distributed demand. $OMV\hat{}$ is the estimated open market value of SGx and K is the capacity constraint of each developer, i.e. each developer can only produce 10 units in a sub-game. The "q_i" denotes the demand for developer i's units and q_t is the total demand for period t. The $n\star$ is the number of developers who offer $p\star$. Π_i denotes the payoff of developer i. Eq 4 implies that:

i) If developer i's price equals to the $p\star$, then it shares the demand with those who sell at $p\star$ in period t;
ii) If developer i's price is higher than $p\star$, then the demand on his units is zero;
iii) If developer i's price is lower than $p\star$, then he gets all the demand in period t

Note that when $p_i = p\star$ and if $q_t / n\star$ is not a round number, the demand is to be allocated to the developers randomly. For example, if q_t is 2 and $n\star$ is 3, then there is to be one player who prices at $p\star$ and gets zero demand. This is randomly selected.

Feature 5 - The rules whereby developers interact in a dynamic Singapore environment repeatedly. It is a dynamic game where developers set and revise their unit price in sequence. For e.g., in *SG1*, *D1* prices his units at $t = 1$ and *D2* prices his units at $t = 2$. This is followed by *D3* and *D4*. *D1* prices his units again at $t = 5$ after *D4* and the sequence is repeated. It enables the developers to observe one another's actions. At the beginning of each period, only one developer in a sub-game can set or reset its price. The payoffs of each developer would be announced at the end of each period. Developing a new residential development project requires 2 periods in order to do the necessary preparation before the project can be launched. Developers are told to regard this game as if it would continue infinitely but of course, the game would not continue infinitely in the experiment. Game 1 would stop at the end of $t = 40$ and Game 2 at $t = 20$ but the playing developers are not informed beforehand. The game is set to reflect the fact that the developers in the real world have no defined ending period, and that they do not act simultaneously. In fact, they can alter price even by an hour later after the other developer's action.

Feature 6 - The structure of the game where the residential development project in Singapore produces limited products and each project has its own capacity constraints. On the basis of 2 games, game 1 comprises 12 sub-games in total that represent the sub-markets of Singapore's private residential development market. The game starts with 3 sub-games (*SG1*, *SG2*, and *SG3*) and each game has 4 players, selling homogeneous residential development units. There are another 9 new sub-games (*SG4* to *SG12*) that represent sub-markets, which have not been developed by any developer before. Each developer develops 10 residential units for sale and to venture into new markets, the developers are required to raise

THE VERSATILITY OF THE REAL ESTATE ASSET CLASS - THE SINGAPORE EXPERIENCE

sufficient funds, say '30 points', in order to develop another 10 units in another sub-game. Developers would get back the '30 points' upon selling all the residential development units in that sub-game, on top of the profits gained but they are not allowed to develop units in the current sub-game. This is to avoid any developer being able to build up any influence in a particular sub-game. Another reason is that the simplified experimental research design seeks to examine the experienced structural pricing behavior by letting the developers play the game several times but not with the same competitors, in order to reduce any possible biases. So, they must invest in another sub-game or do nothing with the funds. For game 2, only *SG1*, *SG2* and *SG3* are opened. Four players are in a fixed play in one of the sub-games *SGs* where once the developers sell sold off all the 10 residential development units, then they would automatically be given another 10 units to sell. Besides the market volatility, everything else is the same with game 1.

Feature 7 - Information conditions for residential development units launched before completion and their unit prices are based on leading indicators. It is industry practice in Asia and Singapore that private residential development units are sold "off-plan", and that these units embody a wide variety of characteristics. Because the units are sold off-plan for a private residential development project, some elements of quality are idiosyncratic and cannot be valued objectively by buyers and sellers (Read, 1988). Buyers and sellers rely on leading indicators of the wider domestic private residential market. In Chapter 2's simplified experimental research design, developers would be given an open market value (OMV) as a rough estimate of the date of anticipated completion. As long as the price is within a given price range, there should be demand for the private residential development sale units.

Feature 8 – Residential Developers in Singapore make decisions to develop under market uncertainty and incomplete information about their rival developers

Feature 9 - Cost advantage is rare within the Singapore private residential development market. In the simplified experimental research design, the playing residential developers are not given full information about one another and market conditions. Each has a different unit cost as summarized in Table 2. The developers only know their own cost condition as indicated in the calculation sheets (see *Appendices*) but they do know that their fellow developers would not have a significant cost advantage over them. Such a setting reflects the fact that the residential developers are not likely to acquire full information about their fellow developers, and that the cost advantage rarely happens in the private residential development market. Additionally, developers do not know the actual demand for each sub-game before setting or resetting their selling prices while demand follows a normal distribution. Developers are informed of the mean, μ_d (SGx) and the variance, σ_d^2 of demand for each sub-game. The "μ_d (SGx)" would be different across the sub-games, and would stay constant over time for simplicity. In contrast, the σ_d^2 would be universal but it would change in game 2. As for new sub-games, SG4 to SG12, there would be 3 possible outcomes due to market conditions, namely the 'average' market, 'above-average' market and 'below-average' market. They differ by the mean demand, μ_d (SGx). If it turns out that the market is 'average', then the mean demand is the same with those of SG1, SG2, and SG3, i.e. μ_d (SGx) = 2. The μ_d (SGx) = 3 and μ_d (SGx) = 1 when the market is 'above-average' and 'below-average' respectively. Market volatility refers to the variance of the entire market, i.e. game, labeled σ_d^2 and that the probability of getting either one of the market conditions is the same, i.e. $P(\mu_d$ (SGi) = 2) = $P(\mu_d$ (SGi) = 4) = $P(\mu_d$ (SGi) = 0) = 1/3. The nature of market conditions is depicted in Fig 4. At the end of each period t, the demand q_t would be announced for each sub-game. When a developer enters into a new sub-game, the estimated OMV would be announced. However, the market condition is informed only when the residential development units are launched, i.e. 2 periods after the developer enters a sub-game SG.

Table 2. Cost per Unit of the Individual Singapore Private Residential Developer in Different Sub-games

Developer	Cost per Unit		
	SG1/4/7/10	SG2/5/8/11	SG3/6/9/12
D1	4	2	1
D2	3	3	1
D3	3	3	1
D4	4	3	0
D5	4	2	1
D6	4	3	0
D7	3	3	1
D8	4	3	0
D9	4	2	1
D10	3	3	1
D11	4	3	0
D12	4	2	1

(Source: Authors, 2009)

On the nature of the interaction for the simplified experimental research design, the private residential development unit purchasers are deemed to be price conscious. Since the residential units are deemed to be homogenous, purchasers buy whichever unit is cheaper. As such, residential developers need to compete with fellow developers to ensure that they can clear their units. They can be cooperative or competitive. If a developer cooperates, i.e. following whatever price set by the previous developer, then it shares the available demand equally for that period.

Fig 4. Decision Tree for the Capital Level of '30 Points'

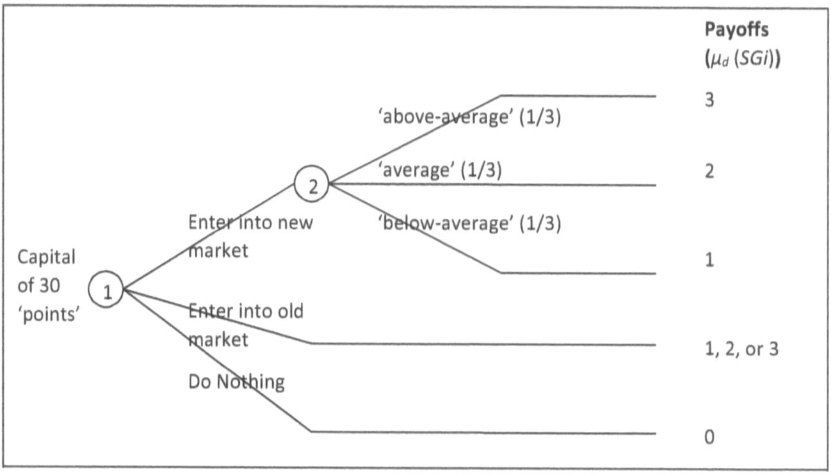

```
                                                                Payoffs
                                                                (μ_d (SGi))

                                    'above-average' (1/3)         3
                                    'average' (1/3)               2
                          ②
                  Enter into new    'below-average' (1/3)
Capital           market                                          1
of 30      ①
'points'          Enter into old
                  market                                          1, 2, or 3

                  Do Nothing
                                                                  0
```

(Source: Authors, 2009 and 2020)

At the same time, it signals to other developer that it is seeking cooperation. A Singapore private residential developer can also undercut the prevailing lowest price so as to get the whole share of demand for that period, then it would signal to others that it is not being cooperative. This is likely to trigger a "price war". Furthermore, no communication among the developers is allowed. Thus, collusion would be difficult. All they can do is to signal to others via pricing strategy and to observe their fellow developers' pricing behavior.

On the several assumptions that are imperative for the simplified experimental research design, they are outlined below:

Homogenous Products. In the real world, private residential development units should be heterogeneous. However, the game assumes that all units in a sub-market are identical. This allows the developers to concentrate on their fellow developers' pricing behavior. Nevertheless, this assumption does not completely violate the heterogeneity feature of the private residential development market. Although the units in a sub-market are not completely identical, they should not have too great discrepancies.

An informationally efficient market. The information flows concerning the prices of the residential development units are efficient, and all purchasers share the same information set. All of the residential development unit purchasers are notified about first-hand information of the selling prices offered by fellow developers.

Purchasers are price conscious and rational. They would only buy the Singapore private residential development units in a sub-game with the lowest price.

The only objective of residential developers is to maximize their wealth. This is the most common objective of a rational private residential developer.

Identical demand distribution across a price range. Because the private residential development sale units are launched and sold off-plan, it is assumed that some idiosyncratic features are not observable by the residential development unit purchasers. Thus, within a reasonable price range, they accept the offered price.

Results and Findings

This section is concerned with the results and findings of the simplified and unique experimental research design to structure behavioral pricing within the context of the Singapore private residential development market. Three research questions, as mentioned earlier, are examined where game 1 is meant for the first two research questions while game 2 is solely meant for the third research question. Detailed results for the experimental research design are provided in the Appendices for information purposes. Under the required private residential development market setting of game 1, the first research question is examined below:

R1.   *Under the private residential development market, what are the equilibrium residential development unit price and the intrinsic structural pricing behavior?*

Intuitively, the pricing decision is simple to comprehend – lower the price and residential development sales go up. However, "when you lower your price, your competitors would match the price or may even undercut you in response, and you would not have any advantage by simply reducing your unit price". It is more complex than such a statement. Fig 5 and its box plots give us some sense of how the **inexperienced residential developers** would price their sale units. They are deemed to be inexperienced because at this stage no element of learning exists. They tend to undercut each other aggressively until it is close to zero profit for their own interest (note that the entire price per unit and the cost per unit are adjusted to the scale from 0 to 10 and 0 to 2 respectively). The first units are sold at around '7 points' and prices are decreasing quite drastically to '2 points'. It is worth noting that developers then begin to realize the consequences of aggressive pricing after reaping a very low profit. They try to raise the selling price in the midst of selling their first 10 units.

They signal their intention through a high enough price and forgo demand for several periods but they fail owing to too many players in a sub-game (or sub-market), which makes it even harder for cooperation. In the last 2 periods, some of the developers are finally able to cooperate with a lesser number of fellow residential developers to monopolize the sub-game *SG* and to sell high in turn. This is because some of the developers have sold off all their residential development sale units, and have moved to the other sub-game *SG*. On the basis of these findings, it supports quite closely the theoretical Bertrand's zero-profit equilibrium.

Fig 5. Pricing Pattern for the 1st 10 Units (the First Development)

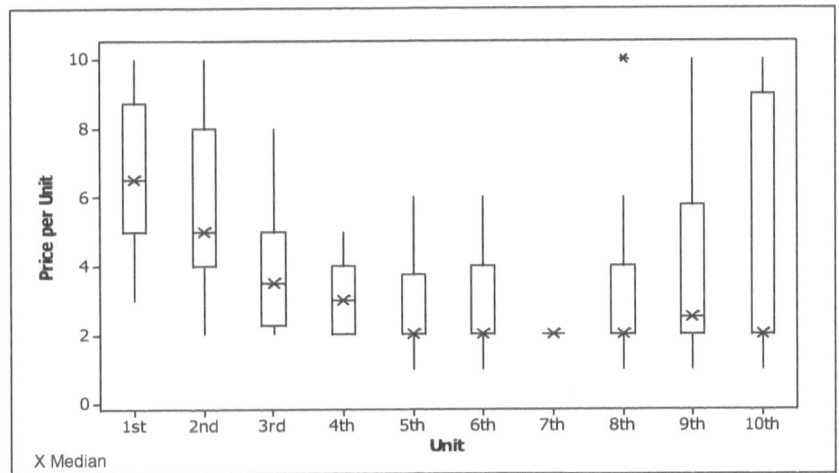

(Source: Authors, 2009 and 2020)

Nevertheless, it would be more precise to examine the behavioral pricing structure of the **experienced residential developers**. The lesson of their first development provides the foundation for them to price prudently and strategically in subsequent private residential developments. Fig 6 and its box plots exhibit the pricing pattern, which stems from the interaction among experienced residential developers.

Fig 6. Pricing Pattern for the Subsequent Private Residential Developments

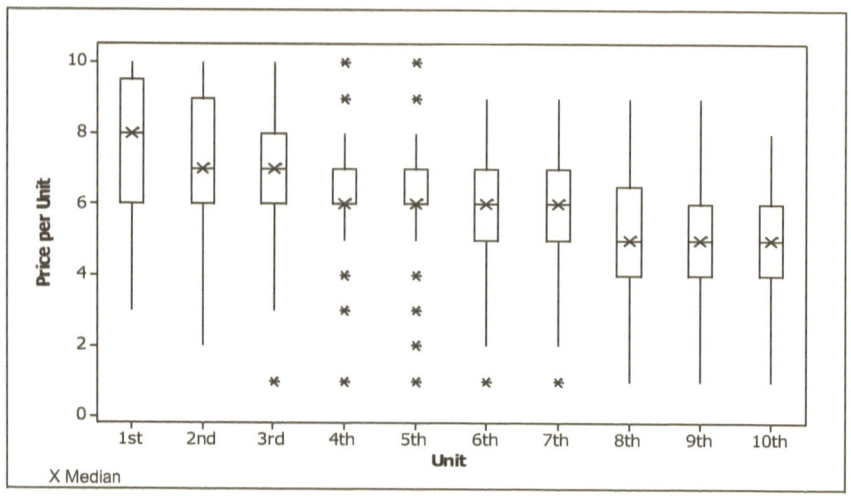

(Source: Authors, 2009 and 2020)

The results are very much different from the previous observations. We observe that prices are more stable and higher on average. Prices begin with around '8 points' and tend to decrease gradually in the first 4 units and to stabilize at '6 points' for the next 4 residential development sale units. Prices drop again for the last few unsold units. Also note that the variation in prices by all the developers is more convergent relative to the behavioral pricing structure of their first development.

Godi and Reyhons (1980) reiterate that in those markets where prices are volatile and demand seems to change almost daily, it is generally difficult to recommend an exact price. Indeed and from the foregoing results, it is inconclusive to indicate an equilibrium price - we cannot find a price that is stable and with no incentive to deviate. However, the results shed light on the intrinsic behavioral pricing structure in the private residential development market. The results point towards collusion and violate the theoretic non-cooperative outcomes of finite games as mentioned earlier. This is owing to the different nature of the finite interaction in Chapter

THE VERSATILITY OF THE REAL ESTATE ASSET CLASS - THE SINGAPORE EXPERIENCE

2's simplified experimental research design. Although the playing residential developers are finitely interacting in a sub-game *SG*, each developer exits the *SG* at a different period depending on when its units are sold completely. When a developer exits the *SG*, the rest of the fellow developers are continuing the game, and there would be new entrants coming in. Simply put, developers play finitely in an infinite game. The incentive for deviation is only applicable to those who are about to leave the game. In addition, as the developers repeat the game they come to realize that collusive pricing strategy is more beneficial. They are more willing to cooperate. Bearing this in mind, the playing residential developers tend to be more defensive. If anyone undercuts the prevailing price then it would try to maintain price for long-term benefit. The rationale is simple - because residential developers know that it is easy to trigger a price war, which in turn causes the prevailing price to drop tremendously but that it would be hard to increase the prevailing price.

These results lead to six key propositions, with the first four propositions obtained from examining the first research question and subsequently one key proposition from examining the second research question, while another key proposition is obtained from examining the third research question.

Proposition 1 - Under the oligopolistic private residential development market, competing residential developers resort to collusive pricing strategy for long-term benefit

The classic Bertrand pricing equilibrium does not occur here. Almost all prices can make positive profits (>0). The results in fact support this notion by Edgeworth (1925), Kreps and Scheinkman (1983) and by Friedman (1971), who reiterate that the classic Bertrand equilibrium does not hold when the features of capacity constraints, the irregularity of return and repeating interactions are introduced to the model. Generally, a private residential development project produces limited new supply owing to high capital outlay, high risk, uncertainties and other specific risk considerations. The limited products give the developers an incentive to share the demand with rivals, and to sell slowly but to seek a high profit per unit. When the private residential development market is uncertain and information about one's rival developers is incomplete, then developers tend to be more conservative. Coupled with the lessons learnt after going through the game several times, the collusive outcomes are more appealing. In general, the results also support proposition 2:

Proposition 2 - Under a game setting with inherent capacity constraints, the irregularity of return andwith repeating interactions introduced, the private residential development sale price would not be in equilibrium, which soon reaches to zero profit

While the overall pricing trend is considerably stable, the playing residential developers seem to have the incentives to deviate for the first and last few residential development sale units. According to the qualitative feedback from the playing residential developers, the price cut in the first few development sale units is possibly because the estimated open market value (OMV) of a mere '5 points' is reasonable beyond which the profit is deemed to be a bonus. Developers prefer to set the highest possible price when they first enter the private residential development market. Thus, there is enough room to undercut price. Despite such possible explanations, price is set against the developer's required rate of return in the Singapore context. Under this behavioral pricing and unless the residential developer monopolizes a new housing product or if demand is remarkably strong, then a typical private residential development would realize stable (equilibrium) pricing and provide a reasonable range for the required rate of return. Proposition 3 is consequently stated.

Proposition 3 – Super abnormal profit is hardly possible in an oligopoly and collusive efforts are more stable at a reasonable price (profit) range

Based on the playing residential developers' feedback, the end effect happens because developers prefer to sell quickly all their few remaining development sale units, so as to get back their initial '30 points', which also amount to the production cost for their next residential development(s). The condition of having the '30 points' refund is meant to enable pricing for the illiquid private residential development market. Such behavioral pricing supports the notion that cash liquidity is a main concern for residential developers. Developers would rather forsake higher profits for shorter time on the market in order to move their private development sale stock. This outcome is consistent with the empirical evidence of Belkin, Hempel, and McLeavey (1976) in that the ratio of selling price to list price is inversely related to time on the market. As a consequence, proposition 4 can be stated below.

Proposition 4 - Besides profit maximizing, residential developers are motivated to sell quickly at a cheap price to generate cash liquidity for their next private residential development(s)

We break down the price-per-unit distribution into three types of market conditions - 'below-average' ($\mu_d = 1$), 'average' ($\mu_d = 2$), and 'above-average' ($\mu_d = 3$) sub-markets. Fig 7 generalizes the breakdown of behavioral pricing under the different market conditions. When demand is low i.e. $\mu_d = 1$, competition is intense and developers tend to price undercut each other. Prices per unit are decreasing quite drastically from '9 points' to '2 points', at which levels profits are zero or nearly zero. In contrast, when demand is good, i.e. $\mu_d = 3$, prices stay at a high level with minimal price change. Price movements tend to be stable while prices are relatively more convergent in the normal market, i.e. $\mu_d = 2$. Such observed trends are consistent with microeconomic theory in which equilibrium prices increase as demand increases.

Fig 7. Pricing Patterns Under Three Residential Development Market Conditions

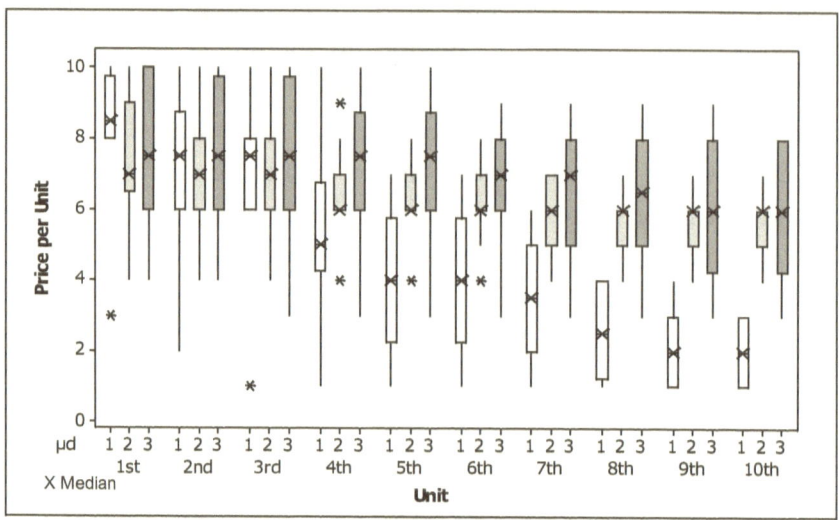

(Source: Authors, 2009 and 2020)

In addition and under the required private residential development market setting of game 1, the second research question is examined as follows:

R2. *In a dynamic private residential development market, is the first mover or the second mover more advantageous?*

We first define the first mover and the second mover as follows:

- The *First mover* is the first playing residential developer, who enters a certain market, which is new and the demand is not known.
- The *Second mover* is the immediate playing residential developer, who enters the new market, ventured by the first mover, and after observing the response of that particular market.

As a general theory, second movers are better off than first movers in a market with incomplete information (Choi & Jagpal, 2004). We next adopt the Wilcoxon matched-pairs, signed-rank test to test whether the first or second mover holds in the private residential development market. However, we find that the second-mover advantage does not seem to hold in our analysis, a behavior akin to industry practice in the Singapore private residential development market.

From Fig 4's decision tree on the capital Level of '30 Points', there are three possibilities pertaining to the demand condition for the new market, namely, 'below-average', 'average', and 'above-average'. The second mover would follow by entering a market with 'average' or 'above-average' demand condition, given that the existing and available market has the 'average' demand condition. What if the market condition is 'below-average'? A rational player would then rather choose to enter an old 'average' market. Taking into consideration opportunity cost and when the market has 'below-average' demand condition, then the "second mover" of that market is a mover that ventures into the other sub-market at a "right period". To be precise, two periods after the first mover enters the market would be the right timing for the second mover to enter, as this is the period just after the observation of the response. Note that some of the first-movers and second-movers of a certain sub-game SG are not selected, owing to the practical limitation of the game arrangements. From Table 3, two parameters are used to test the advantageous position, namely total profit and time on market, for the 10-unit residential development.

Table 3. Total Profits and Time on Market for the First and Second Movers

	First Mover			Second Mover		
Residential Developer (Sub-Game)	Profit ('point')	Time[a] ('Period')	Residential Developer (Sub-Game)	Profit ('point')	Time[a] ('Period')
D1 (SG4)	60	17	D7 (SG9)[b]	41	16

D1 (SG5)	59	20	D5 (SG5)	49	18
D12 (SG7)	60	11	D6 (SG7)	51	13
D3 (SG8)	59	14	D8 (SG8)	46	12
D1 (SG9)	63	9	D7 (SG9)	46	4
D10 (SG10)	51	13	D12 (SG10)	42	9
D5 (SG11)	47	20	D11 (SG7)[b]	46	14
D6 (SG12)	131	10	D2 (SG12)	66	16
Median	59.5	13.5		46	13.5

[a] NB. If there are units unsold in the last period i.e. $t = 40$, it is assumed that each remaining unit takes one period to sell. [b] NOTE: Selected second mover from a different *SG*. (Source: Authors, 2009 and 2020)

In accordance with the studies by Amir and Stepanova (2006) and Choi and Jagpal (2004) we form the following hypotheses:

H1. Total profit gained by the second mover is greater than that of the first mover in every sub-game *SG*.

H2. Time on market for the private residential development sale units of the first mover is longer than that of the second mover in every sub-game *SG*.

H1 and H2 are tested through the Wilcoxon matched-pairs, signed-rank test for which the results are presented in Table 4 and Table 5. Table 4 shows that all 8 new *SG*s have negative ranks. In other words, the profits for first movers are always greater than that for the second movers. This indicates an inclination that first movers are more advantageous than second movers in terms of the profit gained. Table 4 also shows that when the test statistic is based on positive ranks, the z-score is –2.52, and that this value is significant at the probability $p = 0.01$. Therefore, because this value is based on the positive ranks, we conclude that there is sufficient evidence that the first movers' profits are greater than the second movers. The results disprove hypothesis H1.

Table 5 shows further information concerning the ranked scores where 6 out of the 8 *SG*s indicate that the first mover takes a longer period to sell off the 10-unit residential development. The remaining

THE VERSATILITY OF THE REAL ESTATE ASSET CLASS - THE SINGAPORE EXPERIENCE

2 *SGs* indicate otherwise. Table 5 also shows the test statistic, based on the positive ranks, where the z-score is −1.06, and that this value is significant at $p = 0.29$. Therefore, there is insufficient evidence to indicate that the time on market for the first movers' development is longer than that for the second movers' development. The results disprove hypothesis H2. Interestingly, the first set of results even disproves the hypothesized outcomes. Hence, the generalized theory of the second-mover advantage may not seem to hold in the Singapore private residential development market. As a consequence, we can state proposition 5 below.

Table 4. Wilcoxon Matched-Pairs, Signed-Rank Test Results For H1

Ranks

		N	Mean Rank	Sum of Ranks
SECOND - FIRST	Negative Ranks	8[a]	4.50	36.00
	Positive Ranks	0[b]	.00	.00
	Ties	0[c]		
	Total	8		

a. SECOND < FIRST
b. SECOND > FIRST
c. SECOND = FIRST

Test Statistics[b]

	SECOND - FIRST
Z	-2.524[a]
Asymp. Sig. (2-tailed)	.012

a. Based on positive ranks.
b. Wilcoxon Signed Ranks Test

(Source: Authors, 2009 and 2020; SPSS V5)

Table 5. Wilcoxon Matched-Pairs, Signed-Rank Test Results For H2

Ranks

		N	Mean Rank	Sum of Ranks
SECOND_M - FIRST_M	Negative Ranks	6a	4.25	25.50
	Positive Ranks	2b	5.25	10.50
	Ties	0c		
	Total	8		

a. SECOND_M < FIRST_M
b. SECOND_M > FIRST_M
c. SECOND_M = FIRST_M

Test Statisticsb

	SECOND_M - FIRST_M
Z	-1.057a
Asymp. Sig. (2-tailed)	.291

a. Based on positive ranks.
b. Wilcoxon Signed Ranks Test

(Source: Authors, 2009 and 2020; SPSS V5)

Proposition 5 - First-mover advantage is prevalent in the private residential development market in the presence of uncertainty and cost similarities

The second-mover advantage does not seem to hold in the private residential development market within the Singapore context, owing to four reasons. First, private residential developments differ from one another, as construction lags differ along time and with approval time for the residential developments to be launched. Time lag between the first and second movers to launch their residential developments provides the first mover with a period of monopoly power, enabling it to 'grab' a much greater share of demand. Chances of acquiring super abnormal profit are high, an example of this behavior is given by the first mover in sub-game *SG12* of Table 3. In addition and by the time the second mover is launching its residential development sale units, the first mover depresses price while demand is shared among existing residential developers. Secondly and when the private residential development market is unfavorable, most residential developers would resist entering that market. In sub-games *SG4* and *SG11* and where the market is unfavorable, second movers that develop residential sale units in the other old *SGs* do not show any major advantage. This is primarily because *SG4* and *SG11* have less supply in their development stock and face less rival residential developers. Thirdly and unlike the Stackelberg game, Chapter 2's uniquely simplified experimental research design permits first movers to revise their selling price after the second movers' reactions. As such, first and second movers have equal control on prevailing market price. Fourthly, first movers have the flexibility for price setting and benchmarking. Some first movers do intentionally lower the prevailing price to discourage residential developers from entering the market.

The final part of this section examines the third research question below:

R3.   How would behavioral pricing be affected by market uncertainties?

We first compare behavioral pricing in game 1 and game 2 where demand volatilities are given as $\sigma_d^{t\,2} = 1$ and $\sigma_d^{t\,2} = 2$ respectively. To be consistent, only sub-games *SG1*, *SG*, and *SG3* that have the same average demand are taken for this comparison. To capture the experienced playing residential developers' pricing behavior, the first developments in game 1 are neglected. Fig 8 and its box plots depict the results for game 1 and game 2. Two important insights are observed. First, prices under the more volatile markets are stabilizing at prices lower than those under the less volatile markets. Secondly, the greater the volatility then the greater the variation in prices. The results are consistent with the findings by Choi and Jagpal (2004).

Fig 8. Pricing Patterns Under Two Demand Volatilities

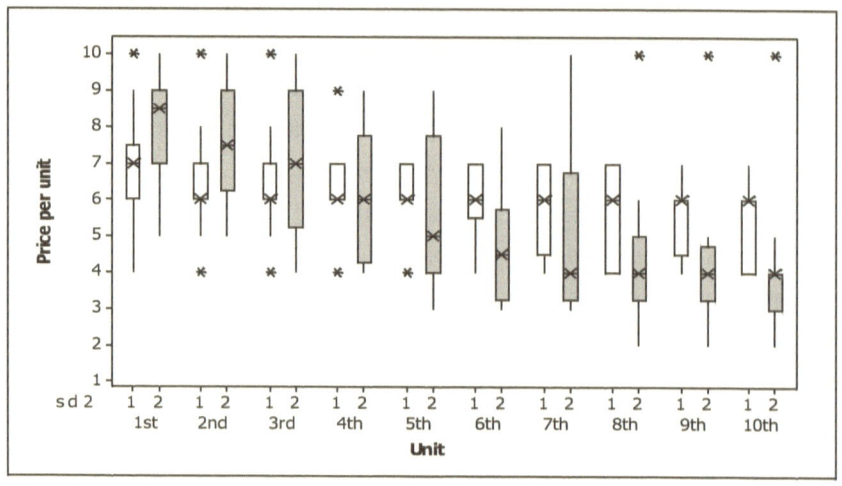

(Source: Authors, 2009 and 2020)

The corresponding hypothesis is next tested through the Mann-Whitney Test:

H3. Prices under more volatile markets are lower than prices under less volatile markets.

H4. Prices under more volatile markets are lower than prices under less volatile markets.

From Table 6, the one-tailed p-value is significant at 0.023 (< 0.05). We can conclude that there is sufficient evidence that prices under more volatile markets are significantly lower than prices under the less volatile markets. As a consequence, proposition 6 can be stated as follows.

Proposition 6 - When demand becomes more uncertain, private residential development sale prices in Singapore are lower albeit with greater variation in prices within the same development.

Table 6. Mann-Whitney Test Results for H3

Mann-Whitney Test
and CI: GAME1, GAME2

N Median
GAME1 130 6.0000
GAME2 120 5.0000
Point estimate for ETA1-ETA2 is 1.0000
95.0 Percent CI for ETA1-ETA2 is (0.0001,1.0002)
W = 17434.0
Test of ETA1 = ETA2 vs ETA1 > ETA2 is significant at 0.0251
The test is significant at 0.0232 (adjusted for ties)

(Source: Authors, 2009 and 2020; Minitab V5)

On the whole, the key features discussed introduced in the uniquely simplified experimental research design, makes the results unique to the private residential development market within the Singapore context. A main insight alludes to the collusion practice as advocated by Chamberlin (1929) to the non-zero profit equilibrium as advocated by Edgeworth (1925), Kreps and Scheinkman (1983) and Friedman (1971). Four other main insights include the 'normal' profit nature of the oligopolistic private residential development market, the importance of cash liquidity, the first-mover advantage and the inverse relationship between private residential development market sale price and its uncertainty.

Concluding Remarks

Chapter 2 looks at the merits of a uniquely simplified experimental research design for the strategic behavioral pricing of the private residential development market under a game theoretic approach, within the context of Singapore. Three research questions are examined where game 1 is meant for the first two research questions while game 2 is solely meant for the third research question. The first research question seeks the observable equilibrium price and its intrinsic behavioral pricing structure under the private residential development market. The results are insightful and conclusive with respect to the collusion structural pricing model where private residential developers cooperate implicitly for long-term benefit. Despite the lacking of conclusive equilibrium prices, it is clear from the results that the zero-profit equilibrium by Bertrand would not be applicable. In addition, residential developers are motivated to deviate from cooperation at the beginning and at the end of successive periods in a sub-market. Relatively high profits, earnable in the first few periods, provide an allowance for them to price undercut others in order to sell faster. For the last few periods, their penalty for deviation is insignificant or zero. For the same reason, they are motivated to deviate.

The second research question is concerned with the relative position of the first mover and the second mover. Because of private residential development market uncertainty and incomplete information, coupled with the non-existence of cost advantage, Chapter 2 reveals that the second mover is not advantageous. Interestingly, the results violate the theoretical results of a Stackelberg game, i.e. the results support the conclusion that the first mover is more advantageous. This is mainly owing to certain features that are absent in the Stackelberg game. Unlike the Stackelberg game, the second mover is envisaged to take a moderately long period to respond while the first mover is allowed to revise its decision after the second mover's actions. Under such an arrangement, the first mover has more control over the second mover. Furthermore, he stands a better chance to gain super abnormal profits, and to sell more quickly his residential development sale units during its monopoly-power period.

The third research question is concerned with the effect of uncertainty on prices. The results show that as the private residential development market uncertainty increases, then private residential development sale prices decrease and the variability in prices increases. Future research may be undertaken on the basis of Chapter

2's findings to examine the dynamic game involving the empirical behavior of residential developers and their purchasers.

Acknowledgement

The author wishes to gratefully acknowledge the initial work carried out for Chapter 2 by Mr HO Tat Wing, a graduate of the NUS Department of Real Estate; and in consultation with Honorary Professor (University of Hertfordshire, Hatfield, UK), Dr HO Kim Hin / David and Professor in Building & Real Estate, Dr HUI Chi Man / Eddie (The Hon Kong Polytechnic, SAR China); during their meaningful brain storming sessions before Professor HO retired from the NUS SDE Department of Real Estate in May 2020.

Chapter 2. Strategic Behavioral Pricing of the Private Residential Development Market - A Simplified Experimental Approach. The <u>Appendices</u>

Appendix A   Derivation of Eq(1) and Eq(2)

<u>Option 1: Invest at $t = 0$</u>

Invest at $t = 0$, Firm i enjoys 2 periods of monopoly market. Then, the Firm i operates in an oligopolistic market for the remaining (T-2) periods, where T is the last period before all the residential units sold.

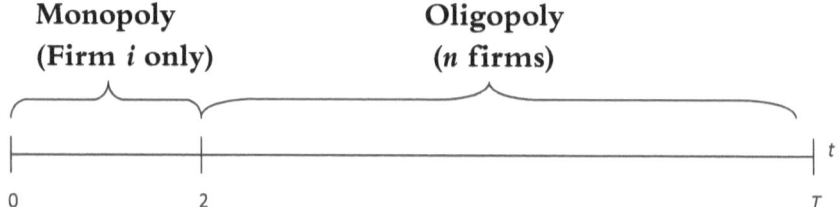

Firm i, the first mover, is uncertain about the demand. The Probabilities of getting the mean demand, q_t = 1, 2, or 3 are the same (i.e. 1/3).

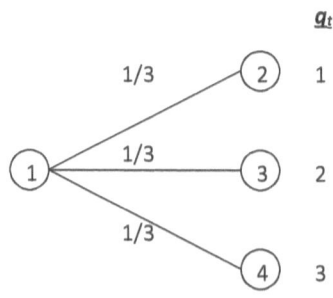

Therefore, the quantities sold in monopoly periods (2 periods) are estimated using equation below:

$$q_{i,\,0\text{-}2} = 1/3\,(1)(2) + 1/3\,(2)(2) + 1/3\,(3)(2) \qquad (i)$$

Quantities sold in oligopoly periods (T-2 periods) are estimated using equation below:

$$q_{i,\,2\text{-}T} = 1/3\,(1)(T\text{-}2)/n + 1/3(2)(T\text{-}2)/n + 1/3(3)(T\text{-}2)/n \qquad (ii)$$

Thus, the total quantities sold for the entire period on the market is the summation of eq(i) and eq (ii):

$$q_{i,0-T} = 1/3\,[2(1) + (T-2)(1)/n] + 1/3\,[2(2) + (T-2)(2)/n] + 1/3\,[2(3) + (T-2)(3)/n]$$

Given the profit per unit is π, then the option value of option 1 is thus estimated using the eq(1):

$$V_0 = \pi\,\{1/3\,[2(1) + (T-2)(1)/n] + 1/3\,[2(2) + (T-2)(2)/n] + 1/3\,[2(3) + (T-2)(3)/n] \qquad (1)$$

Option 2: Invest at $t = 2$

Adopting this option, the firm, say Firm j, operates in an oligopolistic market for the entire time on the market.

The demand condition (mean demand) is known after $t = 2$. During the period from 2 to T, the mean demand, qt will be 1, 2, or 3. Therefore, the quantities sellable can be estimated using equation below:

$q_{j,\ 2-T\ =\ (T-2)}\ qt\ /\ n$, where $qt = 1, 2,$ or 3 \hfill (iii)

Given the profit per unit is π, then the option value of option 2 is thus estimated using the eq(2):

$$V_2 = \pi\ (T-2)\ q_t\ /\ n \qquad (2)$$

Appendix B Instructions for Treatments

Welcome to this experiment. Please read these instructions carefully. In the next 5 to 6 hours you will have to make some pricing decisions in a simulated real estate environment. Although no real money involved, please bear in mind that you should treat the **'point'** as real money and your aim is to **increase your wealth**. But please be quiet during the entire experiment and do not talk to your neighbours. If you have any queries please raise your arm.

You are a developer $D\_\_$ who concentrates on housing development. Besides you there are 11 other firms who engage in the same business. Your task is to decide at which price to sell off your pre-completed units.

Rules of Game

Structure

You will be playing two games: Game 1 and Game 2. Game 1 comprises 12 sub-markets available for you to develop your housing units, i.e. *SG1 to SG12*. This is a dynamic game in which you and your rivals (re)set the selling price in sequence and you will begin your game in one of the *SGs* (please follow the sequence appear on the screen).

All the units in a sub-market are identical. Note that 'purchasers' are price conscious and you only compete with your direct rivals in the same *SG*. So,

iv) if your price is higher than your direct rivals, demand on your units is zero
v) if your price equals to the lowest prevailing price, you share the demand with those who sell at the same price as yours in that period

vi) if your price is lower than all your direct rivals, you gets all the demand in that period

You have zero 'point' (your capital) from the beginning. A capital of **30 'point'** is required for a new development. Other than the *SG(s)* you are currently operating in, you can develop (only) **10 housing units** in any *SGs* or do nothing. Note that it takes 2 periods to construct the foundation works and your units will be launch in the beginning of third period from the period you enter the *SG*. You will get back your 30 'point' invested upon all your units in that *SG* sold on top of the profits you gained.

For Game 2, you will be playing only in a *SG*. Once you sell off all your 10 units you will get another 10 units automatically in the same *SG*. Note that the market volatility are higher than in Game 1.

Demand

You will not know the exact demand before you (re)set your selling price. The demand is normally distributed and the average demand, μ_d (*SGi*) and market volatility, $\sigma_d^{t\,2}$ are publicly available (on screen). The demand of period *t* will be announced at the end of *t* and your quantity sold will also be told. It is worth noting that the μ_d (*SGi*) are different across sub-markets. In contrast, the $\sigma_d^{t\,2}$ are universal.

The demand for new *SGs* is not known. Developers have equal probability (1/3) entering into an 'above-average', 'average', or 'below-average' market. Each of the markets has different μ_d (*SGi*), depending on your luck (see *Figure 1*).You will only be told the μ_d (*SGi*) when your project is launched. (see *Figure 2 for the demand under the 3 market conditions*)

THE VERSATILITY OF THE REAL ESTATE ASSET CLASS - THE SINGAPORE EXPERIENCE

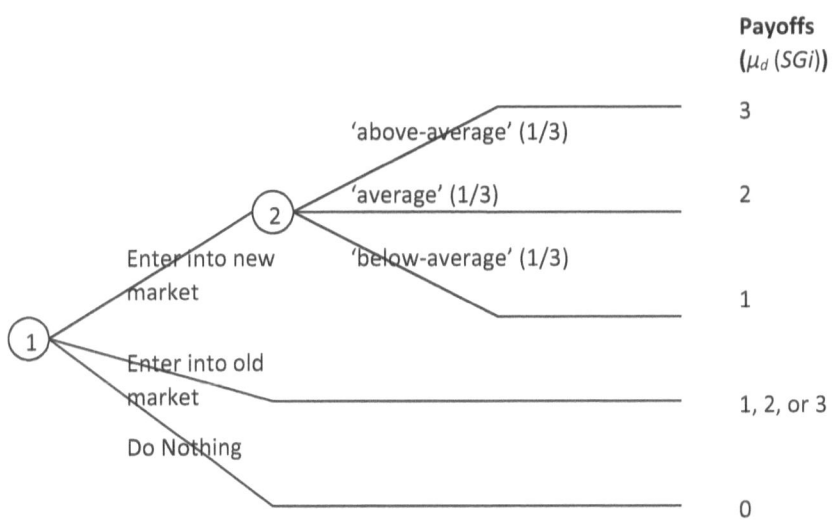

Figure 1: Decision Trees for the Capitals

Price

Because you are selling pre-completed units, your selling price should be based on leading indicator. You will be given **estimated OMV** as at the date of completion. Within a range of 5 'point', your selling price is considered reasonable and there will be demand for your pre-completed units.

Cost

Cost per unit is available in your calculation sheets. Each developer has different cost per unit. But, none of you have significant cost advantage over others.

Profit

Profit per unit is the difference between your price and the cost per unit. (The calculation sheets might be helpful). Your profit in a given period results from multiplying the profit per unit with your quantity sold.

Public Information

The public information channel (on screen) provides:
1) the selling prices set by your rivals;
2) the demand of a *SGi* at period *t*;
3) the housing stocks in the *SGs*;
4) the estimated OMV and the ceiling price beyond which the demand for your units is zero;
5) market conditions (i.e. the average demand, μ_d (*SGi*) and market volatility, σ'^2_d);
6) information about how many units you and your rivals sell in each period;
7) news about which developer(s) enter which *SG* and launch when; and
8) the sequence of moves (developers that can set price at certain period)

Please treat this experiment as an **infinite game**. The experiment will stop at a period that you do not know.

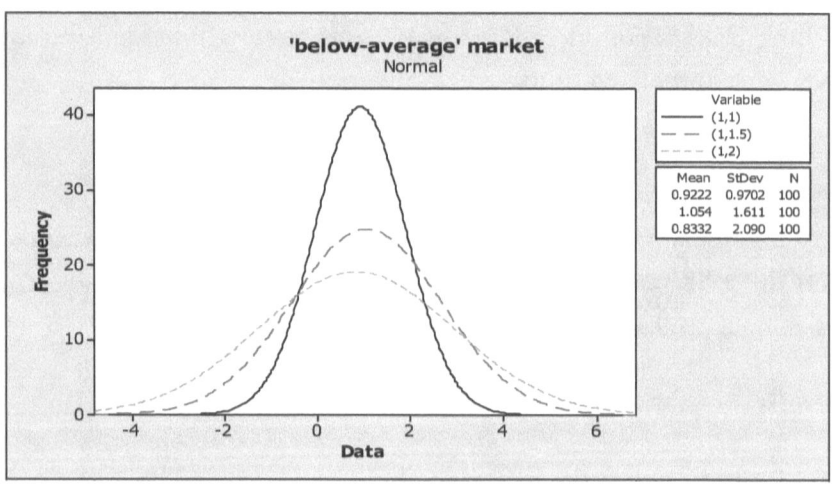

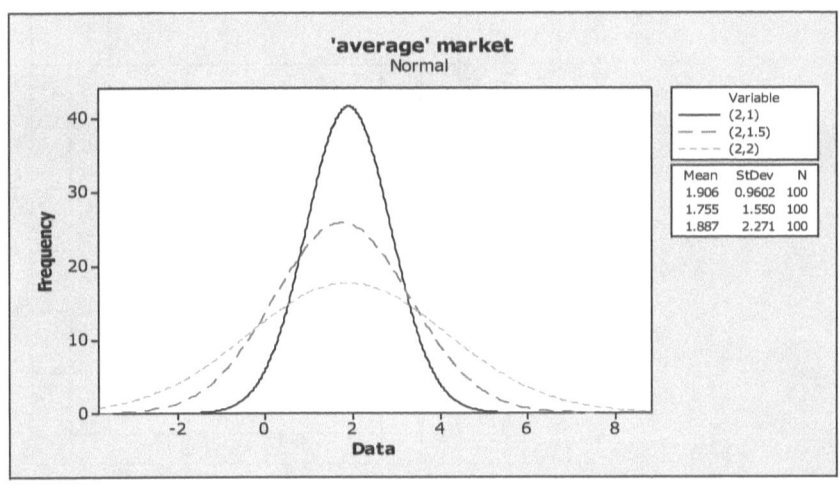

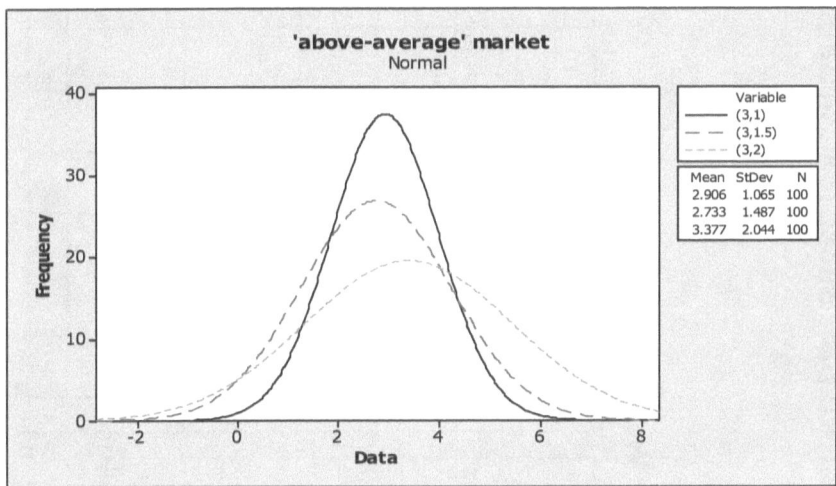

Figure 2: Demand Curves under Three Market Conditions

-End of Instructions-

Appendix C Sample of Calculation Sheet for Participants

CALCULATION SHEET

Developer 1 (D1)

Sub-market (SG1/4/7/10)

t	SGi	Price (unit)	Cost (unit)	Profit (unit)	Units sold	Total Profit	Units left
		4					
		4					
		4					
		4					
		4					
		4					
		4					
		4					

Sub-market (SG2/5/8/11)

t	SGi	Price (unit)	Cost (unit)	Profit (unit)	Units sold	Total Profit	Units left
		2					
		2					
		2					
		2					
		2					
		2					
		2					
		2					

Sub-market (SG3/6/9/12)

t	SGi	Price (unit)	Cost (unit)	Profit (unit)	Units sold	Total Profit	Units left
		1					
		1					
		1					
		1					
		1					
		1					
		1					
		1					

THE VERSATILITY OF THE REAL ESTATE ASSET CLASS - THE SINGAPORE EXPERIENCE

Appendix D Qualitative Questionnaires for the Participants

Questionnaires (Review from the participants)   D __

1. Do you prefer to be the price leader (the first one who enters a new market and price your units) or the price follower (price after observe the market response and your opponents' pricing strategy)? Why?

   _____
   _____
   _____
   _____

2. Given 10 units for sales, how would you strategize your pricing decisions in order to fetch high profit? Why?

   _____
   _____
   _____
   _____

3. Do market uncertainties affect your pricing decision? How does it affect you? Why?

   _____
   _____
   _____
   _____
   _____

Your words are very much appreciated!! Thanks

Appendix E Raw Results

GAME 1
Sequence of action

Period		Sub-markets SG1 SG2 SG3			SG4	SG5	SG6	SG7	SG8	SG9	SG10	SG11	SG12
	OMV^ (max) (μ_d, σ_4^2)	8(13) (2,1)	7(12) (2,1)	5(10) (2,1)	9(14) (1,1)	6(11) (2,1)	6(11) (1,1)	7(12) (2,1)	7(12) (2,1)	4(9) (3,1)	8(13) (3,1)	8(13) (1,1)	5(10) (3,1)
t = 1	Developer	D1	D5	D9									
	Price (Di)	13	7	9									
	Demand	2	3	2									
	Stocks	8	7	8									
t = 2	Developer	D2	D6	D10									
	Price (Di)	12	7	8									
	Demand	1	1	3									
	Stocks	17	16	15									
t = 3	Developer	D3	D7	D11									
	Price (Di)	11	6	7									
	Demand	2	2	1									
	Stocks	25	24	24									
t = 4	Developer	D4	D8	D12									
	Price (Di)	8	5	6									
	Demand	3	2	2									
	Stocks	32	32	32									
t = 5	Developer	D1	D5	D9									
	Price (Di)	7	5	5									
	Demand	3	3	2									
	Stocks	29	29	30									
t = 6	Developer	D2	D6	D10									
	Price (Di)	7	4	5									
	Demand	2	2	1									
	Stocks	27	27	29									
t = 7	Developer	D3	D7	D11									
	Price (Di)	6	7	4									
	Demand	0	2	3									
	Stocks	27	25	26									
t = 8	Developer	D4	D8	D12									
	Price (Di)	6	6	3									
	Demand	2	2	2									
	Stocks	25	23	24									
t = 9	Developer	D1	D5	D9									
	Price (Di)	6	4	3									
	Demand	0	3	1									
	Stocks	25	20	23									
t = 10	Developer	D2	D6	D10	D1								
	Price (Di)	5	4	2	11								
	Demand	1	1	3	0								
	Stocks	24	19	20	10								
t = 11	Developer	D3	D7	D11	D1								
	Price (Di)	5	4	1	11								
	Demand	3	2	0	0								

	Stocks	21	17	20		10			
t = 12	Developer	D4	D8	D12		D1			
	Price (Di)	5	4	5		11			
	Demand	3	3	0		0			
	Stocks	18	14	20		10			
t = 13	Developer	D1	D5	D9		D1			
	Price (Di)	5	4	4		11			
	Demand	1	3	3		1			
	Stocks	17	11	17		9			
t = 14	Developer	D2	D7	D10		D1			
	Price (Di)	5	8	4		11			
	Demand	2	4	1		2			
	Stocks	15	7	16		7			
t = 15	Developer	D3	D8	D11		D1			
	Price (Di)	5	8	4		11			
	Demand	2	3	1		1			
	Stocks	13	4	15		6			
t = 16	Developer	D4	D7	D12		D5			
	Price (Di)	5	8	4		10			
	Demand	2	3	1		1			
	Stocks	11	2	14		15			
t = 17	Developer	D1	D7	D9		D6		D1★	
	Price (Di)	5	12	4		9		9	
	Demand	2	2	3		3		3	
	Stocks	9	0	11		22		7	
t = 18	Developer	D2		D10		D1		D5	
	Price (Di)	4		3		8		8	
	Demand	1		0		2		5	
	Stocks	8		11		20		12	
t = 19	Developer	D3	D10	D11		D5		D1	
	Price (Di)	8	7	3		7		7	
	Demand	1	3	1		2		4	
	Stocks	7	7	10		18		8	
t = 20	Developer	D4	D8	D12		D6		D7★★	D6★
	Price (Di)	4	6	2		6		6	10
	Demand	3	2	3		0		4	2
	Stocks	4	15	7		18		14	8
t = 21	Developer	D1	D10	D9		D1		D5	D1
	Price (Di)	4	6	10		5		6	10
	Demand	4	2	0		1		3	4
	Stocks	1	13	7		17		11	14
t = 22	Developer	D3	D8	D10		D5		D11	D6
	Price (Di)	13	6	2		5		6	10
	Demand	3	1	2		2		2	1
	Stocks	0	12	4		15		19	13
t = 23	Developer		D10	D9	D1★	D6		D1	D2★★
	Price (Di)		6	10	11	4		6	10
	Demand		1	2	1	1		3	2
	Stocks		11	2	9	14		16	21
t = 24	Developer	D9	D8	D9	D6	D1	D12★	D7	D5
	Price (Di)	13	12	10	10	4	12	5	10
	Demand	0	3	1	1	3	2	4	2
	Stocks	10	8	1	18	11	8	12	29
t = 25	Developer	D7	D10	D8	D1★	D5★★ D5	D4	D5 D10★	D1
	Price (Di)	12	11	10	14	10 4	12	5 9	9

THE VERSATILITY OF THE REAL ESTATE ASSET CLASS - THE SINGAPORE EXPERIENCE

	Demand	1	0	4	1	1	1	1	5	4	0
	Stocks	19	8	7	9	27	10	17	7	6	29
t = 26	Developer	D1	D8	D6	D5	D1	D6	D6**	D3*	D11	D4	D5*	D6
	Price (Di)	11	10	10	13	9	4	11	12	6	9	13	9
	Demand	3	0	0	0	1	0	2	3	5	1	0	5
	Stocks	26	8	17	19	26	10	25	7	4	15	10	24
t = 27	Developer	D9	D1	D8	D1	D6	D5	D12	D7	D7**	D3	D1	D2
	Price (Di)	10	9	9	13	9	4	10	11	6	9	12	9
	Demand	0	4	1	1	3	0	2	3	2	4	1	5
	Stocks	26	14	16	18	23	10	23	14	12	21	19	19
t = 28	Developer	D5	D7	D7	D5	D5	D6	D11**	D1	D11	D12**	D5	D5
	Price (Di)	9	9	8	12	8	4	10	10	5	9	11	9
	Demand	1	2	0	2	1	1	3	1	3	2	1	4
	Stocks	35	22	26	16	22	9	30	23	9	29	18	15
t = 29	Developer	D7	D10	D9	D1	D1	D5	D4	D3	D9	D10	D1	D1
	Price (Di)	9	8	7	12	7	4	9	9	5	9	10	8
	Demand	2	1	3	2	0	1	2	1	2	4	2	2
	Stocks	33	21	33	14	22	9	28	22	17	25	16	13
t = 30	Developer	D1	D8	D6	D5	D6	D6	D6	D6**	D10	D4	D5	D6
	Price (Di)	9	8	7	12	7	4	9	8	5	9	9	8
	Demand	3	2	2	0	1	2	2	2	2	1	0	3
	Stocks	30	19	31	14	21	9	26	30	25	24	16	11
t = 31	Developer	D9	D1	D8	D1	D11	D5	D12	D1	D7	D3	D1	D2
	Price (Di)	9	8	7	11	7	4	9	8	5	9	9	8
	Demand	2	1	3	1	2	0	1	2	2	3	0	1
	Stocks	28	18	28	13	29	9	25	28	23	21	16	10
t = 32	Developer	D5	D7	D7	D5	D5	D6	D11	D7	D9	D12	D5	D5
	Price (Di)	9	8	7	10	7	4	9	8	5	9	9	8
	Demand	1	2	3	0	3	1	2	3	4	4	2	1
	Stocks	27	16	25	13	27	8	23	25	19	17	14	9
t = 33	Developer	D7	D8	D9	D1	D1	D5	D4	D3	D10	D10	D1	D1
	Price (Di)	9	8	7	9	7	4	9	8	5	9	9	8
	Demand	2	1	1	1	3	0	2	1	2	2	2	1
	Stocks	25	15	24	12	24	8	21	24	17	15	12	8
t = 34	Developer	D1	D1	D6	D5	D6	D7	D6	D6	D2	D4	D5	D3
	Price (Di)	9	8	7	9	7	4	9	8	5	8	9	8
	Demand	3	2	3	1	1	1	3	0	3	2	1	4
	Stocks	22	13	21	11	23	17	18	24	24	13	11	14
t = 35	Developer	D9	D2	D8	D1	D11	D6	D12	D1	D7	D3	D1	D2
	Price (Di)	9	8	7	9	7	3	8	8	5	8	9	8
	Demand	2	3	2	3	2	1	2	2	3	4	1	3
	Stocks	20	20	19	8	21	16	16	22	21	9	10	11
t = 36	Developer	D5	D7	D7	D5	D5	D5	D11	D7	D9	D12	D5	D8
	Price (Di)	9	8	7	9	7	3	9	8	4	7	8	8
	Demand	1	2	2	0	3	1	2	1	2	3	1	3
	Stocks	19	18	17	8	18	15	14	21	19	6	9	18
t = 37	Developer	D7	D8	D9	D1	D1	D7	D4	D3	D10	D6	D1	D5
	Price (Di)	9	7	6	9	7	3	9	7	4	7	7	8
	Demand	2	2	2	1	2	2	4	2	3	2	1	2
	Stocks	17	16	15	7	16	13	10	19	16	14	8	16
t = 38	Developer	D1	D1	D6	D5	D6	D6	D6	D2	D10	D5	D3
	Price (Di)	8	7	7	9	6	2	8	7	4	6	6	8
	Demand	2	3	3	1	2	1	2	2	2	3	0	2
	Stocks	15	13	12	6	14	12	8	17	14	11	8	14
t = 39	Developer	D9	D2	D8	D1	D11	D5	D11	D1	D7	D3	D1	D2

	Price (Di)	8	8	6	8	6	2	9	7	4	6	5	7
	Demand	3	0	3	2	1	1	2	2	4	3	1	4
	Stocks	12	13	9	4	13	11	6	15	10	8	7	10
$t = 40$	Developer	D5	D7	D7	D5	D5	D7	<u>D4</u>	D7	D2	D6	D5	D8
	Price (Di)	7	8	7	7	6	11	8	7	4	6	6	8
	Demand	2	1	2	3	1	1	3	2	3	4	0	3
	Stocks	10	12	7	1	12	10	3	13	7	4	7	7

▬   Developer who enter the sub-market.
★   First Mover
★★ Second Mover

Game 2

Sequence of action

t		Sub-markets			OMV^(max)	t		Sub-markets			OMV^(max)	t		Sub-markets			OMV^(max)
		SG1 5(10)	SG2 5(10)	SG3 5(10)	(μd, σd²)			SG1 5(10)	SG2 5(10)	SG3 5(10)	(μd, σd²)			SG1 5(10)	SG2 5(10)	SG3 5(10)	(μd, σd²)
		(2,2)	(2,2)	(2,2)	(μd, σd²)			(2,2)	(2,2)	(2,2)	(μd, σd²)			(2,2)	(2,2)	(2,2)	(μd, σd²)
1	Developer	D8	D3	D10	6	6	Developer	D4	D12	D5	11	11	Developer	D11	D6	D9	16
	Price (Di)	10	10	10			Price (Di)	7	6	7			Price (Di)	5	4	4	
	Demand	3	3	0			Demand	2	2	1			Demand	4	4	0	
	Stocks	7	7	10			Stocks	24	24	34			Stocks	16	16	23	
2	Developer	D4	D12	D5	7	7	Developer	D11	D6	D9	12	12	Developer	D7	D1	D2	17
	Price (Di)	9	9	9			Price (Di)	6	6	7			Price (Di)	5	4	4	
	Demand	3	3	0			Demand	2	2	4			Demand	1	1	3	
	Stocks	14	14	20			Stocks	22	22	30			Stocks	15	15	20	
3	Developer	D11	D6	D9	8	8	Developer	D7	D1	D2	13	13	Developer	D8	D3	D10	18
	Price (Di)	9	8	9			Price (Di)	6	5	6			Price (Di)	4	4	4	
	Demand	2	2	0			Demand	2	2	3			Demand	6	6	2	
	Stocks	22	22	30			Stocks	20	20	27			Stocks	9	9	18	
4	Developer	D7	D1	D2	9	9	Developer	D8	D3	D10	14	14	Developer	D4	D12	D5	19

Buyer	Price (Di)	Demand	Stocks	Developer	Price (Di)	Demand	Stocks
5	9	2	30	D8	8	4	26
	7	2	30	D3	7	4	26
	8	5	35	D10	8	0	35
10	5	0	20	D4	5	0	20
	5	0	20	D12	5	0	20
	5	3	24	D5	5	1	23
15	5	0	9	D11	4	6	4
	4	0	9	D6	3	6	4
	3	0	18	D9	3	1	17
20	8	1	24	D7	8	0	34
	6	1	34	D1	6	0	34
	3	6	1	D2	10	0	11

CHAPTER 3

COUNTRY LEGAL ORIGIN OF DIRECT REAL ESTATE RISK PREMIUMS

In addition to country differences across countries, international direct real estate investors face a lack of data and the issues of appraisal smoothing in the available data. Because of these issues, many studies tend to either use securitized real estate data or incomplete, unsecuritized real estate data. Although Barkham and Geltner (1995) as well as Kallberg *et al.* (2002) have found that the direct and indirect markets follow each other closely, others find that direct and indirect real estate investments are not similar. Studies such as that by Seiler *et al.* (1999) show that securitized real estate as in REITs (i.e. the real estate investment trusts) and the un-securitized real estate are not the equivalent from an investor point of view. Giliberto (1993) and Stevenson (2000) have shown that returns on securitized real estate have little correlation with direct real estate but instead are closely related to the common stock market. Therefore, Chapter 3 argues that REITS are not a suitable proxy for private real estate returns to assess the cost of equity for private real estate investments. Ziobrowski and Curcio (1991) use capital gains as proxy for direct real estate returns in Japan. Several studies have used the capitalization rates as proxy for returns to estimate the risk premiums. A decrease in capitalization rate need not imply that there is a decrease in the risk premium, Therefore, the capitalization rates seem to be a poor proxy for risk premium estimation. The lack of transaction-based data, as compared to the relatively large volume of transaction prices in the common stock market, has led to the problem of appraisal smoothing for direct real estate returns. Therefore, Chapter 3 seeks to address the following objectives:

- To estimate the direct real estate total returns for the selective Asian city;
- To estimate the associated risk premiums of key macroeconomic variables, like GDP growth rate and the interest rate, together with the direct real estate specific risk, like vacancy rate for the Asian city concerned;
- To examine the relationship between legal origins, denoting the country aspect. and the direct real estate total returns by the Asian city concerned;
- To examine the relationship between legal origins and the associated direct real estate risk premium of the Asian city concerned;

The first section of Chapter 3 provides the background, the study scope and methodology, the significance of the a Chapter 3 and its objectives. The next (second section) discusses the literature on direct real estate investing risk premiums and the total returns. It also discusses endowment law, country development and the Arbitrage Pricing Theory. The third section discusses the descriptive statistics utilized while looking at the research design in general. The fourth section discusses the findings and analysis of the Chapter 3. The final (fifth) section summarises the Chapter 3 and it offers some suggestions for future work.

The Related Literature

The literature revolves on how risk premiums are estimated for international real estate investing. In particular, the literature looks at whether or not macroeconomic variables and specific real estate risk variables, play significant parts in the overall risk profile of such investing globally. The literature looks at studies that explore whether or not legal origins are significant factors in accounting for the different total returns from various cities globally. On risk premium, Liu and Mei (1992) postulate that two common risk factors help to explain the various expected returns on the different asset classes. These common risk factors can be proxied by a common stock market factor and a bond market factor (Liu & Mei, 1992). Among the implications, the first suggests that the real estate market is already integrated in the common stock and bond markets. An analysis of these latter two markets helps to understand real estate pricing.

Secondly, the implication is that there is no specific real estate risk premium, which is associated with real estate investing (Mei & Lee, 1994). The study by Liu and Mei (1992) differed significantly from an earlier one by Liu, Hartzell, Greig, and Grissom (1990). The Jorion and Schwartz (1986) methodology is adopted by the earlier study to test for the presence of a super risk premium associated with the real estate asset class. The existence of a real estate risk premium is discovered when appraisal-based returns are utilised. Mei and Lee (1994) conclude that real estate contributes to the systematic risk of a portfolio, and that the concept of risk premium can be extended to the real estate asset class. There is the presence of a real estate factor premium on top of a common stock and bond factors in asset pricing. In such a 3-factor world where real estate is now a systematic factor, a real estate exposure is needed to capture the relevant real estate factor premiums (Liu & Mei, 1992). Having ascertained the presence of a real estate risk premium, numerous studies have sought to quantity this premium. Breidenbach, Muller and Schulte (2006) have adopted the CAPM model in assessing the real estate risk premium based on investors' relative risk appetite. Pai and Geltner (2007) reiterate that there is actually different risk premium for different real estate type, with apartments being viewed as the most risky, to be followed by retail and lastly CBD office. They applied the Fama-French model and discovered that there is inherently a larger premium for larger properties. Size and types of direct real estate investments affect the real estate premiums demanded by investors (Pai & Geltner, 2007).

The Country Legal Origin

The idea of how legal origin can affect country structure can be traced back to the Law and Finance theory, which predicts that the historically determined differences in legal traditions help explain international differences in financial systems today (Porta, Silanes, Schleifer, & Vishny, 1998). In particular, the theory focuses on differences between the two most influential legal origins, i.e. the British legal origin and the French legal origin (Hayek, 1960). British legal origin facilitates the ability of private property owners to transact confidently, with positive repercussions on financial development (North & Weingast, 1989). This is opposed to the French legal origin, where state dominance has produced a legal tradition that focuses more on the rights of the state, and less on the rights of individual investors (Hayek, 1960). Legal origin can explain cross-country differences in private property rights protection (Beck, Demirguc-Kunt, & Levine, 2003). It can account for the common stock market development, where countries that originated from the French legal origin, have significantly lower levels of common stock market development than the British legal origin countries (Beck, Demirguc-Kunt, & Levine, 2003). In countries under the French legal origin, we can predict that a direct real estate investment in such countries will garner a higher real premium than otherwise in a British legal origin country (Ho *et al.*, 2007; 2014 & 2016; Lerner & Schoar, 2005).

The Real Estate Data De-Smoothing

Reliability of direct real estate data has to be verified before the risk premium can be assessed. For valuation-based indices, inaccuracy can be inadvertently introduced (Ho *et al.*, 2007; 2014 & 2016). This is caused by the inherent valuation smoothing and temporal aggregations that would mask the true volatility of returns (Matysiak, 1995). Geltner and Webb (1994) find that smoothing is consistent with the optimal interference of the market value of individual properties when the observed price information is noisy. In particular, smoothing in individual appraisal reports results in less informative aggregate price indices. The main root of the problem is ultimately traceable to the nature of direct real estate valuation. As the volume of transactions is limited and the holding periods are usually long, direct real estates' capital values (CVs) are derived from comparison methods. The adverse effect on the accuracy of valuation-based indices, is the smoothening problem of the CVs and temporal aggregation. The relevant de-smoothing technique so adopted is the autoregressive de-lagging model by Geltner and Miller (Ho & Chua, 2007).

It is noteworthy that Chapter 3's data is obtained from the JLL REIS-Asia (Jones Lang Lasalle Real Estate Intelligence-Asia) dataset. The consistent JLL REIS-Asia data set is provided as the chargeable subscription for the JLL REIS-Asia clients. Such a data set is a valuation-based index that contains the TRs of 13 pan-Asia cities located in 8 countries, covering 90 buildings of international grade-A investment quality for each prime office, retail and residential sectors. JLL REIS-Asia only permits the release of historical data from its data set for externally requested research. For Chapter 3 and on good will, JLL REIS-Asia only makes available the historical time period from 2002 Q1 to 2009 Q3 (30 quarters), just long enough to enable meaningful analysis of the direct real estate risk premiums.

The Arbitrage Pricing Theory Model

Chapter 3 adopts the arbitrage pricing theory (APT) model. The APT model is introduced and tested by Ross (1976 and 1977). The APT model estimates the sensitivity of the TR of each direct real estate sector to the fluctuation of macroeconomic variables and specific real estate market risk factors. The APT model is explicit that a direct real estate sector's risk premium should be 0 if it bears no risk. Grissom *et al.* (1987) discover that their study of city and regional macroeconomic markets do capture the risk factors, and that a more robust prediction of TRs can arise from regional APT models. Ling and Naranjo (2002) adopt a 2-stage ordinary least-square regression and found that the specific country factor is significant in explaining the cross-country real estate returns. Bond *et al* (2003) establish that the country specific risk factor is significant for most of the countries under study. The inference is that the overall risk factor in cross-country investments is an agglomeration of variables that include the macroeconomic and specific real estate risk factors (variables).

It is imperative to reiterate that Chapter 3 is meant as the follow-up study that is in contrast to the study by Ho *et al.* (2016), who have estimated betas from the same historical dataset permitted by JLLREIS-Asia, to so obtain risk premiums for relevant macroeconomic variables, direct real estate variables and the regions of Table 1. The multi-factor model is adopted and simplified to eq (1).

ATR = C(1) + C(2)*LGDPF + C(3)*IRF + C(4)*VRF + C(5)*DUM_NA + C(6)*DUM_SA   (1)

Results of the international direct real estate risk premium estimates are presented in Table 1 by macro-economic variables and only by region (i.e. North Asia, South Asia and the US). The French and English legal origins are excluded from Chapter 3 and from Table 1's variable column.

Table 1. International Direct Real Estate Risk Premium Estimates (2003Q1 to 2009Q2)

Variable	Risk premium (%)
Real GDP growth lagged by 1 quarter	-0.7%★
Annual Inflation Rate	-1%★
Vacancy Rate	2.5%★
North Asia (dum_na=1)	7.4%
South Asia (dum_sa=1)	9.1%
Universal (dum_na=dum_sa=0) Risk-Free Rate	7.2%

Risk premiums correspond to those risk factors under the variable column of Table 1. The pooled panel data span the period from 2003Q1 to 2009Q2. ★denotes statistical significance at the 0.01 level. Source: Authors, 2012; Eviews Version 6. Source: Authors, 2016; 2020.

Table 1 shows that the South Asia region has the highest risk premium (9.1%), to be followed by North Asia region (7.4%) and the universal risk-free rate (7.2%). The results may be a function of the different country-specific legal origin, financing, the law for property rights and related tax incentives. Porta *et al.* (1998) alludes to the differences in prevailing international financial systems. Beck *et al.*, (2003) reiterate that the legal origin of countries explains cross-country differences in private real estate rights protection, land acquisition and direct real estate premiums. Unlike the French legal origin, under which the rights of the state dominate individual rights, the British legal origin preserves the sanctity of individual rights (Hayek, 1960), to promote financial development (North and Weingast, 1989). The implication is that countries under the French legal origin have higher risk premiums than those countirs under the English legal origin (Ho *et al.*, 2007; 2014 & 2016).

Given wide differences of the direct real estate risk premiums for cities in the same region, the local-specific institutional milieu, rather than the historical legal origin, underpins the direct real estate risk premiums. For e.g., it is doubtful whether or not the risk exposure owing to the 'yellow-red shirt' political divide in Thailand and the separatist's struggles in The Philippines, is a function of the historical French legal origin. Therefore, the association of legal origin for the institutional environment with the direct real estate risk premium, though real, can be tangential.

Table 2. International Direct Real Estate Risk Premium Estimates (2003Q1 to 2009Q2)

City	Institutional Environment - English (E) / French (F) Legal Origin	Region - North (N) / South (S) Asia	Real Estate Risk Premium
Shanghai	F	N	10.5%
Tokyo	F	N	8.0%
Beijing	F	N	7.7%
Seoul	F	N	3.8%
Manila	F	S	15.2%
Bangkok	F	S	12.2%
Jakarta	F	S	7.5%
Hong Kong	E	N	10.8%
Singapore	E	S	10.1%
Delhi	E	S	8.2%
Mumbai	E	S	7.6%
Kuala Lumpur	E	S	7.2%
Chennai	E	S	6.7%
US	E	-	2.8%

Source: Authors, 2020

From Table 2, Seoul (3.8%) is the safest real estate market in Asia, to be followed by Chennai (6.7%), Kuala Lumpur (7.2%) and Jakarta (7.5%). It is noteworthy though that Mumbai (7.6%) is portrayed to be safer than Tokyo (8.0%), Singapore (10.1%), Shanghai (10.5%) and Hong Kong (10.8%) that are perhaps the most heralded markets in Asia. Similarly, Delhi (8.2%) compares favourably to Tokyo (8.0%) and more favourably to Singapore, Shanghai and Hong Kong (Table 13). It is not surprising that Manila (15.2%) and Bangkok (12.2%) emerge as the riskiest markets in Asia given the wars in 'The Philippines' and the yellow-red shirt political divide in Thailand.

The Data

The predominant model in Chapter 3 adopts the multi-factor APT regression analysis. Macroeconomic and specific real estate risk premiums are duly estimated. The JLL REIS-Asia data is the dataset, made available on good will, for Chapter 3. Table 3 presents the cities concerned and the availability of the dataset for each sector analysis:

Table 3. Summary of cities and the real estate sectors used in study

City	Variable	Office (O)	Residential (R)	Retail (T)
Bangalore	BG	X		
Beijing	BJ	X	X	X
Bangkok	BK	X	X	X
Hong Kong	HK	X	X	X
Jakarta	JK	X	X	X
Kuala Lumpur	KL	X	X	X
Manila	MN	X	X	X
Mumbai	MB	X		
Seoul	SL	X		
Shanghai	SH	X	X	X
Singapore	SG	X	X	X
Taiwan	TW	X		
Tokyo	TK	X		

Total Number of cities		13	8	8
United States	US	X	X	X

Source: Authors, 2020

All data are denoted in US$ terms to facilitate comparison across cities. Real estate variables are taken from the JLL REIS-Asia data that include the capital value, based on NFA (net floor area), the net effective rent and the vacancy rate, which on the whole captures the specific risk for the direct real estate market. The quarterly annual TRs are de-smoothed using the Geltner and Miller auto-regressive, de-lagging model on the assumption of a 100% occupancy rate. This is based on eq (2) from Brown and Matysiak (2000) and (Ho et al., 2007; 2014 &2016).

$$R_t = \frac{CV_t - CV_{t-1} + RV_t}{CV_{t-1}} \qquad (2)$$

, where R_t denotes the return at time t, CV_t denotes the capital value at time t, CV_{t-1} denotes the capital value at time t -1 and RV_t denotes the rental value at time t

Macroeconomic factors, like real GDP growth rate and the inflation rate for the various cities are obtained from the DataStream online database system. The real GDP growth rate is obtained by taking the log difference of the real GDP prices provided by DataStream. The macroeconomic variables will not be de-smoothed as they are not subjected to temporal bias and the seasonality lag. The specific real estate risk factor, namely the vacancy rate, is obtained from the permitted JLL REIS-Asia dataset.

Data De-smoothing and De-lagging

Chapter 3 adopts the autoregressive de-lagging model of Geltner and Miller (2007) to de=smooth the 13 cities' returns that conform to temporal aggregation and the seasonality lag. The un-smoothed return is obtained from eq (3):

$$r_t^* = a_1 r_{t-1}^* + a_4 r_{t-4}^* + (wr_t - w\mu) \qquad (3)$$

, where r_t^* = return in quarter t; r_t = unsmoothed (liquid, or full information) return, characterised by a lack of autocorrelation; a_1, a_4 = factors reflecting autocorrelation (including seasonality, i.e. the fourth-order lag) to be estimated in the auto-regression model; w, μ = a weight and a constant chosen to give the unsmoothed returns the desired mean and volatility; $(wr_t - w\mu)$ = the "residuals" of the auto-regression (zero mean and autocorrelation) = e_t.

Eq (4) is re-expressed as:

$$r_t = \mu + (1/w)e_t \qquad (4)$$

, where e_t is the auto-regression residual and μ is the mean of the unsmoothed return. With the assumption that the temporal lag will not bias the long run mean return, we would obtain a result of $w = (1 - a_1 - a_4)$

The Direct Real Estate Risk Framework

In estimating the direct real estate risk premiums for an international real estate deal under writing, Chapter 3 utilises a summation of the base lending rate: i.e. a direct real estate premium and a specific risk premium that is inherent to a country's direct real estate sector. Such a specific premium includes the liquidity, transparency, definition, and tenure premiums (Ho K. H., 2007). Chapter 3 examines the relationship and risk involved when investing in a country that is either under British (English) Legal Origin or French Legal Origin. The APT model reiterates that there is an equilibrium relationship between returns on risky assets and a small set of macroeconomic factors (variables) that can influence the returns on risky assets significantly. It is assumed that investors take advantage of an arbitrage opportunity by basing their decisions on the beta of an asset with a near identical yield, regardless of their risk aversion and wealth. Compared to the Capital Asset Pricing Model (CAPM), the APT has several key advantages.

First, it is not necessary for returns to be normally distributed. Secondly, several sources of specific risks exist in the economy, rather than just a singular market risk as assumed by CAPM. Chapter 3 adopts the multi-factor APT model owing to its several advantages. The risk factor loadings of the direct real estate returns are estimated in the form of a 2-step multi factor times series and cross-sectional multiple regression analysis models. Real GDP growth rate and annual inflation rate represent the macroeconomic variables used while the vacancy rate represents the direct real estate risk factor. An error term is introduced to capture risks that cannot be explained by these 3 variables.

$$R_{i,t} = R_{i,t}^f + \beta_{1,i} X_{1,i,t}^C + \beta_{2,i} X_{2,i,t} + \beta_{3,i} X_{3,i,t} + \varepsilon_{i,t} \tag{5}$$

, where subscript i indicates the ith real estate sector and t indicates time t; $R_{i,t}$ = total desmoothed returns of a city in real estate sector i; $R_{i,t}^f$ = risk-free rate; $X_{1,i,t}^C$ = the conditional variable, real GDP growth lag 1; $X_{2,i,t}$ = quarterly annual inflation rate; $X_{3,i,t}$ = vacancy rate; $\beta_{k,i}$ = risk of the total returns of real estate sector i to k^{th} economic variable (k = 1, 2, 3) and $\varepsilon_{i,t}$ = error term. The null hypothesis of the multi-factor model is H_0: $\beta_k \neq 0$ (where k = 1, 2, 3). β_k is the sensitivity of real estate total return to the corresponding risk factor k.

Once the betas of each direct real estate sector are obtained, they are utilised as the direct real estate risk factor loadings to estimate the cross-sectional risk premiums. Such risk premiums are represented by the coefficients of the betas in eq (6).

$$\bar{R}_i = C + \lambda_1 \beta_{1,i} + \lambda_2 \beta_{2,i} + \lambda_3 \beta_{3,i} + \lambda_4 DUM\_BC_i + \lambda_5 DUM\_FC_i + \varepsilon_i \tag{6}$$

, where subscript i indicates the ith real estate sector. $\bar{R}$ = average total returns of each city from 2002Q4 to 2009Q2 of each real estate sector i; C = intercept which represents the risk free rate and dummy variable for US; $\beta_{k,i}$ (where k = 1, 2, 3) = betas that are derived from eq (4); λ_k (where k =1, 2, 3) = cross section risk premium to risk factor k; DUM_BC = dummy variable of real estate investment areas sorted by legal origins. DUM_BC=1: British Common Legal Origin. DUM_FC=1: French Civil Legal Origin; ε_i = error term and it captures the risk premiums that are not explained by $\beta_{k,i}$ (where k = 1, 2, 3). The null hypothesis is H_0: $\lambda_k \neq 0$. If λ_k is significantly different from zero, then there is a risk premium for the return of the real estate market on the risk factor k.

Table 4 shows the variables for the estimation of the cross-sectional risk premium model.

Table 4. Variables for the Estimation of Property (Direct Real Estate) Risk Premium Model

Variable	Description
ATR	Quarterly Annual Total Return
GDP	Quarterly Real GDP Growth Rate
IR	Quarterly Annual Inflation Rate
VR	Quarterly Vacancy Rate
DUM_BC	DUM_BC: British Common Law Legal Origin
DUM_FC	DUM_FC: French Civil Law Legal Origin

Source: Author, 2016

Results and Findings

De-smoothing the Office Sector Data

The smoothed total returns are obtained from the JLL REIS=Asia Dataset and are estimated from eqs (2) and (3). The total returns are then de-smoothed via the Geltner and Miller auto-regressive model to account for the temporal bias and the seasonality lag. Table 5 shows the de-smoothing results.

Table 5. Smoothed Office Returns

City\Year	2003	2004	2005	2006	2007	2008	Average
Bangalore	15.98%	15.25%	17.04%	12.33%	24.50%	16.72%	16.97%
Beijing	16.26%	12.67%	12.95%	11.06%	11.51%	16.76%	13.53%
Bangkok	14.87%	13.62%	16.96%	11.55%	12.72%	4.7%	12.40%
Hong Kong	-1.87%	14.07%	15.07%	6.59%	11.00%	11.74%	9.43%
Jakarta	9.76%	8.55%	10.45%	13.22%	8.78%	9.21%	10.00%
Kuala Lumpur	7.92%	2.03%	8.41%	9.42%	10.32%	9.27%	7.90%
Manila	6.94%	7.76%	13.02%	19.2%	17.23%	10.75%	18.87%
Mumbai	15.46%	22.17%	14.74%	27.78%	24.64%	8.41%	12.48%
Seoul	11.15%	8.72%	11.56%	14.08%	12.97%	1.4%	10.62%
Shanghai	6.02%	6.81%	9.75%	10.96%	16.77%	19.70%	11.67%
Singapore	4.23%	6.20%	7.17%	16.21%	27.50%	2.39%	9.98%
Taiwan	2.93%	5.65%	6.73%	7.51%	8.81%	10.51%	8.77%
Tokyo	0.85%	8.02%	12.54%	17.21%	12.87%	1.13%	7.02%

Source: Authors, 2020

From the data, the CBD office sectors of Manila, Bangalore and Beijing recorded the top 3 highest average returns over the years at 18.87%; 16.97%; and 13.53% respectively. This is in spite of the more matured cities like Singapore, Hong Kong and Shanghai, whose returns average around 10% each. We infer that investing in the developing cities office sectors will yield greater returns especially when the city itself is experiencing growth from an influx of financial or manufacturing activities. With more companies and with both multi-national corporations (MNCs) and local players setting up offices, the sector itself will experience boom times. The dataset, though, is a smoothed one and may not reflect the most accurate of scenarios. It is essential to de-smooth the data such that our analysis is not affected by temporal bias and the seasonality lag. Using this treated dataset, we then subject it to the Geltner auto-regressive, de-lagging model to de-smooth it. The regression estimation output for de-smoothing the office total returns is shown in Table 6.

Table 6. Regression estimation output for office data

City	Coefficient	01	04	Residual	R-Squared	Durbin-Watson Stat
Bangalore	0.224145	-0.001146	-0.354109	-0.223745	0.136790	1.926008
Beijing	0.060094	-0.653197	1.492354	6.791262	0.259884	2.077949
Bangkok	0.105862	0.429660	-0.077576	-0.360950	0.165236	1.671020
Hong Kong	0.044525	0.402784	0.218634	-0.119989	0.196569	1.777604
Jakarta	0.069970	0.056254	0.249728	0.553630	0.593844	1.614983
Kuala Lumpur	0.086333	0.199936	-0.349176	0.499571	0.375721	1.528246
Manila	0.056463	0.149356	0.492460	0.221092	0.459202	1.976037
Mumbai	0.056842	0.694707	0.088533	-0.573176	0.347204	2.210962
Seoul	0.035474	0.248903	0.357399	-0.602869	0.217593	1.924995
Shanghai	0.028928	0.846420	-0.045551	-0.240315	0.309121	2.02411
Singapore	0.009960	0.910669	0.222303	-0.284151	0.601051	2.363531
Taiwan	0.041020	-0.069234	0.447331	0.319715	0.304056	2.000632
Tokyo	0.044430	0.739406	-0.175732	-0.199387	0.320936	1.947390

Source: Authors, 2020

The de-smoothed total returns of say the Shanghai office sector can be expressed as:

SHO = 0.028928 + 0.846420 (SHO01) − 0.045551 (SHO04) − 0.240315 (RESID01 SHO)   (6)

Eq (6) can be represented by:

SHO = 0.028928 + 0.846420r_{t-1} − 0.045551 r_{t-4} − 0.240315 e_t (7)

, where r_t = Shanghai Office returns in quarter t; r_{t-1} = Shanghai Office returns lagged by 1 quarter; r_{t-4} = Shanghai Office returns lagged by 4 quarter and e_t = the "residuals" of the auto-regression (zero mean and autocorrelation). Estimation output of the equation displays an adjusted R^2 of 30.9%, with the Durbin-Watson statistic of 2.024 and significant t-ratios for most of the variables.

We can see that the Durbin-Watson stats for the TR values are largely in the range of 1.5 to 2.3. The implication is that there is almost zero auto-correlation that may affect our results, indicating the possibility of more accurate data. The R-Squared figures suggest that de-smoothed returns deviate substantially from the mean, revealing the impact of smoothing effects. The descriptive statistics for the de-smoothed office data TRs are presented in Table 7.

Table 7. Descriptive statistics for de-smoothed office data

City	Period	Observations	Total Returns (Mean)	Total Returns (SD)	Skewness	Kurtosis
Bangalore	03Q3 – 07Q3	17	16.73%	0.0395	0.136790	-0.42982
Beijing	02Q2 – 07Q3	22	12.60%	0.0209	0.259884	4.482536
Bangkok	02Q2 – 07Q3	22	19.52%	0.1179	0.165236	0.677717
Hong Kong	02Q2 – 07Q3	22	10.43%	0.288	0.196569	-0.88345
Jakarta	02Q2 – 07Q3	22	9.82%	0.0764	0.593844	4.173996
Kuala Lumpur	02Q2 – 07Q3	22	7.62%	0.0341	0.375721	1.181536
Manila	02Q2 – 07Q3	22	19.00%	0.3741	0.459202	1.125567
Mumbai	03Q3 – 07Q3	17	21.64%	0.1888	0.347204	0.596045
Seoul	02Q2 – 07Q3	22	8.20%	0.1640	0.217593	2.253709
Shanghai	02Q2 – 07Q3	22	15.88%	0.3341	0.309121	-0.13192
Singapore	02Q2 – 07Q3	22	-3.44%	0.5213	0.601051	7.294487
Taiwan	03Q3 – 07Q3	17	5.98%	0.0372	0.304056	0.676417
Tokyo	02Q2 – 07Q3	22	10.22%	0.1792	0.320936	-0.26161
United States	02Q2 - 09Q3	30	2.11%	0.0478	-	-

Source: Authors, 2020

We notice that the mean returns that are derived from de-smoothed data are different from the mean returns obtained from smoothed data. Clearly, the smoothing effects are apparent in the real estate valuation process. Although the top 3 most attractive places to invest have changed, the theoretical understanding of investing in the growing and developing Asian countries has not. Based on the de-smoothed data, Mumbai, Bangkok, and Manila rank as the most attractive places to invest to reap average returns of around 20%. These 3 key cities are the main financial zones in their respective Asian countries. As the countries evolve economically, the office take-up rates should improve and both capital value and rental gains will increase significantly. The relatively consistent reading of the skewness statistics suggests that we can approximate a normal distribution in our analysis and use of the models.

De-smoothing the Residential Sector Data

The estimated smoothed TRs for the residential sector are provided in Table 8.

Table 8. Smoothed residential returns

City\Year	2003	2004	2005	2006	2007	2008	Average
Beijing	11.02%	13.04%	15.86%	16.98%	17.39%	16.96%	15.21%
Bangkok	13.31%	8.45%	9.27%	10.05%	9.01%	3.35%	8.90%
Hong Kong	2.50%	16.62%	6.27%	2.29%	7.82%	7.66%	7.19%
Jakarta	11.84%	10.06%	11.67%	12.02%	11.23%	11.05%	11.31%
Kuala Lumpur	8.14%	8.74%	10.48%	10.27%	11.82%	8.06%	9.58%
Manila	4.43%	12.41%	11.11%	19.50%	14.42%	9.49%	11.89%
Shanghai	-	-	10.16%	5.87%	9.96%	9.03%	7.39%
Singapore	4.04%	4.83%	4.59%	10.73%	16.49%	3.65%	10.49%

Source: Authors, 2020

Once again, growing cities from developing Asian countries have the highest average TRs. Beijing, Manila and Jakarta rank as the top choices with average returns of 15.21%, 11.89% and 11.31%. Singapore recorded a comparatively high average return of 10.49%. This can be alluded to the fact that Singapore has always been seen as a safe and stable 'haven' for Asian direct real estate investing. Investment activities in the private residential market ensures that Singapore enjoys substantial TRs. We next deploy the Geltner and Miller's auto-regressive, de-lagging model to achieve more accurate data. The resulting regression estimation output for de-smoothing the residential total returns is presented in Table 9.

Table 9. Regression estimation output for the de-smoothed residential data

City	Coefficient	01	04	Residual	R-Squared	Durbin-Watson Stat
Beijing	0.094297	0.658108	-0.304799	-0.348464	0.226509	1.737408
Bangkok	0.034318	0.676914	-0.076914	-0.367861	0.183593	2.082518
Hong Kong	0.075665	0.138893	-0.211129	0.110726	0.096799	2.01378
Jakarta	0.105899	-0.008469	0.065380	-0.049342	0.013113	1.955245
Kuala Lumpur	0.063170	0.202663	0.102186	0.004730	0.057251	2.016512
Manila	0.055844	0.627845	-0.059375	-0.432215	0.117540	2.071291
Shanghai	0.076573	0.267589	-0.281072	0.173500	0.355580	1.661793
Singapore	0.056842	0.694707	0.088533	-0.573176	0.347204	2.210962

Source: Authors, 2020

The Durbin-Watson test statistic resides between the ranges of 1.6 to 2.2, implying that there is almost negligible auto-correlation and providing us with more accurate data. The R-Squared values highlight the smoothing effects and how the data will actually be when they are corrected for the smoothing effects. Wide deviation suggests the presence of de-smoothing and that the reliance on smoothed data will introduce inaccuracy in the analysis. The descriptive statistics for the de-smoothed residential total returns are provided in Table 10.

Table 10. Descriptive statistics for de-smoothed residential data

City	Period	Observations	Total Returns (Mean)	Total Returns (SD)	Skewness	Kurtosis
Beijing	03Q3 – 09Q3	25	14.81%	0.09805	0.606368	0.516588
Bangkok	03Q3 – 09Q3	25	9.71%	0.134663	0.047298	-0.40361
Hong Kong	03Q3 – 09Q3	25	8.83%	0.081521	1.049103	5.472419
Jakarta	03Q3 – 09Q3	25	11.53%	0.032502	-0.57775	1.126059
Kuala Lumpur	03Q3 – 09Q3	25	9.18%	0.043809	-0.53687	0.728011
Manila	03Q3 – 09Q3	25	15.08%	0.198164	0.570976	1.023471
Shanghai	05Q3 – 09Q3	17	35.95%	0.035593	-0.76991	2.503086
Singapore	03Q3 – 09Q3	25	7.82%	0.066256	-1.07943	0.988794
United States	02Q2 - 09Q3	30	2.33%	0.2940	-	-

Source: Authors, 2020

From Table 10, the de-smoothed TRs vary from the smoothed TRs. This further explains the presence of smoothing effects among the appraisal-based indicators. Beijing, Manila and Jakarta still rank as the foremost places to invest in residential real estate. However, it is noted that Shanghai has the highest TRs of 35.95%. This may well be due to the fact that Shanghai has always been the economic and financial hub of China and with the latter's rise in recent years, Shanghai has managed to ride on its 'coat tail' and to achieve such very high TRs.

De-smoothing the Retail sector Data

The estimated smoothed total returns for the retail sector are presented in Table 11.

Table 11. Smoothed retail sector returns

City\Year	2003	2004	2005	2006	2007	2008	Average
Beijing	13.39%	13.79%	16.19%	23.22%	16.49%	18.31%	16.62%
Bangkok	16.00%	12.33%	14.04%	17.72%	18.63%	10.27%	15.74%
Hong Kong	6.50%	20.39%	10.46%	7.21%	8.76%	8.62%	10.66%
Jakarta	17.38%	14.55%	12.45%	19.13%	15.29%	15.51%	15.76%
Kuala Lumpur	10.12%	10.51%	11.70%	11.78%	14.76%	14.44%	11.77%
Manila	9.22%	10.10%	12.17%	16.61%	16.49%	11.98%	12.92%
Shanghai	17.66%	18.13%	14.92%	22.42%	14.15%	17.07%	17.46%
Singapore	8.06%	9.29%	9.11%	13.11%	11.29%	7.96%	10.17%

Source: Authors, 2020

Retail sector TRs wise and from Table 11, all cities record the average of double digit returns. Shanghai and Beijing rank as the top most attractive places to invest. Their attractive TRs can be attributed to China's sustainable trade and robust economic growth. Next, we conduct Geltner and Miller auto-regressive, de-lagging model to de-smooth the data. The regression estimation output for de-smoothing the retail TRs is provided in Table 12.

Table 12. Regression estimation output for the de-smoothed retail data

City	Coefficient	01	04	Residual	R-Squared	Durbin-Watson Stat
Beijing	0.092043	0.713964	-0.231595	-0.638554	0.193992	2.002633
Bangkok	0.116854	0.431464	-0.235797	0.093693	0.236099	1.999392
Hong Kong	0.070406	0.098842	0.121161	0.509671	0.302095	1.907666
Jakarta	0.179895	-0.183612	0.000614	0.181723	0.007375	1.762189
Kuala Lumpur	0.097139	0.274548	-0.078470	-0.008764	0.076921	1.939766
Manila	0.067860	0.776536	-0.293442	-0.422535	0.231756	2.132179
Shanghai	0.174225	0.126695	-0.162922	0.354354	0.255131	2.070980
Singapore	0.049003	0.632463	-0.165728	-0.056952	0.364870	1.898654

Source: Authors, 2020

From Table 12, it is observed that the Durbin-Watson statistic falls within 1.7 to 2.13, implying almost negligible auto-correlation among the data. The R-Squared generally falls within the range of 0.1 to 0.36, implying a wide deviation from the mean once the data is de-smoothed. The descriptive statistics for the de-smoothed retail TRs are presented in Table 13.

Table 13. Descriptive statistics for de-smoothed retail data

City	Period	Observations	Total Returns (Mean)	Total Returns (SD)	Skewness	Kurtosis
Beijing	03Q3 – 09Q3	25	18.05%	0.10163916	1.5844416	6.09907081
Bangkok	03Q3 – 09Q3	25	14.61%	0.06250901	-0.0349725	-0.2169661
Hong Kong	03Q3 – 09Q3	25	10.47%	0.0861724	0.91718977	4.4639117
Jakarta	03Q3 – 09Q3	25	15.14%	0.04712326	0.17598555	0.50703857
Kuala Lumpur	03Q3 – 09Q3	25	12.27%	0.05335112	-1.1765619	2.66778139
Manila	03Q3 – 09Q3	25	13.77%	0.10512844	-0.3837107	0.4545417
Shanghai	03Q3 – 09Q3	25	17.16%	0.04502259	0.85724549	0.59385194
Singapore	03Q3 – 09Q3	25	8.77%	0.07136863	-0.3421468	-0.0533645
United States	02Q2 - 09Q3	30	3.37%	0.170	-	-

Source: Authors, 2020

From Table 13 of the de-smoothed dataset, Shanghai and Beijing still rank as the top two most attractive places to invest in the retail sector. Singapore's retail sector surprisingly came in last in terms of the total average TRs over 6 years. This trend suggests that Singapore's retail sector is approaching saturation and that its TRs are gradually stabilising and evening out.

Empirical Estimation of the Risk Factor Loadings

Under the multi-factor APT model, the systematic risk premiums for the individual direct real estate cities in Asia are estimated. The 2 macroeconomic factors (Real GDP growth rate and annual inflation rate) and 1 direct specific real estate risk variable (vacancy rate) form the 3 risk-factor loads in the model. These risk factor loadings are modelled through the pool-panel ordinary least-square regression analysis. The beta value of each factor is obtained, as presented in Table 14.

Table 14. Definition of Variables

Variable	Description
ATR	Quarterly Annual Total Return (TR)
GDP	Quarterly Real GDP Growth Rate
IR	Quarterly Inflation Rate
VR	Quarterly Vacancy Rate
Universal Risk-Free Rate	7.2%

Source: Authors, 2020

As mentioned earlier, eq (8) is adopted for the analysis of sensitivity of the TR:

$$R_{i,t} = \beta_{1,i} X^C_{1,i,t} + \beta_{2,i} X_{2,i,t} + \beta_{3,i} X_{3,i,t} + \varepsilon_{i,t} \qquad (8)$$

, where subscript i indicates the ith real estate sector and t indicates time t. $R_{i,t}$ = total desmoothed returns of a city in real estate sector i; $X^C_{1,i,t}$ = the conditional variable, real GDP growth lag 1; $X_{2,i,t}$ = quarterly annual inflation rate; $X_{3,i,t}$ = vacancy rate; $\beta_{k,i}$ = sensitivity of the total returns of real estate sector i to k^{th} economic variable (k = 1, 2, 3) and $\varepsilon_{i,t}$ = error term. It captures risks that cannot be explained by the three variables. The null hypothesis of the multi-factor model, from equation (6), is H_0: $\beta_k \neq 0$ (where $k = 1, 2, 3$). β_k is the sensitivity of real estate total return to the corresponding risk factor k.

Eq (8) reflects the change in direct real estate return with respect to the change in GDP growth, inflation rate or the vacancy rate. This pooled-panel ordinary least-square regression model of eq (8) is conducted for the office, residential and retail sectors.

The Empirical Estimation of the Cross-Sectional APT model

The associated betas so derived are deployed as the risk factor loadings for the resulting, multi- factor APT model. These betas measure the sensitivity of the respective variables to the direct real estate TRs. After deploying the risk factor loadings, we can derive the risk premiums from the regressive coefficients of the risk factor loadings in our multi factor APT model. The mean TRs for various cities and their corresponding direct real estate sectors denote the dependent variable of the APT model. Chapter 3 groups by inspection the cities or countries according to their legal origins as presented in Table 15.

Table 15. Grouping of Cities according to legal origins

British Legal Origin	*French Legal Origin*
Bangalore	Bangkok
Hong Kong	Beijing
Kuala Lumpur	Jakarta
Mumbai	Manila
Singapore	Shanghai
United States	Taiwan
	Tokyo

Source: Authors, 2020

From Table 15, the British legal origin refers to the law developed by judges through decisions of the courts. This is in contrast to the French legal origin that adopt statutes via the legislative process.

THE VERSATILITY OF THE REAL ESTATE ASSET CLASS - THE SINGAPORE EXPERIENCE

Cities and/or countries in the Asian region like Singapore, Malaysia, India and Hong Kong adopt the British legal origin as their governing legislation. The other cities, though, adopt the French legal origin, for e.g. the Civil Law legislations in Ottawa, Canada. There are 4 distinct groups for Civil Law, namely, Napoleonic (Jakarta, Manila); Germanistic (Tokyo, Seoul, Bangkok, Taiwan); Scandinavian; and Chinese (Beijing, Shanghai). For Chapter 3's APT model, cities under British legal origin are included collectively as the dummy variable termed 'DUM_BC', while cities under French legal origin are included collectively as the dummy variable termed 'DUM_FC':

$$\bar{R}_i = C + \lambda_1 \beta_{1,i} + \lambda_2 \beta_{2,i} + \lambda_3 \beta_{3,i} + \lambda_4 DUM\_BC_i + \lambda_5 DUM\_FC_i + \varepsilon_i \quad (9)$$

, where subscript i indicates the ith real estate sector. $\bar{R}$ = average total returns of each city from 2003Q1 to 2009Q2 of each real estate sector i; C = intercept which represents the autonomous return; $\beta_{k,i}$ (where k = 1, 2, 3) = betas that are derived from cross-section risk premium to risk factor k. DUM_BC = dummy variable of British legal origin. DUMS1=1: British legal origin. DUM_FC = dummy variable of French legal origins. DUMS2=1: French legal origin; and ε_i = error term that captures the risk premiums that are not explained by $\beta_{k,i}$ (where k = 1, 2, 3).

The null hypothesis is H_0: $\lambda_k \neq 0$. If λ_k is significantly different from zero, then there is a risk premium for the return of the real estate market on the risk factor k. Cities that have British Common Law legal origins are Bangalore, Hong Kong, Kuala Lumpur, Mumbai and Singapore; Cities that have French Civil Law legal origins are Bangkok, Beijing, Jakarta, Manila, Seoul, Shanghai, Taiwan and Tokyo.

The APT model estimations can be expressed in eq (10):

ATR = C(1) + C(2)*LGDPF + C(3)*IRF + C(4)*VRF + C(5)*DUM_BC + C(6)*DUM_FC   (10)

The APT model estimates are presented in Table 14A. To avoid the dummy variable trap problem, the constant term, C, and the

French-Civil-Law dummy (dum fc=1), are retained while allowing the British-Common-Law dummy to be removed. The associated base dummy, i.e. dum fc=0, becomes the base category against which the British-Common-Law dummy is assessed.

Table 16. The APT Model Estimates

Variable	Output
Constant, C	8.2035%*
Real GDP growth	0.6394% ***
Inflation rate	-0.0254%
Vacancy rate	2.7067% *
French Legal Origin (dum_fc=1)	4.1436%**
British Legal Origin (i.e. 8.2035%+0.6394%-0.0254%+2.7067%+0 =11.5242%)	11.5242%**
Universal Risk-Free Rate	7.2%
R-squared	0.375489
Adjusted R-squared	0.261942
Mean dependent var ATR	13.4156%

NB. Significant at the 1% level*; at the 10% level**; at the 29% level***. Source: Authors, 2020

The constant term C, real GDP growth rate, vacancy rate, the French-legal-origin dummy and the British-legal-origin dummy in relation to the French-legal-origin base dummy, are statistically significant in estimating the overall risk premiums of international direct real estate investment in the Asian region. High risk premiums among the 6 risk factors are only observed for vacancy rate (2.7%), the French-legal-origin dummy (4.1%), the British-legal-origin dummy (11.5%) and the constant C (8.2%) of our multi factor APT model, relative to the universal risk-free rate of 7.2%. However, real GDP growth rate is moderately significant with the relatively low risk premium of about 0.6%. It is implicit that the specific real estate risk has a more deterministic role in the overall risk profile of the direct real estate investment in Asia, as compared to macroeconomic variables. It is because the vacancy rate has a much direct impact on the performance of direct real estate investment than the macroeconomic variables.

Real GDP growth rate has a lower risk premium, owing to the fact that the Asia region on the whole has experienced robust and sustainable growth over the past decade. Historical economic performance of the Asia region for the past years means that this region is perceived to be comparatively less risky, and that the risk premiums accorded to the Asia region should be lower than in the past. Interest rate movements suggest a stabilised historical pattern. Generally, they hover around 0% to 5% up to the years 2007 to 2008, where most of the Asian countries' interest rates spike to above 5%. The relatively stable rates for most of the years suggest that lower premium is accorded to this macroeconomic variable.

Coefficients of the British and the French legal origins' dummies are significant at the 10% level for their high risk premiums of about 11.5% and 4.1% respectively. Both legal origins imply an association between legal origin and the direct real estate TRs. This trend is in line with the study by Beck, Kunt and Levine in their "Law, endowments, and Finance" Chapter 3. Their Chapter 3 postulates that historically determined differences in legal origins can predict the difference in the economic development of countries as observed today (Beck, Demirguc-Kunt, & Levine, 2003).

Nevertheless, Chapter 3 suggests that the French legal origin is better perceived for its private direct real estate rights protection, as compared to the British legal origin by international investors in Asian direct real estate. It can be owing to the fact that in the French legal origin, its laws are codified and straightforward, leading to less ambiguous rulings. Instead, the British legal origin is based on case law and it is susceptible to various interpretations. Given the wide differences in risk premiums for cities in the same region, as presented in Table 17, that have similar country nature historical antecedent, it appears that the local-specific country milieu, rather than historical legal antecedent, underpins direct real estate risk premiums. For e.g., it is doubtful whether or not the risk exposure, owing to the 'yellow-red shirt' political divide in Thailand and the separatist's struggles in 'The Philippines', is a function of historical French legal origin antecedent. Therefore, the association of legal origin of the country nature with the direct real estate risk premium, though real, may be tangential.

Nevertheless, one may safely conclude, on the basis of the evidence in Table 17, that Seoul (3.8%) is the safest real estate market in Asia, to be followed by Chennai (6.7%), Kuala Lumpur (7.2%) and Jakarta (7.5%). It is noteworthy though that Mumbai (7.6%) is portrayed to be safer than Tokyo (8.0%), Singapore (10.1%), Shanghai (10.5%) and Hong Kong (10.8%) that are perhaps the most heralded markets in Asia. Similarly, Delhi (8.2%) compares favourably to Tokyo (8.0%) and more favourably to Singapore, Shanghai and Hong Kong (Table 13). Furthermore, it may not surprise any reader that Manila (15.2%) and Bangkok (12.2%) would emerge as the riskiest markets in Asia given the wars in 'The Philippines' and the 'yellow-red shirt' political divide in Thailand.

Table 17. International Direct Real Estate Risk Premium Estimates (2003Q1 to 2009Q2)

City	Country nature - English (E) / French (F) Legal Origin	Region - North (N) / South (S) Asia	Real Estate Risk Premium
Shanghai	F	N	10.5%
Tokyo	F	N	8.0%
Beijing	F	N	7.7%
Seoul	F	N	3.8%
Manila	F	S	15.2%
Bangkok	F	S	12.2%
Jakarta	F	S	7.5%
Hong Kong	E	N	10.8%
Singapore	E	S	10.1%
Delhi	E	S	8.2%
Mumbai	E	S	7.6%
Kuala Lumpur	E	S	7.2%

Chennai	E	S	6.7%
US	E	-	2.8%

Source: Authors, 2020

Although the "Law, endowments and Finance" Chapter 3 has suggested that the British legal origin is perceived to offer better protection, it must be noted that the dependent variable (i.e. the real estate TRs) in such a Chapter 3 is determined by taking the TRs from the public market. TRs from the public markets may well be biased towards countries under British legal origin since the latter normally have more developed common stock market and financial systems. Instead, Chapter 3 utilises the direct real estate TRs from the private market and not from the wider public market. Results suggest that legal origin is a variable that affects the assessment of the riskiness of direct real estate investing in an Asian country and in its risk-return analysis. The French legal origin, with its codified law, is perceived to be more favourable for international real estate investing in the Asia region.

Concluding Remarks

Chapter 3 ascertains the presence of appraisal smoothing. By adopting the Geltner and Miller (2007) 1st and 4th order autoregressive model to de-smooth the direct real estate TRs (total returns), a more robust set of direct real estate total returns can be obtained. The Chapter 3 adopts the multi-factor APT (arbitrage pricing theory) model to examine the correlation of legal origins to an Asian city's direct real estate TRs. Various sensitivities of the direct real estate TRs, i.e. the betas or the risk factor loadings, are estimated with pooled-panel data via multiple regression analysis, resolved by ordinary least-square, and from which the associated risk factor loadings are determined. The 2 main legal origins, i.e. the British legal origin and the French legal origin, are the dummy variables i.e.

'the dummies' in the multi-factor APT model. The coefficients are then estimated and analysed to examine the extent of the correlation.

Given the wide differences in the risk premiums for cities in the same region, as presented in Table 17, that have similar historical country-legal-origin antecedent, it appears that the local-specific country milieu underpins the direct real estate risk premiums. For e.g., it is doubtful whether or not the risk exposure, owing to the 'yellow-red shirt' political divide in Thailand and the separatist's struggles in The Philippines, is a function of the historical French legal origin antecedent. Therefore, the association of the legal origin of the country nature with the direct real estate risk premium, though real, may be tangential.

Although the "Law, endowments and Finance" Chapter 3 suggests that the British legal origin is perceived to offer better direct real estate protection, it should be noted that the dependent variable (i.e. the direct real estate TRs) in such a Chapter 3 is determined by taking the TRs from the public market. TRs from the public markets may well be biased towards countries under the British legal origin since the latter normally have more developed common stock market and financial systems.

However, and in Chapter 3, we utilise the direct real estate TRs from the private market rather than the wider public market. Results imply that legal origin is a variable that affects the assessment of the riskiness of direct real estate investing in an Asian country and in its risk-return analysis. The French legal origin, with its codified law, is perceived to be more favourable for international real estate investing in the Asia region.

Results of the APT model estimates are reproduced from Table 17 below. To avoid the dummy variable trap problem, the constant term, C_1 and the French-legal-origin dummy (dum fc=1), are retained while allowing the British-legal-origin dummy to be removed. The associated base dummy, i.e. dum fc=0 becomes the base category, against which the British legal origin dummy is assessed.

Table 17. APT Model Estimates

Variable	Output
Constant, C	8.2035%*
Real GDP growth	0.6394% ***
Inflation rate	-0.0254%
Vacancy rate	2.7067% *
French Legal Origin (dum_fc=1)	4.1436%**
British Legal Origin	11.5242%**
(i.e. 8.2035%+0.6394%-0.0254%+2.7067%+0 =11.5242%)	
Universal Risk-Free Rate	7.2%
R-squared	0.375489
Adjusted R-squared	0.261942
Mean dependent var ATR	13.4156%

NB. Significant at the 1% level*; at the 10% level**; at the 29% level***. Source: Authors, 2020

Constant term C, real GDP growth rate, vacancy rate, the French-legal-origin dummy and the British-legal-origin dummy in relation to the French-Civil- Law base dummy, are statistically significant in estimating the overall risk premiums of international investing in direct real estate in the Asian region. High risk premiums among the 6 risk factors are only observed for vacancy rate (2.7%), the French-legal-origin dummy (4.1%), the British-legal-origin dummy (11.5%) and the constant C (8.2%) of our multi factor APT model, relative to the universal risk-free rate of 7.2%.

Real GDP growth rate is moderately significant with the relatively low risk premium of about 0.6%. It is implicit that the specific real estate risk has a more deterministic role in the overall risk profile of a direct real estate investing in Asia, as compared to macroeconomic variables. It is because the vacancy rate has a much direct impact on the performance of direct real estate investment than the macroeconomic variables. Real GDP growth rate has a lower risk premium, owing to the fact that the Asia region on the whole has experienced robust and sustainable growth over the past decade. Historical economic performance of the Asia region highlights that this region is perceived to be comparatively less risky, and that the risk premiums accorded to the region should be lower than in the past. Interest rate movements suggest a stabilised historical pattern, generally hovering around 0% to 5% up to the years 2007-2008, where most of the Asian countries' interest rates spike to above 5%. The relatively stable rates for most of these years suggest that lower premium is accorded to this macroeconomic variable.

Nevertheless, Chapter 3 suggests that the French-legal-origin is better perceived for its private direct real estate rights protection by international real estate investors in Asian direct real estate. It can be owing to the fact that in the French-legal-origin, its laws are codified and straightforward, leading to less ambiguous rulings. Instead, the British-legal-origin is based on case laws and it is susceptible to various interpretations.

There are other legal origin systems that fall outside the broad categories of the British and French legal origins, and they can include Muslim Law and Customary Law. To form a more robust and complete set of the direct real estate risk premium empirical model, more studies can be conducted to examine other risk premium variables, such as the cultural factor of a society, and to form a more comprehensive assessment of the relationship between direct real estate investing in an Asian city or country and its legal origin. Research that encompasses a longer study duration should provide for a detailed model, which may include other macroeconomic variables like the unemployment rate and the extent of real estate market transparency.

Acknowledgement: *The Author wishes to gratefully acknowledge the initial work carried out for Chapter 3 by Mr TOH Heng Da / Jacob, a graduate of the NUS Department of Real Estate and the NUS Business School, and in consultation with Honorary Professor (University of Hertfordshire, Hatfield, UK), Dr HO Kim Hin / David; during their meaningful brain storming sessions before Professor HO retired from the NUS SDE Departments of Real Estate and Building in May 2020. Mr TOH is a senior manager of Prologis Ltd, Singapore.*

APPENDICES

Appendix 1: Office regression estimation outputs

Dependent Variable: BGO
Method: Least Squares
Date: 02/22/13   Time: 01:58
Sample (adjusted): 2003Q3 2007Q3
Included observations: 17 after adjustments

Variable	Coefficient	Std. Error	t-Statistic	Prob.
C	0.224145	0.104357	2.147867	0.0512
BGO01	-0.001146	0.485215	-0.002361	0.9982
BGO04	-0.354109	0.338986	-1.044611	0.3152
RESID01_BGO	-0.223745	0.444999	-0.502800	0.6235

R-squared	0.136790	Mean dependent var	0.167305
Adjusted R-squared	-0.062412	S.D. dependent var	0.067324
S.E. of regression	0.069394	Akaike info criterion	-2.295721
Sum squared resid	0.062601	Schwarz criterion	-2.099671
Log likelihood	23.51363	Hannan-Quinn criter.	-2.276233
F-statistic	0.686689	Durbin-Watson stat	1.926008
Prob(F-statistic)	0.576016		

Dependent Variable: BJO
Method: Least Squares
Date: 02/22/13   Time: 02:13
Sample (adjusted): 2003Q2 2007Q3
Included observations: 8 after adjustments

Variable	Coefficient	Std. Error	t-Statistic	Prob.
C	0.060094	0.860087	0.069870	0.9477
BJO01	-0.653197	0.871772	-0.749275	0.4954
BJO04	1.492354	6.322710	0.236031	0.8250
RESID01_BJO	6.791262	16.53618	0.410691	0.7023

R-squared	0.259884	Mean dependent var	0.137288
Adjusted R-squared	-0.295203	S.D. dependent var	0.078062
S.E. of regression	0.088840	Akaike info criterion	-1.697114
Sum squared resid	0.031570	Schwarz criterion	-1.657393
Log likelihood	10.78845	Hannan-Quinn criter.	-1.965014
F-statistic	0.468185	Durbin-Watson stat	2.077949
Prob(F-statistic)	0.720432		

Dependent Variable: BKO
Method: Least Squares
Date: 02/22/13   Time: 02:03
Sample (adjusted): 2003Q2 2007Q3
Included observations: 18 after adjustments

Variable	Coefficient	Std. Error	t-Statistic	Prob.
C	0.105862	0.064371	1.644553	0.1223
BKO01	0.429660	0.355827	1.207496	0.2472
BKO04	-0.077576	0.250192	-0.310067	0.7611
RESID01_BKO	-0.360950	0.232245	-1.554175	0.1425

R-squared	0.165236	Mean dependent var		0.143892
Adjusted R-squared	-0.013642	S.D. dependent var		0.055630
S.E. of regression	0.056009	Akaike info criterion		-2.733493
Sum squared resid	0.043917	Schwarz criterion		-2.535633
Log likelihood	28.60144	Hannan-Quinn criter.		-2.706211
F-statistic	0.923733	Durbin-Watson stat		1.671020
Prob(F-statistic)	0.454895			

Dependent Variable: HKO
Method: Least Squares
Date: 02/22/13   Time: 02:05
Sample (adjusted): 2003Q2 2007Q3
Included observations: 18 after adjustments

Variable	Coefficient	Std. Error	t-Statistic	Prob.
C	0.044545	0.033519	1.328943	0.2051
HKO01	0.402784	0.267001	1.508551	0.1536
HKO04	0.218634	0.219328	0.996837	0.3358
RESID01_HKO	-0.119989	0.231311	-0.518733	0.6120

R-squared	0.196569	Mean dependent var		0.091496
Adjusted R-squared	0.024405	S.D. dependent var		0.093863
S.E. of regression	0.092710	Akaike info criterion		-1.725548
Sum squared resid	0.120332	Schwarz criterion		-1.527687
Log likelihood	19.52993	Hannan-Quinn criter.		-1.698265
F-statistic	1.141754	Durbin-Watson stat		1.777604
Prob(F-statistic)	0.366384			

```
Dependent Variable: JKO
Method: Least Squares
Date: 02/22/13   Time: 02:06
Sample (adjusted): 2003Q2 2007Q3
Included observations: 18 after adjustments
```

Variable	Coefficient	Std. Error	t-Statistic	Prob.
C	0.069970	0.028163	2.484447	0.0262
JKO01	0.056254	0.223767	0.251396	0.8052
JKO04	0.249728	0.154805	1.613177	0.1290
RESID01 JKO	0.553630	0.164768	3.360066	0.0047

R-squared	0.593844	Mean dependent var		0.102936
Adjusted R-squared	0.506810	S.D. dependent var		0.025959
S.E. of regression	0.018230	Akaike info criterion		-4.978324
Sum squared resid	0.004653	Schwarz criterion		-4.780464
Log likelihood	48.80492	Hannan-Quinn criter.		-4.951042
F-statistic	6.823164	Durbin-Watson stat		1.614983
Prob(F-statistic)	0.004597			

```
Dependent Variable: KLO
Method: Least Squares
Date: 02/22/13   Time: 02:07
Sample (adjusted): 2003Q2 2007Q3
Included observations: 18 after adjustments
```

Variable	Coefficient	Std. Error	t-Statistic	Prob.
C	0.086333	0.026231	3.291307	0.0054
KLO01	0.199936	0.254618	0.785240	0.4454
KLO04	-0.349176	0.224891	-1.552647	0.1428
RESID01 KLO	0.499571	0.270450	1.847183	0.0860

R-squared	0.375721	Mean dependent var		0.075563
Adjusted R-squared	0.241947	S.D. dependent var		0.042435
S.E. of regression	0.036946	Akaike info criterion		-3.565571
Sum squared resid	0.019110	Schwarz criterion		-3.367711
Log likelihood	36.09014	Hannan-Quinn criter.		-3.538289
F-statistic	2.808629	Durbin-Watson stat		1.528246
Prob(F-statistic)	0.078005			

```
Dependent Variable: MBO
Method: Least Squares
Date: 02/22/13   Time: 02:16
Sample (adjusted): 2003Q3 2007Q3
Included observations: 17 after adjustments
```

Variable	Coefficient	Std. Error	t-Statistic	Prob.
C	0.056842	0.085371	0.665820	0.5172
MBO01	0.694707	0.269700	2.575851	0.0230
MBO04	0.088533	0.295211	0.299899	0.7690
RESID01_MBO	-0.573176	0.363367	-1.577402	0.1387

R-squared	0.347204	Mean dependent var		0.216382
Adjusted R-squared	0.196558	S.D. dependent var		0.108883
S.E. of regression	0.097597	Akaike info criterion		-1.613613
Sum squared resid	0.123828	Schwarz criterion		-1.417562
Log likelihood	17.71571	Hannan-Quinn criter.		-1.594125
F-statistic	2.304775	Durbin-Watson stat		2.210962
Prob(F-statistic)	0.124779			

```
Dependent Variable: MNO
Method: Least Squares
Date: 02/22/13   Time: 02:08
Sample (adjusted): 2003Q2 2007Q3
Included observations: 18 after adjustments
```

Variable	Coefficient	Std. Error	t-Statistic	Prob.
C	0.056463	0.033722	1.674342	0.1162
MNO01	0.149356	0.423064	0.353034	0.7293
MNO04	0.492460	0.299771	1.642789	0.1227
RESID01_MNO	0.221092	0.323289	0.683883	0.5052

R-squared	0.459202	Mean dependent var		0.131109
Adjusted R-squared	0.343317	S.D. dependent var		0.063620
S.E. of regression	0.051555	Akaike info criterion		-2.899212
Sum squared resid	0.037211	Schwarz criterion		-2.701351
Log likelihood	30.09290	Hannan-Quinn criter.		-2.871929
F-statistic	3.962557	Durbin-Watson stat		1.976037
Prob(F-statistic)	0.030806			

Dependent Variable: SGO
Method: Least Squares
Date: 02/22/13   Time: 02:09
Sample (adjusted): 2003Q2 2007Q3
Included observations: 18 after adjustments

Variable	Coefficient	Std. Error	t-Statistic	Prob.
C	0.009960	0.049989	0.199248	0.8449
SGO01	0.910669	0.622962	1.461837	0.1659
SGO04	0.222303	0.551109	0.403373	0.6928
RESID01_SGO	-0.284151	0.682282	-0.416471	0.6834

R-squared	0.601051	Mean dependent var		0.117746
Adjusted R-squared	0.515562	S.D. dependent var		0.090355
S.E. of regression	0.062889	Akaike info criterion		-2.501774
Sum squared resid	0.055370	Schwarz criterion		-2.303914
Log likelihood	26.51597	Hannan-Quinn criter.		-2.474492
F-statistic	7.030729	Durbin-Watson stat		2.363531
Prob(F-statistic)	0.004075			

Dependent Variable: SHO
Method: Least Squares
Date: 02/22/13   Time: 02:09
Sample (adjusted): 2003Q2 2007Q3
Included observations: 18 after adjustments

Variable	Coefficient	Std. Error	t-Statistic	Prob.
C	0.028928	0.048504	0.596402	0.5604
SHO01	0.846420	0.348424	2.429284	0.0292
SHO04	-0.045551	0.430623	-0.105780	0.9173
RESID01_SHO	-0.240315	0.216509	-1.109954	0.2857

R-squared	0.309121	Mean dependent var		0.097789
Adjusted R-squared	0.161075	S.D. dependent var		0.051716
S.E. of regression	0.047368	Akaike info criterion		-3.068593
Sum squared resid	0.031413	Schwarz criterion		-2.870733
Log likelihood	31.61734	Hannan-Quinn criter.		-3.041311
F-statistic	2.088012	Durbin-Watson stat		2.020411
Prob(F-statistic)	0.147828			

```
Dependent Variable: SLO
Method: Least Squares
Date: 02/22/13   Time: 02:10
Sample (adjusted): 2003Q2 2007Q3
Included observations: 18 after adjustments
```

Variable	Coefficient	Std. Error	t-Statistic	Prob.
C	0.035474	0.069238	0.512355	0.6164
SLO01	0.248903	0.348961	0.713267	0.4874
SLO04	0.357399	0.287011	1.245244	0.2335
RESID01_SLO	-0.602869	0.328299	-1.836340	0.0876

R-squared	0.217593	Mean dependent var		0.116800
Adjusted R-squared	0.049935	S.D. dependent var		0.046247
S.E. of regression	0.045078	Akaike info criterion		-3.167724
Sum squared resid	0.028448	Schwarz criterion		-2.969864
Log likelihood	32.50952	Hannan-Quinn criter.		-3.140442
F-statistic	1.297837	Durbin-Watson stat		1.924995
Prob(F-statistic)	0.314081			

```
Dependent Variable: TKO
Method: Least Squares
Date: 02/22/13   Time: 02:11
Sample (adjusted): 2003Q2 2007Q3
Included observations: 18 after adjustments
```

Variable	Coefficient	Std. Error	t-Statistic	Prob.
C	0.044430	0.028951	1.534667	0.1472
TKO01	0.739406	0.316205	2.338380	0.0347
TKO04	-0.175732	0.236952	-0.741636	0.4706
RESID01_TKO	-0.199387	0.239610	-0.832132	0.4193

R-squared	0.320936	Mean dependent var		0.102249
Adjusted R-squared	0.175422	S.D. dependent var		0.073483
S.E. of regression	0.066728	Akaike info criterion		-2.383267
Sum squared resid	0.062336	Schwarz criterion		-2.185406
Log likelihood	25.44940	Hannan-Quinn criter.		-2.355985
F-statistic	2.205536	Durbin-Watson stat		1.947390
Prob(F-statistic)	0.132761			

Dependent Variable: TPO				
Method: Least Squares				
Date: 02/22/13 Time: 02:11				
Sample (adjusted): 2003Q2 2007Q3				
Included observations: 18 after adjustments				
Variable	Coefficient	Std. Error	t-Statistic	Prob.
C	0.041020	0.021130	1.941334	0.0726
TPO01	-0.069234	0.250397	-0.276497	0.7862
TPO04	0.447331	0.203821	2.194718	0.0455
RESID01_TPO	0.319715	0.428044	0.746921	0.4675
R-squared	0.304056	Mean dependent var		0.059765
Adjusted R-squared	0.154925	S.D. dependent var		0.039365
S.E. of regression	0.036188	Akaike info criterion		-3.607056
Sum squared resid	0.018334	Schwarz criterion		-3.409196
Log likelihood	36.46351	Hannan-Quinn criter.		-3.579774
F-statistic	2.038852	Durbin-Watson stat		2.000632
Prob(F-statistic)	0.154685			

Source: EViews version 7

Appendix 2: Residential regression estimation outputs

Dependent Variable: BJ
Method: Least Squares
Date: 02/26/13   Time: 00:05
Sample (adjusted): 2003Q3 2009Q3
Included observations: 25 after adjustments

Variable	Coefficient	Std. Error	t-Statistic	Prob.
C	0.094297	0.060319	1.563319	0.1329
BJ01	0.658108	0.352669	1.866078	0.0761
BJ04	-0.304799	0.256119	-1.190068	0.2473
RESID01_BJ	-0.348464	0.352642	-0.988152	0.3343

R-squared	0.226509	Mean dependent var	0.140211
Adjusted R-squared	0.116010	S.D. dependent var	0.063476
S.E. of regression	0.059680	Akaike info criterion	-2.653984
Sum squared resid	0.074796	Schwarz criterion	-2.458964
Log likelihood	37.17480	Hannan-Quinn criter.	-2.599894
F-statistic	2.049876	Durbin-Watson stat	1.737408
Prob(F-statistic)	0.137634		

Dependent Variable: BK
Method: Least Squares
Date: 02/26/13   Time: 00:06
Sample (adjusted): 2003Q3 2009Q3
Included observations: 25 after adjustments

Variable	Coefficient	Std. Error	t-Statistic	Prob.
C	0.034318	0.029692	1.155806	0.2607
BK01	0.676914	0.344061	1.967426	0.0625
BK04	-0.076956	0.232319	-0.331250	0.7437
RESID01_BK	-0.367861	0.337365	-1.090394	0.2879

R-squared	0.183593	Mean dependent var	0.079925
Adjusted R-squared	0.066964	S.D. dependent var	0.054839
S.E. of regression	0.052971	Akaike info criterion	-2.892504
Sum squared resid	0.058924	Schwarz criterion	-2.697484
Log likelihood	40.15630	Hannan-Quinn criter.	-2.838413
F-statistic	1.574160	Durbin-Watson stat	2.082518
Prob(F-statistic)	0.225364		

Dependent Variable: HK
Method: Least Squares
Date: 02/26/13   Time: 00:07
Sample (adjusted): 2003Q3 2009Q3
Included observations: 25 after adjustments

Variable	Coefficient	Std. Error	t-Statistic	Prob.
C	0.075665	0.032368	2.337613	0.0294
HK01	0.138893	0.462308	0.300433	0.7668
HK04	-0.211129	0.286854	-0.736014	0.4699
RESID01_HK	0.110726	0.482454	0.229506	0.8207

R-squared	0.096799	Mean dependent var	0.071169
Adjusted R-squared	-0.032229	S.D. dependent var	0.092265
S.E. of regression	0.093740	Akaike info criterion	-1.750937
Sum squared resid	0.184531	Schwarz criterion	-1.555917
Log likelihood	25.88672	Hannan-Quinn criter.	-1.696847
F-statistic	0.750215	Durbin-Watson stat	2.013718
Prob(F-statistic)	0.534413		

Dependent Variable: JK
Method: Least Squares
Date: 02/26/13   Time: 00:07
Sample (adjusted): 2003Q3 2009Q3
Included observations: 25 after adjustments

Variable	Coefficient	Std. Error	t-Statistic	Prob.
C	0.105899	0.048016	2.205491	0.0387
JK01	-0.008469	0.357775	-0.023671	0.9813
JK04	0.065380	0.215551	0.303314	0.7646
RESID01_JK	-0.049342	0.288640	-0.170947	0.8659

R-squared	0.013113	Mean dependent var	0.112292
Adjusted R-squared	-0.127871	S.D. dependent var	0.024319
S.E. of regression	0.025827	Akaike info criterion	-4.329180
Sum squared resid	0.014007	Schwarz criterion	-4.134160
Log likelihood	58.11475	Hannan-Quinn criter.	-4.275090
F-statistic	0.093012	Durbin-Watson stat	1.955245
Prob(F-statistic)	0.963071		

Dependent Variable: KL
Method: Least Squares
Date: 02/26/13   Time: 00:08
Sample (adjusted): 2003Q3 2009Q3
Included observations: 25 after adjustments

Variable	Coefficient	Std. Error	t-Statistic	Prob.
C	0.063170	0.043556	1.450321	0.1617
KL01	0.202663	0.434526	0.466399	0.6457
KL04	0.102186	0.293192	0.348528	0.7309
RESID01_KL	0.004730	0.438716	0.010781	0.9915

R-squared	0.057251	Mean dependent var	0.091492
Adjusted R-squared	-0.077427	S.D. dependent var	0.031400
S.E. of regression	0.032593	Akaike info criterion	-3.863816
Sum squared resid	0.022308	Schwarz criterion	-3.668796
Log likelihood	52.29770	Hannan-Quinn criter.	-3.809726
F-statistic	0.425097	Durbin-Watson stat	2.016512
Prob(F-statistic)	0.737025		

Dependent Variable: MN
Method: Least Squares
Date: 02/26/13   Time: 00:08
Sample (adjusted): 2003Q3 2009Q3
Included observations: 25 after adjustments

Variable	Coefficient	Std. Error	t-Statistic	Prob.
C	0.055844	0.042975	1.299450	0.2079
MN01	0.627845	0.385933	1.626821	0.1187
MN04	-0.059375	0.228631	-0.259697	0.7976
RESID01_MN	-0.432215	0.356210	-1.213373	0.2385

R-squared	0.117540	Mean dependent var	0.112984
Adjusted R-squared	-0.008526	S.D. dependent var	0.080316
S.E. of regression	0.080658	Akaike info criterion	-2.051554
Sum squared resid	0.136619	Schwarz criterion	-1.856534
Log likelihood	29.64443	Hannan-Quinn criter.	-1.997464
F-statistic	0.932370	Durbin-Watson stat	2.071291
Prob(F-statistic)	0.442520		

Dependent Variable: SG
Method: Least Squares
Date: 02/26/13   Time: 00:08
Sample (adjusted): 2003Q3 2009Q3
Included observations: 25 after adjustments

Variable	Coefficient	Std. Error	t-Statistic	Prob.
C	0.067481	0.023816	2.833495	0.0100
SG01	1.102674	0.368501	2.992319	0.0069
SG04	-0.787457	0.318778	-2.470235	0.0222
RESID01_SG	-0.880458	0.612623	-1.437194	0.1654

R-squared	0.444140	Mean dependent var		0.067013
Adjusted R-squared	0.364731	S.D. dependent var		0.079698
S.E. of regression	0.063522	Akaike info criterion		-2.529199
Sum squared resid	0.084737	Schwarz criterion		-2.334179
Log likelihood	35.61499	Hannan-Quinn criter.		-2.475109
F-statistic	5.593099	Durbin-Watson stat		1.374043
Prob(F-statistic)	0.005572			

Dependent Variable: SH
Method: Least Squares
Date: 02/26/13   Time: 00:09
Sample (adjusted): 2005Q3 2009Q3
Included observations: 17 after adjustments

Variable	Coefficient	Std. Error	t-Statistic	Prob.
C	0.076573	0.023329	3.282313	0.0059
SH01	0.267589	0.284387	0.940932	0.3639
SH04	-0.281072	0.193485	-1.452683	0.1700
RESID01_SH	0.173500	0.357831	0.484866	0.6358

R-squared	0.355580	Mean dependent var		0.068552
Adjusted R-squared	0.206867	S.D. dependent var		0.037610
S.E. of regression	0.033495	Akaike info criterion		-3.752513
Sum squared resid	0.014585	Schwarz criterion		-3.556463
Log likelihood	35.89636	Hannan-Quinn criter.		-3.733025
F-statistic	2.391057	Durbin-Watson stat		1.661793
Prob(F-statistic)	0.115710			

Source: EViews version 7

Appendix 3: Retail sector regression estimation outputs

Dependent Variable: BJT
Method: Least Squares
Date: 02/26/13   Time: 19:30
Sample (adjusted): 2003Q3 2009Q3
Included observations: 25 after adjustments

Variable	Coefficient	Std. Error	t-Statistic	Prob.
C	0.092043	0.051099	1.801259	0.0860
BJT01	0.713964	0.331000	2.156993	0.0427
BJT04	-0.231595	0.224807	-1.030198	0.3146
RESID01_BJT	-0.638554	0.301212	-2.119949	0.0461
R-squared	0.193992	Mean dependent var		0.171826
Adjusted R-squared	0.078849	S.D. dependent var		0.044894
S.E. of regression	0.043087	Akaike info criterion		-3.305526
Sum squared resid	0.038987	Schwarz criterion		-3.110506
Log likelihood	45.31908	Hannan-Quinn criter.		-3.251436
F-statistic	1.684782	Durbin-Watson stat		2.002633
Prob(F-statistic)	0.200754			

Dependent Variable: BKT
Method: Least Squares
Date: 02/26/13   Time: 19:30
Sample (adjusted): 2003Q3 2009Q3
Included observations: 25 after adjustments

Variable	Coefficient	Std. Error	t-Statistic	Prob.
C	0.116854	0.045844	2.548945	0.0187
BKT01	0.431464	0.272077	1.585817	0.1277
BKT04	-0.235797	0.233152	-1.011349	0.3234
RESID01_BKT	0.093693	0.275925	0.339561	0.7376
R-squared	0.236099	Mean dependent var		0.142506
Adjusted R-squared	0.126971	S.D. dependent var		0.052764
S.E. of regression	0.049301	Akaike info criterion		-3.036114
Sum squared resid	0.051042	Schwarz criterion		-2.841094
Log likelihood	41.95142	Hannan-Quinn criter.		-2.982023
F-statistic	2.163495	Durbin-Watson stat		1.999392
Prob(F-statistic)	0.122568			

Dependent Variable: HKT				
Method: Least Squares				
Date: 02/26/13 Time: 19:31				
Sample (adjusted): 2003Q3 2009Q3				
Included observations: 25 after adjustments				

Variable	Coefficient	Std. Error	t-Statistic	Prob.
C	0.070406	0.033592	2.095897	0.0484
HKT01	0.098842	0.285245	0.346517	0.7324
HKT04	0.121161	0.220109	0.550460	0.5878
RESID01_HKT	0.509671	0.312867	1.629033	0.1182
R-squared	0.302095	Mean dependent var		0.095654
Adjusted R-squared	0.202394	S.D. dependent var		0.073415
S.E. of regression	0.065566	Akaike info criterion		-2.465862
Sum squared resid	0.090278	Schwarz criterion		-2.270842
Log likelihood	34.82327	Hannan-Quinn criter.		-2.411771
F-statistic	3.030020	Durbin-Watson stat		1.907666
Prob(F-statistic)	0.052072			

Dependent Variable: JKT				
Method: Least Squares				
Date: 02/26/13 Time: 19:31				
Sample (adjusted): 2003Q3 2009Q3				
Included observations: 25 after adjustments				

Variable	Coefficient	Std. Error	t-Statistic	Prob.
C	0.179895	0.101644	1.769845	0.0913
JKT01	-0.183612	0.511878	-0.358703	0.7234
JKT04	0.000614	0.343546	0.001787	0.9986
RESID01_JKT	0.181723	0.470320	0.386381	0.7031
R-squared	0.007357	Mean dependent var		0.152647
Adjusted R-squared	-0.134449	S.D. dependent var		0.058498
S.E. of regression	0.062307	Akaike info criterion		-2.567850
Sum squared resid	0.081525	Schwarz criterion		-2.372830
Log likelihood	36.09813	Hannan-Quinn criter.		-2.513760
F-statistic	0.051881	Durbin-Watson stat		1.762189
Prob(F-statistic)	0.983966			

Dependent Variable: KLT
Method: Least Squares
Date: 02/26/13   Time: 19:32
Sample (adjusted): 2003Q3 2009Q3
Included observations: 25 after adjustments

Variable	Coefficient	Std. Error	t-Statistic	Prob.
C	0.097139	0.052085	1.865018	0.0762
KLT01	0.274548	0.361362	0.759759	0.4558
KLT04	-0.078470	0.265924	-0.295083	0.7708
RESID01_KLT	-0.008764	0.345960	-0.025332	0.9800

R-squared	0.076921	Mean dependent var		0.119986
Adjusted R-squared	-0.054947	S.D. dependent var		0.040722
S.E. of regression	0.041826	Akaike info criterion		-3.364936
Sum squared resid	0.036738	Schwarz criterion		-3.169916
Log likelihood	46.06171	Hannan-Quinn criter.		-3.310846
F-statistic	0.583317	Durbin-Watson stat		1.939766
Prob(F-statistic)	0.632534			

Dependent Variable: MNT
Method: Least Squares
Date: 02/26/13   Time: 19:32
Sample (adjusted): 2003Q3 2009Q3
Included observations: 25 after adjustments

Variable	Coefficient	Std. Error	t-Statistic	Prob.
C	0.067860	0.035413	1.916223	0.0690
MNT01	0.776536	0.313371	2.478008	0.0218
MNT04	-0.293442	0.244614	-1.199610	0.2437
RESID01_MNT	-0.422535	0.269703	-1.566670	0.1321

R-squared	0.231756	Mean dependent var		0.123245
Adjusted R-squared	0.122007	S.D. dependent var		0.050742
S.E. of regression	0.047546	Akaike info criterion		-3.108577
Sum squared resid	0.047474	Schwarz criterion		-2.913557
Log likelihood	42.85721	Hannan-Quinn criter.		-3.054487
F-statistic	2.111687	Durbin-Watson stat		2.132179
Prob(F-statistic)	0.129209			

Dependent Variable: SGT
Method: Least Squares
Date: 02/26/13   Time: 19:33
Sample (adjusted): 2003Q3 2009Q3
Included observations: 25 after adjustments

Variable	Coefficient	Std. Error	t-Statistic	Prob.
C	0.049003	0.039593	1.237683	0.2295
SGT01	0.632463	0.317312	1.993190	0.0594
SGT04	-0.165728	0.293703	-0.564271	0.5785
RESID01_SGT	-0.056952	0.401751	-0.141759	0.8886

R-squared	0.364870	Mean dependent var	0.088033
Adjusted R-squared	0.274138	S.D. dependent var	0.048100
S.E. of regression	0.040980	Akaike info criterion	-3.405830
Sum squared resid	0.035266	Schwarz criterion	-3.210810
Log likelihood	46.57288	Hannan-Quinn criter.	-3.351740
F-statistic	4.021372	Durbin-Watson stat	1.898654
Prob(F-statistic)	0.020849		

Dependent Variable: SHT
Method: Least Squares
Date: 02/26/13   Time: 19:36
Sample (adjusted): 2003Q3 2009Q3
Included observations: 25 after adjustments

Variable	Coefficient	Std. Error	t-Statistic	Prob.
C	0.174225	0.069733	2.498478	0.0208
SHT01	0.126695	0.308739	0.410362	0.6857
SHT04	-0.162922	0.218877	-0.744352	0.4649
RESID01_SHT	0.354354	0.299560	1.182917	0.2501

R-squared	0.255131	Mean dependent var	0.168312
Adjusted R-squared	0.148721	S.D. dependent var	0.047574
S.E. of regression	0.043894	Akaike info criterion	-3.268415
Sum squared resid	0.040461	Schwarz criterion	-3.073395
Log likelihood	44.85519	Hannan-Quinn criter.	-3.214325
F-statistic	2.397624	Durbin-Watson stat	2.070980
Prob(F-statistic)	0.096771		

Appendix 4 – The Multi Factor APT Model

Dependent Variable: ATR				
Method: Least Squares				
Date: 06/23/16 Time: 02:13				
Sample: 1 29				
Included observations: 27				
Variable	**Coefficient**	**Std. Error**	**t-Statistic**	**Prob.**
Constant, C	0.082035	0.020529	3.996048	0.0006
GDP	0.006394	0.005941	1.076262	0.2935
IR	-0.000254	0.002020	-0.125704	0.9011
VR	0.027067	0.008601	3.146842	0.0047
DUM_FC	0.041436	0.024084	1.720474	0.0994
R-squared	0.375489	**Mean dependent var**		0.134156
Adjusted R-squared	0.261942	**S.D. dependent var**		0.067535
S.E. of regression	0.05802	**Akaike info criterion**		-2.690495
Sum squared resid	0.074058	**Schwarz criterion**		-2.450525
F-statistic	3.30689	**Durbin-Watson stat**		2.096053
Prob(F-statistic)	0.028913			

Source: EViews Version 7 and author, 2016

Appendix 5 – GDP growth rate

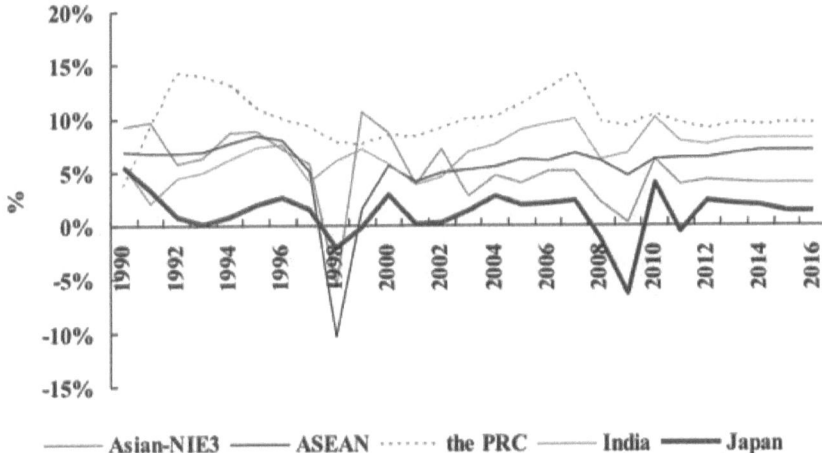

Source: Asian Development Bank Institute (http://www.asiapathways-adbi.org/2012/01/introduction-to-asia-pathways/) and Author, 2016

Appendix 6 – Interest rate movements for 13 cities

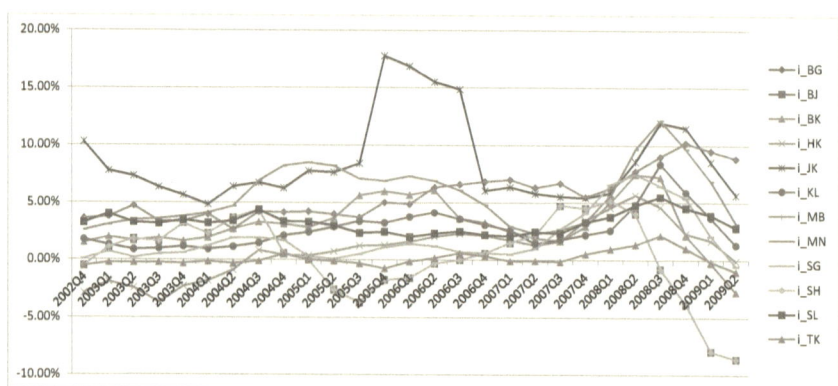

Source: Author, 2016

CHAPTER 4

THE RISK-RETURN BEHAVIOR OF REAL ESTATE MEZZANINE INVESTMENT (REMI) – THE SINGAPORE EXPERIENCE

For decades, investors have utilized varying combinations and structures of debt and equity to finance real estate investments. Real estate mezzanine investment (REMI) was introduced in the advanced economies in the early 1990s, when real estate capital became scarce, prompting significant investment opportunities for alternative capital structures. REMI became an important source of capital in Singapore, one of East Asia's rapidly growing economy, for direct commercial real estate acquisitions, development and refinancing. Traditional first mortgage providers had become reluctant to finance projects at loan-to-value (LTV) ratios in excess of 65%. REMI is debt capital that gives the lender (investor) the rights to convert to an ownership in the direct real estate asset if the loan is not paid back in time and in full. It is generally subordinated to a bank's senior and junior debts and is senior only to the equity owner's position in the direct real estate asset. As REMI is provided to a borrower quickly with little due diligence on the part of the investor and with little or no collateral on the physical real estate asset, such REMI is aggressively priced with a substantial spread over a bank's loan rate. The challenge for the REM investor is to price the REMI appropriately on a risk-adjusted return principle, to provide adequate compensation for the risk taken. Chapter 4 is prompted by three key motivations:

- REMI is a relatively new financial innovation in Asia. Many issues relating to how it is structured are not rigorously examined. An in-depth examination should throw new light on the REMI over traditional sources of financing.
- Owing to its short history, traditional empirical methods cannot be adopted while modern derivative theory may offer more REMI insights.
- Singapore's relatively stable real estate market albeit its speculative boom periods of 1994-1996 and 2006-2008, provides a good context to examine the REMI risk-return behavior.

As an intermediate debt piece in the capital structure, REMI provides a return exceeding that of senior debt. The increased return comes at the expense of increased risk because REM investors are risk averse. If today's price is below expectation then REM investors should be remunerated for bearing the increased risk. To price REMI general, the expected values need to be adjusted for the REM investor's risk preferences and with discounted rates that vary between investors. However, an individual's risk preference is difficult to quantify. In the complete market and with no arbitrage opportunities, the probabilities of future values can be adjusted once and for all, such that the future values incorporate all the investor's risk premia. The resulting probability distribution denotes the risk-neutral probabilities, whereby every asset can be priced simply by taking its expected payoff (Ho et al., 2003 and 2007). Three pertinent research question can be posed:

- What are the REMI risky factors?
- How will these factors affect the REMI return within the context of the Singapore real estate market?
- What is the risk-adjusted return once the risky factors are taken into consideration?

Hence, Chapter 4 thus adopts the discrete-time binomial asset tree model in association with risk neutral pricing to discuss the *ex-ante* REMI. The empirical treatment involves the rigorous discrete-time forecasting of Singapore's prime office sector rent and capital value, given its market conditions and assumptions. Subsequently, the REMI total returns are discussed under the probability-weighted average cash flow approach. In particular, the series of natural default probabilities are envisaged, corresponding to the respective REMI original interest rates.

The Related Literature

Holding period returns (HPRs) for mezzanine loan investment is shown by sensitivity and simulation analyses to generate high double digit expected (Ho & Sing, 2003). Its initial 6- year anticipated return is consistent with the achievable annual rate of HPRs of 25%-40% for mezzanine loan investment in the US commercial mortgage market. Mezzanine loan investment offers high expected risk-adjusted returns a potential investment opportunity in the Singapore office sector. Mezzanine's HPR excess return of 100 basis point relative to the primary debt's HPR, may well be at least 100 basis point to adequately compensate the mezzanine loan investor. Some limitations of the study:

- In the discounted cash flow (DCF) framework for simulating the projected holding period returns, excessive high rates of return are obtained towards the end of the loan period.

- The lack of mezzanine debt "comparables" in Singapore is a significant problem but not too severe.
- Due to the confidential nature of direct real estate asset, firms seem unwilling to disclose their asset underwriting and operational parameters but choose to give a close estimate.
- The study assumes minimal transaction cost that does not take into consideration other costs that may be relevant in the computation of returns. Therefore, actual returns may be even lower as the impact of the other cost is omitted from the analysis.

Nevertheless, it is noteworthy that the Government of Singapore Investment Corporation (GIC) suffers the large write-down of its US$575 million mezzanine loan investment in 2009, and the additional investment equity loss of US$100 million (Chan, 2010). Both investments are backed by Manhattan's "Stuyvesant Town and Peter Cooper Village", the 80-acre 11,000-unit mixed use apartment complex on 1st Avenue, between 14th Street and 23rd street in Manhattan. Such a large direct teal estate complex, built in the 1940s, is purchased for US$5.4 billion in 2006 by Tishman Speyer Properties and the private equity powerhouse Black Rock unit. These two owners owe hundreds of millions of US$ to their tenants by New York's Court of Appeals ruling. Unable to raise rents, these two owners default on their loan and to declare bankruptcy when loan restructuring fails. This large apartment complex plunged by >half to less than US$2 billion. Therefore, GIC's global real estate portfolio slumps by more than 20 per cent in S$ terms for the financial year ended on 31 March 2009. However, GIC said in September 2009 that it recovers more than half of those foregoing loses.

The REMI denotes that layer of financing between a company's senior debt and its equity. REMI is a unique debt capital that grants the lender-investor the right(s) to convert that debt capital to an equity ownership if this debt capital is not paid back on time and in full. Structurally, the REMI is subordinate to the senior debt but that the REMI is senior to equity or common stock. As the REMI is provided to the borrower with limited due diligence on the part of the lender-investor and with little or no collateral, such REMI is aggressively priced with a higher required investment return. The return may be in the form of higher interest rate or equity participation. Compared to equity, REMI may offer the advantages of a lower transaction cost, no management control and a predefined exit arrangement. When the mezzanine investor earns much of its returns that are tied directly to the performance of the borrowing company (instead of through equity ownership), the investor then participates in the success or failure of that company. The returns are limited to the REMI life arrangement. This way, the REMI can eliminate outside ownership and management control issues that often concern entrepreneurs, and that the REMI does not dilute shareholders' equity (Ho et al., 2003 and 2017).

Although there are disparities among REMIs in the capital market, there are four key common characteristics:

- REMI is a junior debt that is subordinate to the senior debt.
- Repayment is a bullet type, i.e., the loan principal is repaid at maturity.
- Owing to subordination, REMI risk is higher that of senior loan. Therefore, the REM investor demands a higher yield, compared to the senior debt yield.
- REMI has an inherent yield that includes a cash interest, which is higher than that of the senior debt cash interest. REMI's cash interest can be a fixed or floating rate. Besides the cash interest, the REM investment yield consists of an equity component. Such an equity component grants the REM investor the right(s) to take over the direct real estate asset from the original owner, if and only if the REMI interest is not or fully paid up.

Institutional and private investors find REMIs to be relatively secure investment vehicles because of the privilege of having a first call or priority position over the borrower and the equity investor (Ho

& Sing, 2003). From the investor's perspective, the REM investor is preferred to the equity investor because if the borrower defaults, then the REM investor has the ability to foreclose and pay off the first mortgagee, and so owns the direct real estate asset for a lower transaction cost. The REM investor can achieve higher returns that are adjusted for its high risk. From the borrower's perspective, the REM debt capital is more flexible than bank debt, and that such debt capital is less expensive and dilutive than equity. However, private REMI securities are the lowest ranking debt obligation in a borrower's capital structure and that such REM securities contain a very loose covenant package. REMI securities can be used by a borrower to achieve higher gearing (i.e., LTV ratio) levels and returns on the equity structure.

There are different forms of REM investment with different functions. On subordinated debt, the most straightforward case, the REM investor provides a subordinated debt to the direct real estate asset owner. The investor usually receives a fixed-income yield for operational, fully leased direct real estate assets that generate adequate cash flow to service a mortgage, and that provide a return to the equity owner. Sponsors seek REMI to leverage their returns or limit their at-risk equity.

On subordinated debt with delayed payment, interest payments on private REMI securities involve a cash-pay portion and a pay-in-kind (PIK) portion. The total stated interest rate return usually ranges between 14% and 16%, with the cash-pay portion generally ranging between 12% and 14% while the remainder of the interest portion is in the PIK. Such an investment structure is arranged by REM borrowers, who do not want to disburse cash flow during the original real estate development life-cycle stage.

On the subordinated debt with equity warrants, the equity kicker is a contingent common equity by way of warrants or a conversion option, to which registration rights are typically attached. Warrants are the most common form of the equity component of a REMI issue. The exercise price of the warrant is nominal or at least substantially below the market value of the borrower-company's common stock.

The warrant holds some value that is at least equal to the difference between the market value of the common stock and the exercise price. Such warrants have at least a ten-year term each and represent a minority stake to the issuer. The REM investor may require a "put" option on the warrant and on any common stock purchased with the warrant. The equity kicker is adopted in real estate development projects in the (pre) construction stage, with well-developed plans and budgets for development and subsequent stabilization through to lease up. Sponsors seek REMI to fund a portion of the construction costs and to leverage their return or to free up equity.

The performance participating junior mortgage of a REMI is used for non-stabilized or value-added direct real estate assets, wherein the cash flows have not stabilized or wherein the direct real estate asset is undervalued for some identifiable reason. Sponsors seek this REMI type to execute the value-add investment strategy in order to enhance cash flows.

On the REMI market, Watkins et al. (2003) provide a comprehensive review. As a financing innovation, REMI emerged in the early 1990's. During the 1980's, a typical real estate deal is financed with a combination of senior debt and equity, as the senior lenders provide a high leveraged mortgage to tax-induced investors, thereby limiting the need for REMI. Primary lenders do not desire junior mortgages because a junior mortgagee is likely to raise legal obstacles to the senior lender's remedies in the event of default. This REMI use has no claim on the underlying direct real estate asset but secured through a pledge by the borrowers for their equity.

In the early 1990's, many senior debt holders experienced difficulties in foreclosing mortgaged direct real estate assets that are also subject to a junior mortgage. Banks then adopt a more conservative approach to lending while the senior debtors are only willing to provide loans up to a certain loan-to-value (LTV) ratio, with interest rates softening in the last ten years. An increasing gap emerges in the capital market structure between borrowers and traditional lenders. Such gap creates risks for new investments in the form of constrained liquidity while opportunities emerge for investors to earn higher risk-adjusted returns through investment vehicles, designed to exploit the gap. REMI so provides an alternative financing means to raise capital. The REMI market can take the pressure off the CMBS (commercial mortgage backed securities) issuers, the rating agencies, the B-piece buyers and direct real estate asset. The REMI market can place the mezzanine equity risks with the emerging and appropriate institutions, entering the market.

REMI can be construed to be "a range of risks rather than a vehicle or structure" (Petch, 1997). Table 1 outlines three major types of REMI and the securitized REMI. Each type has different LTV ratios that expose them to different risk factors with different expected returns. Stabilized direct real estate assets are main candidates for the REMI as their cash flows can support a LTV ratio greater than that of the typical senior debt. Two primary situations for mezzanine investment pertain to a buyer, who seeks financing related to acquiring a direct real estate asset while the owner wants to take equity out of his direct real estate asset. In other words, the owners of stabilized direct real estate assets seek the REMI to leverage their returns and to limit their "at-risk" capital (Watkins et al., 2003).

Debt financing ought to be combined with equity to arrive at an optimal financing point, whereby any increase of the debt to equity ratio is considered risky, resulting in a fall in the profitability of the investment. Various models are developed to estimate the optimal point of financing for, e.g., the capital asset pricing model. McDonald (2007) examines the optimal leverage when REMI is available, and he finds that investors may use REMI even if the REMI interest rate exceeds the target after-tax rate of return on equity. Nevertheless, real estate developers and investors have continually used REMIs in order to possibly reach the optimal point of the debt-to-equity ratio. A limit on the loan principal issued is typically imposed by banks and financial institutions to curb any lending amounting to 100% of the loan principal. Then, the investors and developers are required to make up for the shortfall in the required loan principal through secondary financing.

Table 1. Main Types of Real Estate Mezzanine Investment (REMI)

Mezzanine Investment Type	Property Characteristics	Typical Deal Structures	Total Return Expectations*	Key Risk Issues
Stabilized	• Existing cash flow • Limited lease-up risk • Minor rehabilitation or repositioning	• 70% to 85% LTV piece • No participation in cash flow or residual value • 3 to 7-year term • Exit through refi or mortgage amortization. • Cash flow sweep/lockbox	14% to 18% IRR	• Severe value decline • Magnitude and timing of cash flow • Interest rate risk • Quality of underwriting • Management control
Value – Added	• Some existing cash flow • Moderate rehabilitation, repositioning. • Moderate to substantial lease-up, releasing required • Completed property will represent 75% to 80% loan to value based upon the total capital structure	• 70% to 95% LTC piece • 10% to 15% interest rate, with participation in cash flow and/or residual value • 18 month to 3-year term • Exit through refi or sale • Value creation should allow return of 100% of capital through refi.	18% to 25% IRR	• Severe value decline • Magnitude and timing of cash flow • Interest rate risk • Quality of underwriting • Exit timing • Management control
Development	• No existing cash flow • To-be-built property • Completed property will represent 75% - 80% loan to value based upon the total capital structure	• 70% to 95% LTC piece • Participation in cash flow and residual value • 3 year term • Exit through refi, sale, or "presale" • Value creation should allow return of 100% of capital through refi.	20% to 30% IRR	• Significant value decline • Magnitude and timing of cash flows • Financial risk • Quality of underwriting • Exit timing • Development risk • Construction risk • Management control
Securitized	• Mortgages securitized by a pool of properties. • Existing cash flow • Stabilized underlying assets	• 70% to 75% LTV tranche of CMBS • 10-year term	20% to 25% IRR	• Severe value decline • Financial risk • Quality of underwriting • Management quality • Cross-defaulted first loss • Management Control

*Returns presume leverage at the property level but not at the "fund" or investor level. Returns are net of 1% asset management fee and 20% of profits typically paid to sponsor.
Source: The Muldavin Company.

Authors, 2020.

REMI Default and Remedy

REMI has the priority of cash flows in between the first mortgage lenders and the equity owners. In the event of borrower default, REM investors have the option to assume the first mortgage obligation or alternatively, the REM investors can choose to walk away from the bad investment without obligation. There are usually three REMI scenarios outlined herewith:

- <u>Scenario 1</u>. If the cash flow after the REMI interest is positive, implying that the NOI (net operating income) is enough to cover both the interest of the senior loan and the REMI. The REM investor collects the deemed interest plus the principal at the end of the REMI's term.

- Scenario 2. If the cash flow after the REMI interest is negative but that the cash flow after the senior loan interest is positive, the implication is that the REMI is in default while the associated senior loan is safe. In "Scenario 2", the REM investor takes over the direct real estate asset, and the cash flow to the REM investor is then that cash flow after netting off the senior loan interest quantum, but adding on the residual capital value after deducting the senior loan at the end of the REMI's loan term.
- Scenario 3. If the cash flow after the senior loan interest is negative, implying that the senior loan and the REMI are in default. In "Scenario 3", the direct real estate asset is liquidated and the REM investor gets back the residual value of the direct real estate asset, after deducting the associated senior loan quantum. If the capital value of the direct real estate asset under "Scenario 3" are even lower than the senior loan principal, then the REM investor gets nothing.

In practice, there is an inter-creditor agreement between the senior mortgage lender and the REM investor, with the threshold issue relating to the REM investor's ability to realize its collateral. It is therefore that ability to take over the borrower's position and to become the owner of the direct real estate asset. The REMI's success or failure may well depend upon the terms of the inter-creditor agreement with the mortgage lender, because the REMI ultimately has the mere right to step into the shoes of the borrower in the event of problems. Typical provisions can those outlined below. In a typical REMI structure, the mortgage (senior) borrower is a bankruptcy-remote single-purpose entity (SPE), in the form of a partnership or a limited liability company, and with the following key features:

- Notification of non-payment or default on the first mortgage - the senior lender must give notice to the REM investor of any default under the senior loan.

- The right to cure any default on the first mortgage - the REM investor wants to protect itself by taking over the direct real estate asset, and by not allowing the senior lender to foreclose.
- The senior lender takes no action if the borrower defaults under the REMI i.e. there have been no cross-default provision in the senior loan terms.

The REMI Key Market-Wide Risks

REMI are similar to those found in other real estate investments but that they incorporate debt and equity risk characteristics, depending on the particular REMI type and structure (Ballard & Muldavin, 2000; Watkins et al., 2003). The key market risk factors consist of the unavoidable market-wide real estate and capital markets risk, affecting the REMI return volatility. The capital market risk denotes the risk that capitalization rates increase and that capital values decline, leading to the investors' inability or unwillingness to pay off their financed positions. Real estate market risk denotes the market-wide risk that real estate market conditions change for the worse and that market rents decline, leading to the inability to pay off the in-place interest obligations. It is argued that REM investors are oversimplifying the real estate market dynamics.

In contrast to the early 1990's, real estate markets are in a state of relative supply and demand balance, enabling REM investors to comfortably predict stable or strong real estate market conditions for the next several years (Rosen & Anderson, 1999). Many real estate markets seem to be moving back and forth around their peak and equilibrium positions, as supply seeks to meet growing, changing demand. Enhancing information availability to all real estate market participants should help to avoid any sustained overbuilding in real estate markets. The implication is that the real estate markets are more efficient and less volatile than the situation historically (Mueller, 2000). The impact of a normal economic downturn on real estate markets is likely to be mild (Louargand, 2000).

Other risks are non-market wide like financial risk, and such risks are highly constrained in terms of being hedged or mitigated like the risk on the quality of underwriting and tenant risk. Tenant risk: denotes that risk when tenants fail to make timely rental payment. It is usually mitigated via a tenancy deposit. Risk on the quality of underwriting denotes that risk, controlled through conducting careful direct real estate asset valuation from several independent appraisers. Interest rate risk denotes the risk from rising interest rates, which in turn increases default probability. The interest rate risk is hedged via interest rate derivatives. Financial risk is a highly specific non-market wide risk due to the REMI being inherently levered but the REMI merely forms a small slice of the capital structure (typically between 5% and 20%). Financial risk is subordinate to other financing means such that the full mezzanine principal loss occurs before the first dollar loss occurs to the senior position. The smaller the piece of the capital structure that is represented by the REMI, then the more severe the REM principle loss becomes.

REMI Pricing

REMI is like any other investment opportunity and before investing, it is essential to understand the expected (*ex ante*) risks and return from asset pricing models. The capital asset pricing models of Sharpe (1964), Linter (1965) and Mosin (1966) envisage the systematic risk, i.e. market-wide risk, is to be reflected in the return premium and is therefore the primary determinant of asset price. Ross (1976) and Roll (1977) criticize the early single factor models while Roll and Ross (1980) provide an alternative view, with more variables entering the return generating process. While the REMI return expectation is subject to the common factors in the macro economy, the return varies significantly based upon the structure of a particular REMI. Required return rises as the level of lease-up risk increases and that the returns rise as the loan-to-value ratio rises. The required return is influenced by the REMI type and size, the financial strength of the direct real estate asset and the borrower as well as the certainty of the exit strategy. When evaluating a REMI strategy, the investor has to determine whether or not the increased yield(s) justify the commensurate risk(s) (Ballard & Muldavin, 2000).

The REMI success also depends on the manager's ability to identify correctly those situations where the risk of losing the REMI's principal is limited, and where the potential for equity or for the accrued interest appreciation is high. The deal team targets REMIs in smaller companies that may have volatile performance, less experienced management, fewer liquidity options and the need for additional capital. Success for such companies may be subject to factors over which the company's management team has little or no control, including changes in technologies, markets, competition, government regulations and the health of the economy. While the REMI portfolio may have numerous REMIs, the portfolio performance may be adversely affected by the results of a few investments. Additionally, the REMI deal team structures some control on its REMIs through board participation, representation rights and stringent loan documentation. Typically, the REMI deal team is to be a minority shareholder in each company within the REMI portfolio. The deal team is therefore unable to exercise full REMI management control.

REMI Forward Looking Pricing

The challenge is how to price the REMI to compensate for the risk undertaken by investors? So far, there is virtually no formal valuation model for pricing REMI. We need a forward-looking measure of risks and so examine the REMI. Common *ex ante* approaches include the Monte Carlo risk simulation model, the vector auto regression (VAR) model and the discrete-time binomial asset tree Model. The Monte Carlo risk simulation model first proposed by Metropolis and Ulam (1949), takes into account the distributions and the associated probabilities for the input variables and the model generates a probability distribution of future values. Such simulation provides a range of possibilities for the future outcomes. However, the limitation is that the results are only as good as the input variables, and we need to pre-specify the unique distributions of the deployed input variables. The VAR model is commonly used for forecasting systems with respect to the interrelated time series. The VAR model sidesteps the need for structural modeling by treating every endogenous variable in the system as a function of the lagged values of all the endogenous variables in the system. Advocated by Sims (1980) to be a theory-free method to estimate economic relationships, and similar to Monte Carlo simulation model, the VAR model is limited by its inputs.

Another model that is less impacted by input variables is the discrete time-based binomial asset tree model by Cox et. al. (1979). An important assumption is that the probability of each price change follows the risk-neutral probability. By simulating asset price on a "discrete time" basis, the next period asset value is estimated through multiplying the upward and downward factors with their respective risk-neutral probabilities for the two nodal branches. Being risk neutral implies that investors value risk at a constant value, and that they accept exactly the same interest rate for all assets. However, actual market prices are affected by the willingness to pay for the risk undertaken. Implementing the discrete-time binomial asset tree model with real world probabilities is the resolution (Cox & Rubinstein, 1985; Baz & Strong, 1997). Although such a model avoids the inputs and focuses on the characteristics of the output itself, the drawback is its "discrete-time" basis. Therefore, the ability to forecast an accurate probability of default is limited and is only possible to forecast the "jump point" when the default is likely to happen (Ho, 2007).

The Discrete-Time Binomial Asset Tree (DTBAT) Model

The DTBAT model first constructs the office rental-expectation binomial tree from a unique real estate market analysis (REMA) of the Singapore prime office space under "The Data" section of Chapter 4, with the starting nodal rent set at S$12 per sq ft per month (psfpm). Subsequent quarter's upward and downward rents are forecasted by multiplying this S$12 psfpm by the upward and downward factors as shown in Table 2, with the associated risk neutral probabilities. The process is repeated for 16 quarters, assuming a 4-year term for the senior loan and the REMI. Secondly, the office capital value (CV)-expectation binomial tree is constructed in a similar manner with the starting nodal CV of S$2,200 psf. (See Appendices I & II for details of the two discrete-time binomial asset trees of the prime office market rent and CV in Singapore.)

Then for each node, the net operating income (NOI) is estimated, taking account of the prime office market rent, the assumed LTV ratio and the interest rates. The NOI is compared with the senior loan interest and the REMI interest to see whether or not any default occurs (see Appendices 1, 1A). As afore mentioned in the "REMI *Default and Remedy*" sub-section, the REMI leads to the earlier three 'Scenarios'. The probability-weighted average cash flow for each path of the DTBAT model can be modeled. At maturity date, the prime office market CV DTBAT is matched with the respective nodes from the prime office market rental tree, to estimate the last REMI cash flow. Total return is measured as the yield to maturity (YTM) of the weighted-average cash flow. For e.g. if the NOI of the direct real estate portfolio follows Scenario 1 and no default occurs, then the REMI YTM is equal to its interest rate. If any of the default scenarios occur, then the YTM is lower than the interest rate. The default risk is measured by the spread between the YTM and the interest rate YTM.

The Data

The steady state Singapore real estate market provides the appropriate context for examining the REMI risk-return behavior. In addition, there are 20 real estate investment trusts (REITs) listed on the Singapore Stock Exchange, which has a total market capitalization of over S$46 billion. Private real estate property funds that include Morgan Stanley, Goldman Sachs, Macquarie, Lehman Brothers, ING, AIG and Pacific Star, are actively invested in the Singapore real estate market. With total investment sales of over S$20 billion and S$40 billion for 2006 and 2007 respectively, and assuming that 10% of the investments are funded by the REMI market, the market size is large at around S$2-4 billion.

Office Real Estate Market Analysis (REMA)

On the office REMA, Figs 1 & 2 depict the quarterly average market rent and CV (capital value) of Singapore's prime office sector from 1993 to 2007. The data is obtained from the international real estate consultancy, DTZ Leong Research Asia, Singapore. The data indicates that during the study period the Singapore prime office sector has experienced several cycles, enabling the estimation of the upward and downward factors and their respective risk neutral probabilities. The data indicates that market rents and CVs tend to move in the same direction, and that such a relationship is problematic under the REMI's default risk. So, when the direct real estate sector goes into a severe downturn, the resulting low cash flow from a direct real estate asset leads to rising defaults for that REMI's asset. The REM investor is prompted to take over the direct real estate asset owner's equity. The severe weakening of the direct real estate asset's CV results in a very low or even zero equity for the REMI (Ho, 2007 and 2017).

Table 2 presents the associated data descriptive statistics. Quarterly average rent has a mean of S$7.39 psfpm, with a standard deviation of 2.32. To estimate the up and down factors (u and d respectively), the quarterly rental growth factor (1 + growth rate) is divided into 2 groups, i.e. greater or smaller than 1, and then the average of each group is estimated. To normalize the growth factors, the average of each group is divided by the square root of their product. The risk neutral probability is estimated via the number of upward growths versus the downward growth. The estimation method is repeated for the prime office CV utilizing the DTZ Leong quarterly data (see Appendix III details for information).

Fig 1. Average Sector Rent & Growth Rate for Singapore's Prime Office

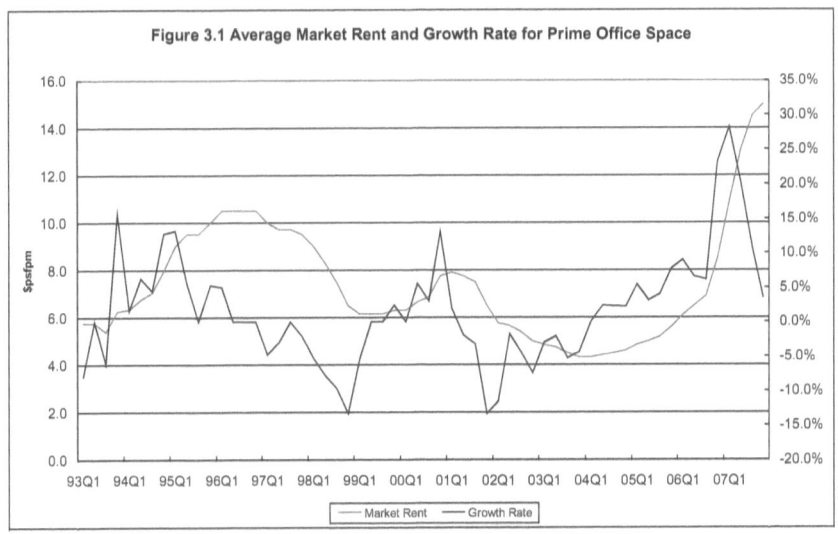

Source: DTZ Leong Research Asia and Authors, 2020.

Figure 2. Average Sector Capital Value (CV) for Singapore's Prime Office

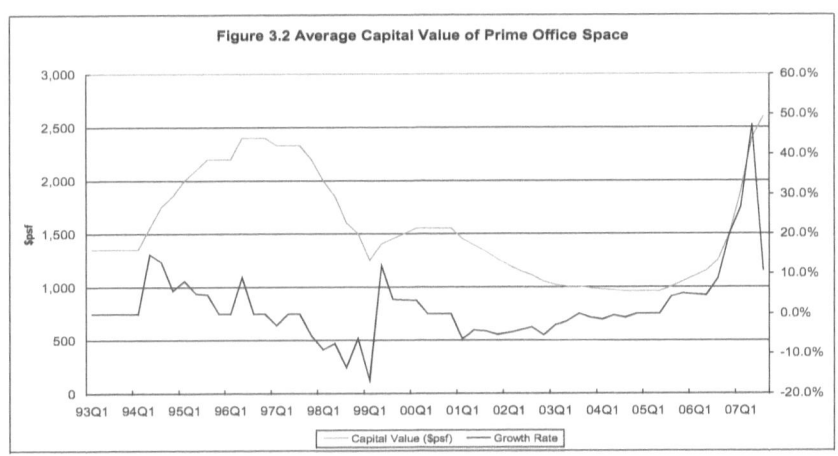

Source: DTZ Leong Research Asia and Authors, 2020.

From Table 2 and for the prime office rent, the upward growth factor is estimated to be 1.07 with a risk neutral probability of 58.3%. The downward growth factor is estimated to be 0.93 with a probability of 46.6%. The implication is that for the 72 quarters of rents, about 53.4% of the quarters experience a rental increase from the previous quarter, and with the average increase of 7.7%. The remaining 46.6% of the quarters experience a rental decrease of rent from the previous quarter, and with the average decrease of 7.2%. The growth factor numbers imply that Singapore's prime office rents have been highly volatile along a slight upward trend. The prime office CVs average S$1,565 psm and with the standard deviation of 528. The associated upward growth factor is 1.07 while its upward risk neutral probability is 50.0%. Prime office CV growth conforms to the mean-reversion process but with highly volatile changes quarter-on-quarter.

Table 2. Descriptive Statistics for Prime Office Sector Quarterly Average Rent & CV

Ave Rent (S$psfpm)	7.39	Ave CV (S$psf)	1,565
Std dev of Rent	2.32	Std dev of CV	503
Growth Factor (u)	1.07	Growth Factor (u)	1.07
Growth Factor (d)	0.93	Growth Factor (d)	0.93
Risk Neutral Probability (p)	58.3%	Risk Neutral Probability (p)	50.0%

Source: DTZ Leong Research Asia and Authors; 1990-2007, 2020.

On prime office natural vacancy, Grenadier (1995) and Khor (2000) define Singapore's prime office sector to be an equilibrium level of space inventory, attributable to a matching process between landlord and tenant. Office landlords hold an optimal buffer stock of prime office space to meet future leasing contingencies. Such a process is akin to the concept of natural unemployment rate in that the natural vacancy rate arises because of imperfect market information, which gives rise to friction in the prime office sector. Central to Khor's findings is that Singapore's prime office sector natural vacancy rate fluctuates around the 10% level. It is found that the prime office sector natural vacancy rate is between 10% and 12%. Other domestic survey findings on market sentiment indicate that the majority of building landlords and real estate consultants hold the common perception that the prime office sector natural vacancy rate is about 10%. Therefore, the natural vacancy of 10% is adopted in Chapter 4 and for its three planned "Scenarios".

Market Assumptions

Once the market rent of the Singapore prime office sector and its natural vacancy rate are available, then the revenue from the direct real estate portfolio is estimated. Operating expenses for a direct real estate asset are estimated to be S$1 psfpm for service charge, typical of the office sector, while a prevailing 10% property tax is imposed on income in Singapore. After netting off operating expenses from revenue is the net operating income (NOI) (see Appendix 1A). Domestic commercial banks usually require the borrower to hedge interest rate risk for the senior loan, and that the fixed interest rate of 4.0% p.a. typical of the domestic commercial banking sector is paid every quarter. Similarly, the REMI fixed interest rate is paid every quarter.

Results and Findings

This section discusses the empirical analysis to enable the discrete-time, binomial asset tree model estimation. In particular and based on the market assumptions, a series of natural default probabilities is envisaged corresponding to the respective REMI interest rates. The impact of LTV ratio pertaining to the senior loan and the REMI on the total return (TR) is examined. In general, a stable spread (of about 1.36%) exists between the REMI's original interest rate and its real TR. At different LTV ratios, such a spread tends to be stable for each different LTV ratio. The spread increases as the senior-loan LTV ratio increases and the spread conforms to a "staircase shape".

The results are generally consistent in that the market risk (i.e., real estate market risk and capital market risk), and the financial risk (i.e., the LTV ratio concerning the senior loan and the REMI), are the main risk factors affecting the REMI total return.

The REMI Discrete Default Probability

Initially a prime office portfolio is assumed that is 65% financed by that senior bank loan, based on a consensus among direct real estate investors and pertaining to an LTV ratio of 60% to 70% for a typical bank loan on a Singapore prime office building. 20% of that bank loan is typically financed by REMI. The interest rate of the senior loan is fixed at 4% p.a. It is observed that the REMI TR in terms of its interest rate ranges from 5.0% to 8.0% p.a. Given the estimated NOI assumptions in the foregoing real estate market analysis (REMA) and market assumptions, the market rent is estimated at which the borrower is to default on the REMI. Then focusing on the lowest boundary of the binomial asset tree (BAT) of the prime office market rent (see Appendices I & 1A), the default probability for a given REMI interest rate is estimated. However, owing to its "discrete time" nature, a main limitation of the BAT model is that it merely forecast the "discrete" default probability for a range of inputs. Accordingly, for that range of the REMI interest rate of between 5.0% and 8.0% p.a., there are three default probability categories as presented in Table 3 below.

Based on the common senior loan's LTV ratio specific to the Singapore prime office sector, the default probabilities are deemed to be the natural default probabilities for the domestic REMI. The natural default probability is attributed to the real estate and capital markets risk. In particular, a high REMI interest rate of 7.1% to 8.0% p.a. is required for the high default probability of 17.4%, while a 150 bps lower REMI interest rate is required for the lower default risk at 7.2%. An even lower REMI interest rate, close to the senior loan interest rate, requires the relatively lowest default probability of 3.0%.

Table 3. Default Probability under Different REMI Interest-Rate Ranges

REMI Interest Rate, p.a.	Default Probability
7.1%-8.0%	17.4%
5.5%-7.0%	7.2%
Below 5.0%	3.0%

Source: Authors, 2020.

The REMI TR (Total Return)

The REMI TR is measured by the yield to maturity (YTM) of the weighted average cash flow from the BAT paths. Figure 3 below depicts the REMI YTM and with the REMI interest rate as the X-axis. The spread between the REMI interest rate and the REMI TR is plotted, to see how much the REMI YTM drops from the original REMI interest rate, owing to the default risk. From Figure 3, the YTM of REMI increases as the original interest rate increases but it is lower than the original interest rate owing to default risk. One meaningful finding from Fig 3 is that the spread between the REMI interest rate and the REMI YTM, is stable (at around 1.34%-1.38% p.a.) for the different interest rates, owing to default risk. In particular, the other sets of the LTV ratio, concerning the senior loan and REMI, show that the spread is still generally stable.

It is explicit that the REMI default probability is stable once the market risk (i.e., the real estate and capital markets risk) and the financial risk (represented by the LTV ratio for the senior loan and the REMI), are controlled. Similar to the natural default probability, the stable spread between the REMI interest rate and the REMI YTM, are regarded to be the natural default spread that is specific to the Singapore prime office sector. Therefore, under a common structure, the REMI for such a prime office sector is to generate the REMI TR, which is about 1.36% lower than the original REMI interest rate.

The REMI TR with Different Senior Loan LTV Ratios

The REMI TR is next examined in relation to different senior loan LTV ratios. As expected, the REMI TR falls as the senior loan LTV ratio rises, Figure 4 below depicts the REMI YTM as against the different senior loan LTV ratio. The REMI's 20% LTV ratio and the REMI interest rate of 6.0% p.a. are assumed. Then the REMI TR of 5.8% is very close to the original REMI interest rate of 6.0%, when the senior loan LTV ratio is relatively low at 45%. As the senior-loan LTV ratio rises, the REMI YTM falls. For a senior-loan LTV ratio of 75%, the REMI's spread between the REMI original interest rate and the REMI YTM rises to over 3.0%. It is clear that the financial risk, owing to the senior loan's inherent leverage, is a significant factor affecting the REMI TR. Thus, the higher the senior loan inherent leverage, then the higher the financial risk.

Fige 3. Total Return for Mezzanine Investment with Fixed LTV Ratios

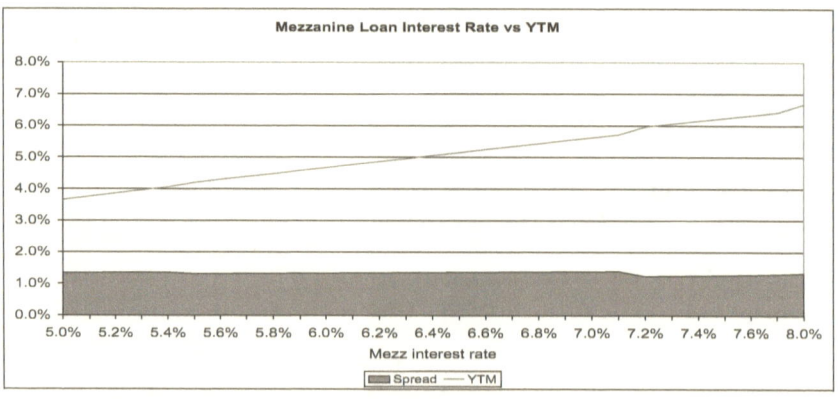

Source: Authors, 2020.

Fig 4. Total Return of Mezzanine with Different Senior Loan LTV

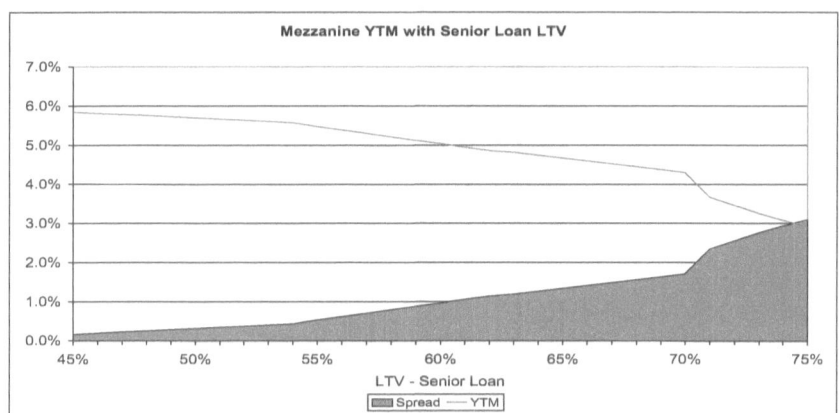

Source: Authors, 2020.

The REMI TRs with Different Senior Loan LTV Ratios and Different REMI Interest Rates

To examine the joint effect of financial risk, owing to the senior loan leverage and the different REMI interest rate on the REMI TR, the results in Figure 5 below are so depicted. Consistent with the foregoing results, the REMI TR as measured by the REMI YTM, falls as the senior loan TV ratio rises. The spread between the REMI interest rate and the REMI YTM is found to change with the different senior-loan LTV ratio (see Fig 6).

Such a spread conforms to a "staircase shape" 3-D (dimensional) plot with roughly the same spread for the different REMI interest rates, given the the senior loan LTV ratio's narrow range. The spread also increases as the senior loan LTV ratio rises. It is therefore inferred that the financial risk, measured by the existing senior loan LTV ratio, is the main cause of the REMI default probability, given the constant market risk.

Fig 5. REMI TR with Different Senior Loan LTV Ratios and REMI Interest Rates

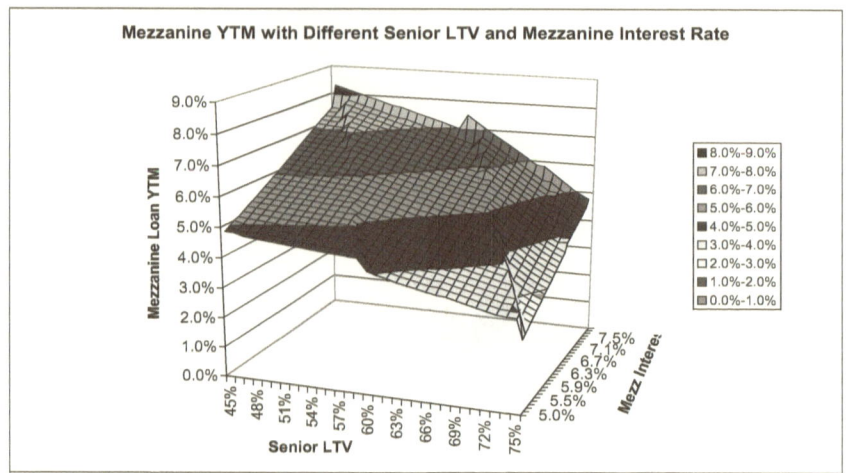

Source: Authors, 2020.

Fig 6. Spread Between the REMI Interest Rate and the REMI TR Under Different Senior Loan LTV Ratios And REMI Interest Rates

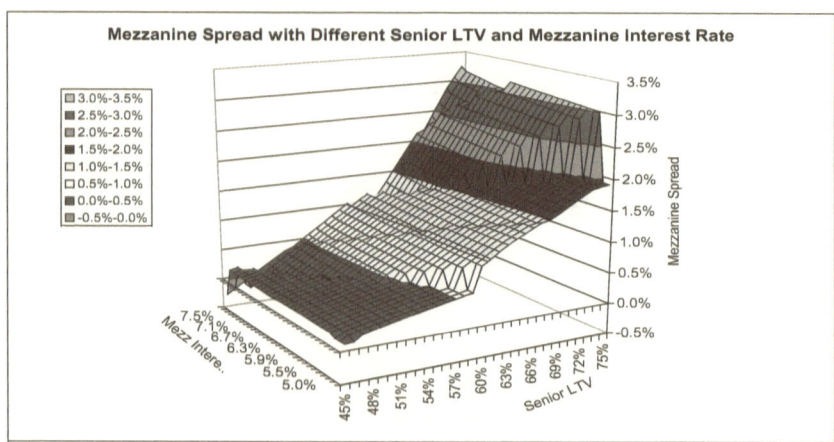

Source: Authors, 2020.

Concluding Remarks

The REMI is a new financial instrument for the real estate market in Asia although it would provide superior returns than those for usual typical commercial bank loans. The resultant risk exposure becomes relatively high. The Singapore real estate market has experienced robust growth over the past several years, with a fast-growing real estate investment trust (REIT) market and the teeming emergence of private equity fund investments. As a result, Chapter 4 is appropriately motivated to examine the risk-return behavior of mezzanine investment.

A discrete-time binomial asset tree model in association with risk neutral probabilities is estimated for the *ex ante examination* of the REMI. The empirical analysis involves a rigorous discrete-time forecasting of the market rent and capital value expectations of the prime office market in Singapore, given the conditions and assumptions unique to this market. Subsequently, the total return (TR) for mezzanine investment is investigated under a probability-weighted average cash flow approach.

In particular, a series of natural default probabilities is envisaged, corresponding to the respective REMI-investment interest rates. The impact of loan-to-value (LTV) ratio pertaining to the senior loan and the REMI on the total return for the mezzanine investment is examined. It is found that a generally stable spread (of about 1.36%) exists between REMI's original interest rate and its real total return. When Chapter 4 looks at different LTV ratios, the results show that such a spread tends to be stable for each different LTV ratio. This spread increases as the senior-loan LTV ratio increases and it follows a "staircase shape" 3-D (3-dimensional) plot. The results are generally consistent in that the market risk, i.e., real estate market risk and capital market risk, and the financial risk, represented by the LTV ratio concerning the senior loan and the mezzanine investment, are the main risk factors that affect the return for REMI.

Chapter 4 introduces a unique valuation model that examines the *ex ante* risk-return behavior of REMI specific to Singapore's prime office market. It introduces a rigorous straightforward model approach easily implemented in industry by adopting risk neutral pricing in a discrete-time binomial asset tree model. The results affirm that when we value a REMI, we need to be merely concerned with the inherent leverage that arises from the existing senior loan. A higher return would therefore be required to compensate for the higher financial risk and real estate market risk on the risk-adjusted return principle. While limited to Singapore, Chapter 4 can be extended to include other key cities and their real estate markets in Asia. A cross-city comparative study can be conducted to evaluate and contrast the risk-return behavior of REMI across the Asian region, in particular the key capital cities of interest.

Acknowledgement

The authors wish to gratefully acknowledge the initial work carried out for Chapter 4 by Ms HE Yun Fan, the higher MSc degree by research graduate of the NUS Department of Real Estate); and in consultation with Honorary Professor (University of Hertfordshire, Hatfield, UK), Dr HO Kim Hin / David and Associate Professor in Management (Dr) Javier Calero CUERVO (University of Macau, SAR China); during their meaningful brain storming sessions before Professor HO retired from the NUS SDE Department of Real Estate in May 2020.

THE VERSATILITY OF THE REAL ESTATE ASSET CLASS - THE SINGAPORE EXPERIENCE

Appendix I: Binomial Tree for Market Rent

Binomial Tree:

	Market Rent	Capital Value
u	1.0773	1.08055
d	0.928236507	0.92545
p	58%	50%

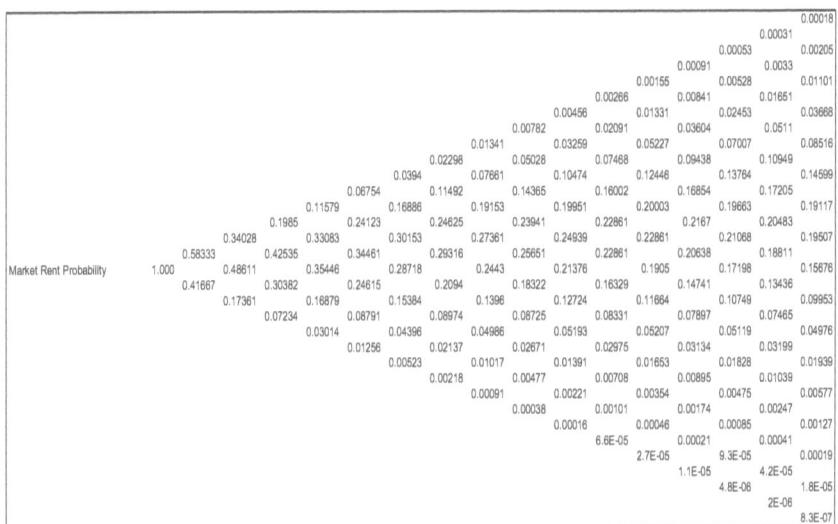

Appendix IA: Mezzanine Cash Flows, NOI, LTV & the Interest Rates

cap value	2200		
area	1		
Occupancy	90%		
Rental	12.000	9.84	7.12
svg	1.000		
proptax	10%		
noi	104.640		
LTV	65%		
interest	57.200	4%	
cash after i	47.440		
mezz	20%	133.33%	
interest	26.4	6.0%	
cash after i	21.040		

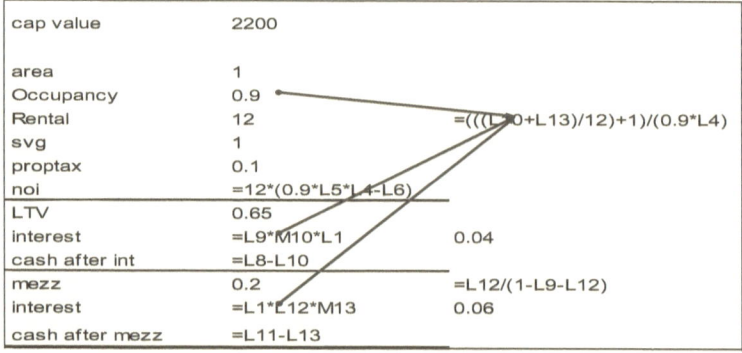

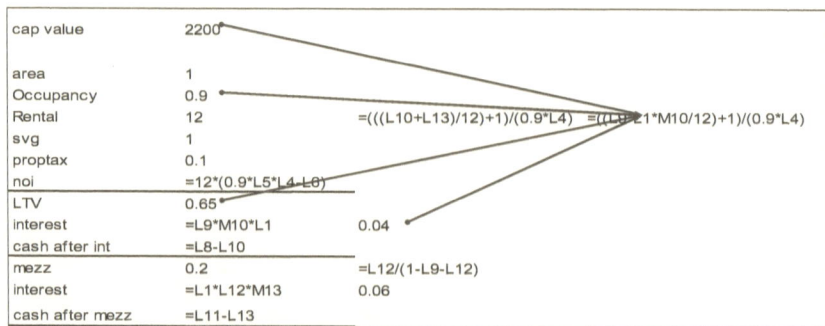

THE VERSATILITY OF THE REAL ESTATE ASSET CLASS - THE SINGAPORE EXPERIENCE

Mezzanine Cash Flow	6.6	6.6 6.6	6.6 6.6	6.6 6.6 7.3	6.6 6.6 6.6 5.6	6.6 6.6 6.6 7.3 3.9 2.4	6.6 6.6 6.6 5.6 3.9 1.0	6.6 6.6 6.6 7.3 3.9 2.4	6.6 6.6 6.6 5.6 3.9 1.0	6.6 6.6 6.6 7.3 3.9 2.4	6.6 6.6 6.6 5.6 3.9 1.0	6.6 6.6 6.6 7.3 3.9 2.4	6.6 6.6 6.6 5.6 3.9 1.0	6.6 6.6 6.6 7.3 3.9 2.4	446.6 6.6 6.6 6.6 6.6 6.6 6.6 6.6 6.6 6.6 6.6 189.3 2.4
Probability Weighted Average	-440	6.60	6.60	6.65	6.57	6.63	6.53	6.59	6.50	6.56	6.47	6.53	6.45	6.51	6.43	6.49	422
Interest rate	6%																
YTM	4.67%																

LTV	65%	45%	46%	47%	48%	49%	50%	51%	52%	53%	54%	55%	56%	57%	58%	59%	60%
YTM	4.67%	5.84%	5.81%	5.78%	5.76%	5.73%	5.70%	5.66%	5.63%	5.60%	5.57%	5.47%	5.39%	5.30%	5.2%	5.9%	5.04%
Interest Rate	1%	0%	0%	0%	0%	0%	0%	0%	0%	0%	0%	1%	1%	1%	1%	1%	1%
Mezz LTV	20%	10.0%	11%	11.0%	12%	12.0%	13%	13.0%	14%	14.0%	15%	15.0%	16%	16.0%	17%	17.0%	18%
YTM	5%	5%	0.05379	0.05375	0.05371	0.05368	0.0536627	0.0538786	0.0495203	0.0496606	0.0488387	0.0485221	0.0483091	0.0480286	0.0478196	0.0475805	0.04737095
		1%	1%	1%	1%	1%	1%	1%	1%	1%	1%	1%	1%	1%	1%	1%	1%
		40%	43%	46%	49%	52%	56%	59%	63%	67%	71%	75%	79%	84%	89%	94%	100%
Mezz Interest	6%	5.00%	5.10%	5.20%	5.30%	5.40%	5.50%	5.60%	5.70%	5.80%	5.90%	6.00%	6.10%	6.20%	6.30%	6.40%	6.50%
YTM	5%	3.7%	3.8%	3.9%	4.0%	4.1%	4.2%	4.3%	4.4%	4.5%	4.6%	4.7%	4.8%	4.9%	5.0%	5.0%	5%
		1.34%	1.34%	1.34%	1.34%	1.35%	1.31%	1.31%	1.32%	1.32%	1.33%	1.33%	1.34%	1.34%	1.35%	1.35%	1.36%
		1.25%	1.28%	1.30%	1.33%	1.35%	1.38%	1.40%	1.43%	1.45%	1.48%	1.50%	1.53%	1.55%	1.58%	1.60%	1.63%
		0	0	0	0	0	0	0	0	0	0	0	0	0	0	0	0
Interest Mezz		6%	6%	6%	6%	6%	6%	6%	6%	6%	6%	6%	6%	6%	6%	6%	6%
		1	2	3	0	0	0	0	0	0	0	0	0	0	0	0	0
		1	2	3	4	5	6	7	0	0	0	0	0	0	0	0	0
	9.84	7.12															
Default Prob Mezz	3.0%																
Default Prob Senior Loan	0.1%																

Appendix II: Binomial Tree for Capital Value

Quarter

0	1	2	3	4	5	6	7	8	9	10	11	12	13	14	15	16
																7,599
															7,032	
														6,508		6,508
													6,023		6,023	
												5,574		5,574		5,574
											5,158		5,158		5,158	
										4,774		4,774		4,774		4,774
									4,418		4,418		4,418		4,418	
								4,089		4,089		4,089		4,089		4,089
							3,784		3,784		3,784		3,784		3,784	
						3,502		3,502		3,502		3,502		3,502		3,502
					3,241		3,241		3,241		3,241		3,241		3,241	
				2,999		2,999		2,999		2,999		2,999		2,999		2,999
			2,776		2,776		2,776		2,776		2,776		2,776		2,776	
		2,569		2,569		2,569		2,569		2,569		2,569		2,569		2,569
	2,377		2,377		2,377		2,377		2,377		2,377		2,377		2,377	
2,200		2,200		2,200		2,200		2,200		2,200		2,200		2,200		2,200
	2,036		2,036		2,036		2,036		2,036		2,036		2,036		2,036	
		1,884		1,884		1,884		1,884		1,884		1,884		1,884		1,884
			1,744		1,744		1,744		1,744		1,744		1,744		1,744	
				1,614		1,614		1,614		1,614		1,614		1,614		1,614
					1,493		1,493		1,493		1,493		1,493		1,493	
						1,382		1,382		1,382		1,382		1,382		1,382
							1,279		1,279		1,279		1,279		1,279	
								1,184		1,184		1,184		1,184		1,184
									1,096		1,096		1,096		1,096	
										1,014		1,014		1,014		1,014
											938		938		938	
												868		868		868
													804		804	
														744		744
															688	
																637

Capital Value Probability

0	1	2	3	4	5	6	7	8	9	10	11	12	13	14	15	16
																0.00002
															0.00003	
														0.00006		0.00024
													0.00012		0.00046	
												0.00024		0.00085		0.00183
											0.00049		0.00159		0.00320	
										0.00098		0.00293		0.00555		0.00854
									0.00195		0.00537		0.00952		0.01389	
								0.00391		0.00977		0.01611		0.02222		0.02777
							0.00781		0.01758		0.02686		0.03491		0.04166	
						0.01563		0.03125		0.04395		0.05371		0.06110		0.06665
					0.03125		0.05469		0.07031		0.08057		0.08728		0.09164	
				0.06250		0.09375		0.10938		0.11719		0.12085		0.12219		0.12219
			0.12500		0.15625		0.16406		0.16406		0.16113		0.15710		0.15274	
		0.25000		0.25000		0.23438		0.21875		0.20508		0.19336		0.18329		0.17456
	0.50000		0.37500		0.31250		0.27344		0.24609		0.22559		0.20947		0.19638	
1.000		0.50000		0.37500		0.31250		0.27344		0.24609		0.22559		0.20947		0.19638
	0.50000		0.37500		0.31250		0.27344		0.24609		0.22559		0.20947		0.19638	
		0.25000		0.25000		0.23438		0.21875		0.20508		0.19336		0.18329		0.17456
			0.12500		0.15625		0.16406		0.16406		0.16113		0.15710		0.15274	
				0.06250		0.09375		0.10938		0.11719		0.12085		0.12219		0.12219
					0.03125		0.05469		0.07031		0.08057		0.08728		0.09164	
						0.01563		0.03125		0.04395		0.05371		0.06110		0.06665
							0.00781		0.01758		0.02686		0.03491		0.04166	
								0.00391		0.00977		0.01611		0.02222		0.02777
									0.00195		0.00537		0.00952		0.01389	
										0.00098		0.00293		0.00555		0.00854
											0.00049		0.00159		0.00320	
												0.00024		0.00085		0.00183
													0.00012		0.00046	
														0.00006		0.00024
															0.00003	
																0.00002

THE VERSATILITY OF THE REAL ESTATE ASSET CLASS - THE SINGAPORE EXPERIENCE

Capital Value after pay down $ 2200.00											
											6169
										5602	5602
									5078	5078	5078
								4593	4593	4593	4593
							4144	4144	4144	4144	4144
						3728	3728	3728	3728	3728	3728
					3344	3344	3344	3344	3344	3344	3344
				2988	2988	2988	2988	2988	2988	2988	2988
			2659	2659	2659	2659	2659	2659	2659	2659	2659
		2354	2354	2354	2354	2354	2354	2354	2354	2354	2354
	2072	2072	2072	2072	2072	2072	2072	2072	2072	2072	2072
1811	1811	1811	1811	1811	1811	1811	1811	1811	1811	1811	1811
1569	1569	1569	1569	1569	1569	1569	1569	1569	1569	1569	1569
1346	1346	1346	1346	1346	1346	1346	1346	1346	1346	1346	1346
1139	1139	1139	1139	1139	1139	1139	1139	1139	1139	1139	1139
947	947	947	947	947	947	947	947	947	947	947	947
770	770	770	770	770	770	770	770	770	770	770	770
606	606	606	606	606	606	606	606	606	606	606	606
454	454	454	454	454	454	454	454	454	454	454	454
314	314	314	314	314	314	314	314	314	314	314	314
184	184	184	184	184	184	184	184	184	184	184	184
63	63	63	63	63	63	63	63	63	63	63	63
0	0	0	0	0	0	0	0	0	0	0	0
	0	0	0	0	0	0	0	0	0	0	0
		0	0	0	0	0	0	0	0	0	0
			0	0	0	0	0	0	0	0	0
				0	0	0	0	0	0	0	0
					0	0	0	0	0	0	0
						0	0	0	0	0	0
							0	0	0	0	0
								0	0	0	0
									0	0	0
										0	0
											0

Appendix III: Market Rent, CV, u, d & rISK nUETRAL pROBABILITIES

Year	Qtr			Raffles Place	CCC					
93	Q1		93Q1	6.75	-8.0%					
93	Q2		93Q2	6.75	0.0%					
93	Q3		93Q3	6.40	-5.1%					
93	Q4		93Q4	6.25	16.7%	0.93913		0.93913	1	
94	Q1		94Q1	6.35	1.6%	1.157407	1.157407		1	1
94	Q2		94Q2	6.75	6.3%	1.016	1.016		1	
94	Q3		94Q3	7.05	4.4%	1.062992	1.062992		1	
94	Q4		94Q4	7.95	12.8%	1.044444	1.044444		1	
95	Q1		95Q1	9.00	13.2%	1.12766	1.12766		1	
95	Q2		95Q2	9.50	5.6%	1.132075	1.132075		1	
95	Q3		95Q3	9.50	0.0%	1.055556	1.055556		1	
95	Q4		95Q4	10.00	5.3%	1				
96	Q1		96Q1	10.50	5.0%	1.052632	1.052632		1	
96	Q2		96Q2	10.50	0.0%	1.05	1.05		1	
96	Q3		96Q3	10.50	0.0%	1				
96	Q4		96Q4	10.50	0.0%	1				
97	Q1		97Q1	10.00	-4.8%	0.952381		0.952381		1
97	Q2		97Q2	9.70	-3.0%	0.97		0.97		1
97	Q3		97Q3	9.70	0.0%	1				
97	Q4		97Q4	9.50	-2.1%	0.979381		0.979381		1
98	Q1		98Q1	9.00	-5.3%	0.947368		0.947368		1
98	Q2		98Q2	8.30	-7.8%	0.922222		0.922222		1
98	Q3		98Q3	7.50	-9.6%	0.903614		0.903614		1
98	Q4		98Q4	6.50	-13.3%	0.866667		0.866667		1
99	Q1		99Q1	6.15	-5.4%	0.946154		0.946154		1
99	Q2		99Q2	6.15	0.0%	1				
99	Q3		99Q3	6.15	0.0%	1				
99	Q4		99Q4	6.30	2.4%	1.02439	1.02439		1	
2000	Q1		00Q1	6.30	0.0%	1				
2000	Q2		00Q2	6.65	5.6%	1.055556	1.055556		1	
2000	Q3		00Q3	6.85	3.0%	1.030075	1.030075		1	
2000	Q4		00Q4	7.75	13.1%	1.131387	1.131387		1	
2001	Q1		01Q1	7.90	1.9%	1.019355	1.019355		1	
2001	Q2		01Q2	7.75	-1.9%	0.981013		0.981013		1
2001	Q3		01Q3	7.50	-3.2%	0.967742		0.967742		1
2001	Q4		01Q4	6.50	-13.3%	0.866667		0.866667		1
2002	Q1		02Q1	5.75	-11.5%	0.884615		0.884615		1
2002	Q2		02Q2	5.65	-1.7%	0.982609		0.982609		1
2002	Q3		02Q3	5.40	-4.4%	0.955752		0.955752		1
2002	Q4		02Q4	5.00	-7.4%	0.925926		0.925926		1
2003	Q1		03Q1	4.85	-3.0%	0.97		0.97		1
2003	Q2		03Q2	4.75	-2.1%	0.979381		0.979381		1
2003	Q3		03Q3	4.50	-5.3%	0.947368		0.947368		1
2003	Q4		03Q4	4.30	-4.4%	0.955556		0.955556		1
2004	Q1		04Q1	4.30	0.0%	1				
2004	Q2		04Q2	4.40	2.3%	1.023256	1.023256		1	
2004	Q3		04Q3	4.50	2.3%	1.022727	1.022727		1	
2004	Q4		04Q4	4.60	2.2%	1.022222	1.022222		1	
2005	Q1		05Q1	4.85	5.4%	1.054348	1.054348		1	
2005	Q2		05Q2	5.00	3.1%	1.030928	1.030928		1	
2005	Q3		05Q3	5.20	4.0%	1.04	1.04		1	
2005	Q4		05Q4	5.60	7.7%	1.076923	1.076923		1	
2006	Q1		06Q1	6.10	8.9%	1.089286	1.089286		1	
2006	Q2		06Q2	6.50	6.6%	1.065574	1.065574		1	
2006	Q3		06Q3	6.90	6.2%	1.061538	1.061538		1	
2006	Q4		06Q4	8.50	23.2%	1.231884	1.231884		1	
2007	Q1		07Q1	10.90	28.2%	1.282353	1.282353		1	
2007	Q2		07Q2	13.10	20.2%	1.201835	1.201835		1	
2007	Q3		07Q3	14.50	10.7%	1.10687	1.10687		1	
2007	Q4		07Q4	15.00	3.4%	1.034483	1.034483		1	
									28	20
		stdev		7.39 2.322107		avg u Avg D		1.08 0.93	0.94	
						p		58.3% 1.008226		
								1.071163 0.933568		

THE VERSATILITY OF THE REAL ESTATE ASSET CLASS - THE SINGAPORE EXPERIENCE

Year	QTR		CVs, Raffles Place S$ psf pm	QOQ	YOY					
1993	Q1	93Q1	1,350	0.0%						
	Q2	93Q2	1,350	0.0%					1	
	Q3	93Q3	1,350	0.0%					1	
	Q4	93Q4	1,350	0.0%					1	
1994	Q1	94Q1	1,350	0.0%	0.0%				1	
	Q2	94Q2	1,550	14.8%	14.8%	1.148148	1.148148		1	
	Q3	94Q3	1,750	12.9%	29.6%	1.129032	1.129032		1	
	Q4	94Q4	1,850	5.7%		1.057143	1.057143		1	
1995	Q1	95Q1	2,000	8.1%	48.1%	1.081081	1.081081		1	
	Q2	95Q2	2,100	5.0%	35.5%	1.05	1.05		1	
	Q3	95Q3	2,200	4.8%	25.7%	1.047619	1.047619		1	
	Q4	95Q4	2,200	0.0%	18.9%				1	
1996	Q1	96Q1	2,200	0.0%	10.0%				1	
	Q2	96Q2	2,400	9.1%	14.3%	1.090909	1.090909		1	
	Q3	96Q3	2,400	0.0%	9.1%				1	
	Q4	96Q4	2,400	0.0%					1	
1997	Q1	97Q1	2,330	-2.9%	5.9%	0.970833		0.970833		1
	Q2	97Q2	2,330	0.0%	-2.9%				1	
	Q3	97Q3	2,330	0.0%	-2.9%				1	
	Q4	97Q4	2,200	-5.6%	-8.3%	0.944206		0.944206		1
1998	Q1	98Q1	2,000	-9.1%	-14.2%	0.909091		0.909091		1
	Q2	98Q2	1,850	-7.5%	-20.6%	0.925		0.925		1
	Q3	98Q3	1,600	-13.5%	-31.3%	0.864865		0.864865		1
	Q4	98Q4	1,500	-6.3%	-31.8%	0.9375		0.9375		1
1999	Q1	99Q1	1,250	-16.7%	-37.5%	0.833333		0.833333		1
	Q2	99Q2	1,400	12.0%	-24.3%	1.12	1.12		1	
	Q3	99Q3	1,450	3.6%	-9.4%	1.035714	1.035714		1	
	Q4	99Q4	1,500	3.4%	0.0%	1.034483	1.034483		1	
2000	Q1	00Q1	1,550	3.3%	24.0%	1.033333	1.033333		1	
	Q2	00Q2	1,550	0.0%	10.7%				1	
	Q3	00Q3	1,550	0.0%	6.9%				1	
	Q4	00Q4	1,550	0.0%	3.3%				1	
2001	Q1	01Q1	1,450	-6.5%	-6.5%	0.935484		0.935484		1
	Q2	01Q2	1,390	-4.1%	-10.3%	0.958621		0.958621		1
	Q3	01Q3	1,330	-4.3%	-14.2%	0.956835		0.956835		1
	Q4	01Q4	1,260	-5.3%	-18.7%	0.947368		0.947368		1
2002	Q1	02Q1	1,200	-4.8%	-17.2%	0.952381		0.952381		1
	Q2	02Q2	1,150	-4.2%	-17.3%	0.958333		0.958333		1
	Q3	02Q3	1,110	-3.5%	-16.5%	0.965217		0.965217		1
	Q4	02Q4	1,050	-5.4%	-16.7%	0.945946		0.945946		1
2003	Q1	03Q1	1,020	-2.9%	-15.0%	0.971429		0.971429		1
	Q2	03Q2	1,000	-2.0%	-13.0%	0.980392		0.980392		1
	Q3	03Q3	1,000	0.0%	-9.9%				1	
	Q4	03Q4	990	-1.0%	-5.7%	0.99		0.99		1
2004	Q1	04Q1	975	-1.5%	-4.4%	0.984848		0.984848		1
	Q2	04Q2	970	-0.5%	-3.0%	0.994872		0.994872		1
	Q3	04Q3	960	-1.0%	-4.0%	0.989691		0.989691		1
	Q4	04Q4	960	0.0%	-1.5%				1	
2005	Q1	05Q1	960	0.0%	-1.0%				1	
	Q2	05Q2	1,000	4.2%	4.2%	1.041667	1.041667		1	
	Q3	05Q3	1,050	5.0%	9.4%	1.05	1.05		1	
2006	Q1	06Q1	1,100	4.8%	14.6%	1.047619	1.047619		1	
	Q2	06Q2	1,150	4.5%	19.8%	1.045455	1.045455		1	
	Q3	06Q3	1,250	8.7%	25.0%	1.086957	1.086957		1	
	Q4	06Q4	1,500	20.0%	42.9%	1.2	1.2		1	
2007	Q1	07Q1	1,900	26.7%	72.7%	1.266667	1.266667		1	
	Q2	07Q2	2,400	47.4%	143.5%	1.263158	1.263158		1	
	Q3	07Q3	2,600	10.7%	148.0%	1.083333	1.083333		20	21
		07Q4	2,500							
			1,565			u	1.095616	0.948398		
			503.1522			d	0.912729			
						p	50%	0.487805		
							1.039074			
						u	1.074818			
						d	0.93039			

183

CHAPTER 5

THE CONCLUSION

Chapter 5 summarises the book's findings and highlights the contributions and recommendations made. Chapter 1 develops a rigorous model of private housing market price dynamics within behavioral theory. A key assumption is that the investors are a heterogeneous mix of the disposition and momentum types. The decision-making of the two types' investors shows different sensitivities to housing market price changes. This Chapter sheds light on the behavioral explanation of empirical estimates for housing market price's autocorrelation and mean reversion time path, as in the recent study by Gao, Lin and Na (2009) and Titman, Wang and Yang (2014). The interaction between the two types of investors and the aggregate effect of their behavior are important determinants of the private housing market price dynamics.

Chapter 1 highlights the definition and interpretation of the patterns (features) of the private housing market price dynamics, in accordance with the disposition-momentum behavioral theory. The Chapter categorizes the private housing market price dynamics into four patterns, including the price bubble via the composite autocorrelation and mean-reversion parameters, within the disposition-momentum domain, i.e. convergent or divergent and oscillatory or not oscillatory, as established by Capozza *et al.* (2004). The Chapter empirically investigates the features of the Singapore private housing market price dynamics and interprets them within both the autocorrelation-mean reversion and the disposition-momentum domains. The private housing market price dynamics exhibit a variety of features over different periods with variant autocorrelation and mean reversion parameters: during the longer period (1982 to 2007). Then there is the convergence without oscillation, which in effect is the reaction to price shocks while in the shorter, so-called "speculative" period (from 1990 to 2001). The private housing market price dynamics display convergent oscillation rather than divergence. It is found that the characteristics of the private housing market upturn around 2006 differ from those of the 1990s' boom-and-recovery, which had been slower and that the magnitude of the price gain tend to be lower. In both periods (around 2006 and the 1990s' boom-and-recovery), the disposition investors prevail, as compared to the momentum investors of the Singapore private housing market. Furthermore, the Chapter's model offers a stylized investment market, in which the fundamental value changes exogenously. Such a stylized investment market provides potential evidence that investor behavior is endogenously crucial in explaining the private housing market price dynamics. The average autocorrelation parameter in this Chapter is approximately 0.7. The instantaneous adjustment parameter is almost zero with a large p-value, suggesting that during both periods i.e. around 2006 and the 1990s' boom-and-recovery, almost 100% of housing price adjustments occur gradually over time. The housing market prices merely converge to the 2-3% range of the total adjustment each year, from 1982 to 2007; to the 3-4% range from 1990 to 2001. A key implication for investors is that the boom around 2006 of the Singapore private housing market does not provide as large a magnitude as that from the price gain in the 1990's boom-and-recovery, viewed from a long-term perspective. However, the Singapore private housing market seems to be low risk, offering stable returns, thanks to virtually no divergence, even in the speculative 1990s. Given that the disposition investors prevail in the private housing market, the best way to invest is to consider the momentum strategy and to avoid the herd behavior for profit sustainability. For policy makers, the Singapore private housing market is over-damped in the long run. Moreover, the disposition investors predominate this private housing market, and that their behavior contributes to the market mechanism, which automatically adjusts the private housing market prices. The implication is to consider the appropriateness of relaxing government intervention in the Singapore private housing market, to make it more efficient.

Chapter 2 looks at the merits of a uniquely simplified experimental research design for the strategic behavioural pricing of the private residential development market under a game theoretic approach, within the context of Singapore. Three research questions are examined where game 1 is meant for the first two research questions while game 2 is solely meant for the third research question. The first research question seeks the observable equilibrium price and its intrinsic behavioural pricing structure under the private residential development market. The results are insightful and conclusive with respect to the collusion structural pricing model where private residential developers cooperate implicitly for long-term benefit. Despite the lacking of conclusive equilibrium prices, it is clear from the results that the zero-profit equilibrium by Bertrand would not be applicable. In addition, residential developers are motivated to deviate from cooperation at the beginning and at the end of successive periods in a sub-market. Relatively high profits, earnable in the first few periods, provide an allowance for them to price undercut others in order to sell faster. For the last few periods, their penalty for deviation is insignificant or zero. For the same reason, they are motivated to deviate.

Chapter 3 ascertains the presence of appraisal smoothing. By adopting the Geltner and Miller (2007) 1st and 4th order autoregressive model to de-smooth the direct real estate TRs (total returns), a more robust set of direct real estate total returns can be obtained. The Chapter 3 adopts the multi-factor APT (arbitrage pricing theory) model to examine the correlation of legal origins to an Asian city's direct real estate TRs. Various sensitivities of the direct real estate TRs, i.e. the betas or the risk factor loadings, are estimated with pooled-panel data via multiple regression analysis, resolved by ordinary least-square, and from which the associated risk factor loadings are determined. The 2 main legal origins, i.e. the British legal origin and the French legal origin, are the dummy variables i.e. 'the dummies' in the multi-factor APT model. The coefficients are then estimated and analysed to examine the extent of the correlation.

Given the wide differences in the risk premiums for cities in the same region that have similar historical country-legal-origin antecedent, it appears that the local-specific country milieu underpins the direct real estate risk premiums. For e.g., it is doubtful whether or not the risk exposure, owing to the 'yellow-red shirt' political divide in Thailand and the separatist's struggles in The Philippines, is a function of the historical French legal origin antecedent. Therefore, the association of the legal origin of the country nature with the direct real estate risk premium, though real, may be tangential.

Although the "Law, endowments and Finance" Chapter 3 suggests that the British legal origin is perceived to offer better direct real estate protection, it should be noted that the dependent variable (i.e. the direct real estate TRs) in such a Chapter 3 is determined by taking the TRs from the public market. TRs from the public markets may well be biased towards countries under the British legal origin since the latter normally have more developed common stock market and financial systems. However, and in Chapter 3, we utilise the direct real estate TRs from the private market rather than the wider public market. Results imply that legal origin is a variable that affects the assessment of the riskiness of direct real estate investing in an Asian country and in its risk-return analysis. The French legal origin, with its codified law, is perceived to be more favourable for international real estate investing in the Asia region.

Results of the APT model estimates are reproduced from Table 17 below. To avoid the dummy variable trap problem, the constant term, C_2 and the French-legal-origin dummy (dum fc=1), are retained while allowing the British-legal-origin dummy to be removed. The associated base dummy, i.e. dum fc=0 becomes the base category, against which the British legal origin dummy is assessed.

Table 17. APT Model Estimates

Variable	Output
Constant, C	8.2035%*
Real GDP growth	0.6394% ***
Inflation rate	-0.0254%
Vacancy rate	2.7067% *
French Legal Origin (dum_fc=1)	4.1436%**
British Legal Origin	11.5242%*
i.e. 8.2035%+0.6394%-0.0254%+2.7067%+0 =11.5242%	
Universal Risk Free Rate	7.2%
R-squared	0.375489
Adjusted R-squared	0.261942
Mean dependent var ATR	13.4156%

NB. Significant at the 1% level*; at the 10% level**; at the 29% level***.
Source: Authors, 2019

Constant term C, real GDP growth rate, vacancy rate, the French-legal-origin dummy and the British-legal-origin dummy in relation to the French-Civil- Law base dummy, are statistically significant in estimating the overall risk premiums of international investing in direct real estate in the Asian region. High risk premiums among the 6 risk factors are only observed for vacancy rate (2.7%), the French-legal-origin dummy (4.1%), the British-legal-origin dummy (11.5%) and the constant C (8.2%) of our multi factor APT model, relative to the US risk free rate of 7.2%. Real GDP growth rate is moderately significant with the relatively low risk premium of about 0.6%. It is implicit that the specific real estate risk has a more deterministic role in the overall risk profile of a direct real estate investing in Asia, as compared to macroeconomic variables. It is because the vacancy rate has a much direct impact on the performance of direct real estate investment than the macroeconomic variables. Real GDP growth rate has a lower risk premium, owing to the fact that the Asia region on the whole has experienced robust and sustainable growth over the past decade. Historical economic performance of the Asia region highlights that this region is perceived to be comparatively less risky, and that the risk premiums accorded to the region should be lower than in the past. Interest rate movements suggest a stabilised historical pattern, generally hovering around 0% to 5% up to the years 2007-2008, where most of the Asian countries' interest rates spike to above 5%. The relatively stable rates for most of these years suggest that lower premium is accorded to this macroeconomic variable. Nevertheless, Chapter 3 suggests that the French-legal-origin is better perceived for its private direct real estate rights protection by international real estate investors in Asian direct real estate. It can be owing to the fact that in the French-legal-origin, its laws are codified and straightforward, leading to less ambiguous rulings. Instead, the British-legal-origin is based on case laws and it is susceptible to various interpretations.

Chapter 4 introduces the real estate mezzanine investment (REMI), a new financial instrument for the real estate market in Asia, although it would provide superior returns than those for usual typical commercial bank loans. The resultant risk exposure becomes relatively high. The Singapore real estate market has experienced robust growth over the past several years, with a fast-growing real estate investment trust (REIT) market and the teeming emergence of private equity fund investments. As a result, Chapter 4 is appropriately motivated to examine the risk-return behavior of mezzanine investment. A discrete-time binomial asset tree model in association with risk neutral probabilities is estimated for the *ex ante examination* of the REMI. The empirical analysis involves a rigorous discrete-time forecasting of the market rent and capital value expectations of the prime office market in Singapore, given the conditions and assumptions unique to this market. Subsequently, the total return (TR) for mezzanine investment is investigated under a probability-weighted average cash flow approach.

In particularly, a series of natural default probabilities is envisaged, corresponding to the respective REMI-investment interest rates. The impact of loan-to-value (LTV) ratio pertaining to the senior loan and the REMI on the total return for the mezzanine investment is examined. It is found that a generally stable spread (of about 1.36%) exists between REMI's original interest rate and its real total return. When Chapter 4 looks at different LTV ratios, the results show that such a spread tends to be stable for each different LTV ratio. This spread increases as the senior-loan LTV ratio rises and it follows a "staircase shape" 3-D (3-dimensional) plot. The results are generally consistent in that the market risk, i.e., real estate market risk and capital market risk, and the financial risk, represented by the LTV ratio concerning the senior loan and the mezzanine investment, are the main risk factors that affect the return for REMI. When we value a REMI, we need to be merely concerned with the inherent leverage that arises from the existing senior loan. A higher return would therefore be required to compensate for the higher financial risk and real estate market risk on the risk-adjusted return principle. While limited to Singapore, a cross-city comparative study can be conducted to evaluate and contrast the risk-return behavior of REMI across the Asian region, in particular the key capital cities of interest. Lastly, Chapter 5 concludes this book.

REFERENCES

Chapter 1

Lim, C.Y and associates (1988). Policy options for the Singapore economy. Singapore: McGraw Hill Book Co.

Liu, T.K. (2002) Urbanizing Singapore: Optimizing Resources: Mega Cities Lecture 6, Megacities Foundation c/o S@M stedebouw & architectuurmanagement, Herengracht, 23, 1015 BA Amsterdam, The hague,The Netherlands.

D.C. Stafford (1978) The economics of housing policy. Great Britain: Croom Helm London.

Paul N. Balchin (1981) Housing policy and housing needs. London: The Macmillan Press Ltd.

P. Malpass and A. Murie (1999) Housing policy and practice (5th ed.). London: The Macmillan Press Ltd.

Balchin, Bull and Kieve (1995) Urban land economics and public policy (5th ed.). England: Macmillan Distirbution Ltd

Tan, Augustine H. H. and Phang S. Y. (1991) The Singapore Experience in Public

Housing, Occasional Chapter 1 9. Singapore: Times Academic Press for the Centre for Advanced Studies.

Tan, E.K. (2012) Public Housing & New Town Planning & Design in Singapore Lecture, MSc RE5013 Urban Policy & Real Estate Markets, Department of Real Estate, School of Design & Environment, National University of Singapore.

Tan, S.Y. (1998). Private Ownership of Public Housing in Singapore. Singapore: Times Academic Press.

Low, Linda and Aw, T.C. (1997). Housing a healthy, educated and wealthy nation through the CPF. Singapore: Times Academic Press for the Institute of Policy Studies.

Ooi, G. L. and Kwok, K. (1997). City & the State: Singapore's Built Environment Revisited. Singapore: Oxford University Press for the Institute of Policy Studies.

Yeh H. K. (1985). Households and housing. Singapore: Department of Statistics.

Joseph F. Healey (2002). Statistics A tool for social research (6th ed.) CA, USA:
Wadsworth/ Thomson learning.

Hair, Anderson, Tatham and Black (1998). Multivariate Data Analysis (5th ed.) New Jersey: Prentice Hall.

George, D. and Mallery, P. (2001). SPSS for Windows step by step (3rd ed.) USA: Allyn & Bacon.

D. Fisher (2001). Intermediate macroeconomics : a statistical approach. Singapore River Edge, NJ : World Scientific.

Bénassy, J.P. (2002). The macroeconomics of imperfect competition and nonclearing markets : a dynamic general equilibrium approach. Massachusetts Institute of Technology Press, Cambridge, Mass.

King, J.E.(2002). A history of post Keynesian economics since 1936. Northampton, MA : Edward Elgar Publishing

Norusis, Marija J. (2002). SPSS 11.0 Guide to Data Analysis. New Jersey: Prentice Hall.

Norusis, Marija J. (2000). SPSS 10.0 Guide to Data Analysis. New Jersey: Prentice Hall.

Tan, Willie (2001). Practical Research Methods: With Applications in Building and Real Estate. Singapore: Prentice Hall.

Tan, Willie (2001). Practical Research Methods. Singapore: Prentice Hall.

Tan, Willie (1995). Housing Markets and Public Policy: Singapore: SBEM Book Series.

Sterman, J. (2000). Business dynamics/: System thinking and modeling for a complex world. McGraw-Hill. New York.

B. Richmond and S. Peterson (2000). An introduction to systems thinking (5th ed.). US: High Performance Systems Inc.

B. Richmond and M Paich (1997). Business applications (4th ed.). US: High Performance Systems Inc.

Economics Survey of Singapore 2002. Ministry of Trade and Industry.

Economics Survey of Singapore 2001. Ministry of Trade and Industry

Housing and Development Board annual report 1984/1985

Housing and Development Board annual report 1985/1986

Housing and Development Board annual report 1986/1987

Housing and Development Board annual report 1987/1988

Housing and Development Board annual report 1988/1989

Housing and Development Board annual report 1989/1990

Housing and Development Board annual report 1990/1991

Housing and Development Board annual report 1991/1992

Housing and Development Board annual report 1992/1993

Housing and Development Board annual report 1993/1994

Housing and Development Board annual report 1994/1995

Housing and Development Board annual report 1995/1996

Housing and Development Board annual report 1996/1997

Housing and Development Board annual report 1997/1998

Housing and Development Board annual report 1998/1999

Housing and Development Board annual report 1999/2000

Housing and Development Board annual report 2000/2001

Housing and Development Board annual report 2001/2002.

Wong K. and Yeh H.K. (1995). Housing a Nation, 25 Years of Public Housing in Singapore. Singapore: Maruzen Asia for Housing and Development Board.

Yeh H. K. (1975). Public Housing in Singapore, a multi-disciplinary study. Singapore: Singapore University Press for Housing and Development Board.

T. O'Sullivan and K. Gibb (2003). Housing economics and public policy. UK. Blackwell Science Ltd.

Ho, K.H.D; Teh, R.Y.C; Tham K.W. and Briffett, C (1997). The greening of Singapore National Estate, *HABITAL International*, Vol. 21, No. 1, pp 107-121.

Ho, K.H.D; Ho, M.W and Hui, C.M.E. (2002). Modelling the dynamic structure between port throughput and capacity policy – the port of Hong Kong.

Phang, S. Y.(2003). Housing Policy, Wealth and the Singapore Economy. *Housing Studies*, 16(4), 443-459.

Sterman, J. (2001). System Dynamics Modeling: Tools for learning in a complex world. *California Management Review*, Vol 43, No 4

Meen, G. (2003). Housing, random walks, complexity and the macroeconomy. *Real Estate Issues,* Chapter 6.

Quek, T. (2003, December, 7) If demand is bad, HDB won't build. *The Straits Times, Singapore.*

Leong, P.K.(2003, October, 10) HDB now to focus on basics. *The Straits Times, Singapore.*

2003 Centaur Communications Limited (2003, September, 8) Singapore opens its doors. *International Money Marketing*

Leong, C. T. (2003, August, 17). CPF cut will hit highly mortgaged most. *The Sunday Times.* Leong P. Y. (2003, August, 15). Affordability of flats a concern in this economic gloom. *The Straits Times.*

Kwak, S. (1995). Policy analysis of Hanford Tank farm operations with system dynamic approach. Ph.D thesis, Department of Nuclear Engineering, Massachusetts Institute of Technology, Cambridge, Mass.

Chapter 2

D.C. Stafford (1978). The economics of housing policy. Great Britain: Croom Helm London

Paul N. Balchin (1981) Housing policy and housing needs. London: The Macmillan Press Ltd.

P. Malpass and A. Murie (1999) Housing policy and practice (5th ed.). London: The Macmillan Press Ltd.

Balchin, Bull and Kieve (1995) Urban land economics and public policy (5th ed.). England: Macmillan Distirbution Ltd

Tan, S.Y. (1998). Private Ownership of Public Housing in Singapore. Singapore: Times Academic Press.

Low, Linda and Aw, T.C. (1997). Housing a healthy, educated and wealthy nation through the CPF. Singapore: Times Academic Press for the Institute of Policy Studies.

Ooi, G. L. and Kwok, K. (). City & the State: Singapore's Built Environment Revisited. Singapore: Oxford University Press for the Institute of Policy Studies.

Yeh H. K. (1985). Households and housing. Singapore: Department of Statistics.

Joseph F. Healey (2002). Statistics A tool for social research (6th ed.) CA, USA:
Wadsworth/ Thomson learning.

Hair, Anderson, Tatham and Black (1998). Multivariate Data Analysis (5th ed.) New Jersey: Prentice Hall.

George, D. and Mallery, P. (2001). SPSS for Windows step by step (3rd ed.) USA: Allyn & Bacon.

D. Fisher (2001). Intermediate macroeconomics : a statistical approach. Singapore River Edge, NJ : World Scientific.

Bénassy, J.P. (2002). The macroeconomics of imperfect competition and nonclearing markets : a dynamic general equilibrium approach. Massachusetts Institute of Technology Press, Cambridge, Mass.

King, J.E.(2002). A history of post Keynesian economics since 1936. Northampton, MA : Edward Elgar Publishing

Norusis, Marija J. (2002). SPSS 11.0 Guide to Data Analysis. New Jersey: Prentice Hall.

Tan, Willie (2001). Practical Research Methods: With Applications in Building and Real Estate. Singapore: Prentice Hall.

Tan, Willie (2001). Practical Research Methods. Singapore: Prentice Hall.

Tan, Willie (1995). Housing Markets and Public Policy: Singapore: SBEM Book Series.

Sterman, J. (2000). Business dynamics/: System thinking and modeling for a complex world. McGraw-Hill. New York.

B. Richmond and S. Peterson (2000). An introduction to systems thinking (5th ed.). US: High Performance Systems Inc.

Wong K. and Yeh H.K. (1995). Housing a Nation, 25 Years of Public Housing in Singapore. Singapore: Maruzen Asia for Housing and Development Board.

Yeh H. K. (1975). Public Housing in Singapore, a multi-disciplinary study. Singapore: Singapore University Press for Housing and Development Board.

T. O'Sullivan and K. Gibb (2003). Housing economics and public policy. UK. Blackwell Science Ltd.

Ho, K.H.D; Teh, R.Y.C; Tham K.W. and Briffett, C (1997). The greening of Singapore National Estate, *HABITAL International*, Vol. 21, No. 1, pp 107-121.

Ho, K.H.D; Ho, M.W and Hui, C.M.E. (2002). Modelling the dynamic structure between port throughput and capacity policy – the port of Hong Kong.

Sterman, J. (2001). System Dynamics Modeling: Tools for learning in a complex world. *California Management Review*, Vol 43, No 4

Meen, G. (2003). Housing, random walks, complexity and the macroeconomy. *Real Estate Issues,* Chapter 6.

Liu, T.K. Urbanising Singapore. Optimising Resources. Megacities Lecture 2002, The hague, Nethelands, November 2002.

Quek, T. (2003, December, 7) If demand is bad, HDB won't build. *The Straits Tim.e*

Leong, P.K.(2003, October, 10) HDB now to focus on basics. *The Straits Time.*

2003 Centaur Communications Limited (2003, September, 8) Singapore opens its doors. *International Money Marketing*

Chapter 3

Brueggeman, W., Fisher J. (2005). *Real estate finance and investment.* (12th Edition).Boston: McGraw-Hill/Irwin.

Davis, K., Harper, I. (1993). (Ed) (1989). *Privatization in Singapore: the political and administrative implications.* Singapore: Longman.

Glen, A. (2001) Corporate financial management. (2nd Edition). New York: Prentice Hall.

Levy, H., Sarnat, M. (1994). *Capital investment and financial decisions.* (5th Edition). UK: Prentice Hall.

Housing and Development Board annual report 2000/2001
Housing and Development Board annual report 2001/2002.

Republican Policy Committee. (2003). *Problems at fannie mae and freddie mac: Too big to fall.* Jon kyl. Retrieved 28 January 2005 from http://rpc.senate.gov.

Singapore Development Board (2003/2004) Financial statement Chuang Kwong Yong: Auditor General Singapore. Retrieved 20 December 2004 from http://www.hdb.gov.sg.

Street TRACK STI. (2003) Straits time index fund annual report 30 june 2003.

PricewaterhouseCoopers. Retrieved 29 February 2005 from http://www.streettracks.com.sg

Thynne, I. and Ariff, M. (Ed) (1989). *Privatisation: the financial implications.* Sydney: Australian Print Group.

Wallison, P. (Ed.) (2001). *Serving two masters yet out of control fannie mae and freddie mac.* Washington: AEI Press.

Chapter 4

Amy Khor. (2000) A Study of the Natural Vacancy Rate in Singapore's office Market. *Journal of Real Estate Research*, 17(4), 329-338. https://doi.org/10.1080/09599910010001448

Arditti, F. D. (1996). *Derivatives: A comprehensive resource for options, futures, interest rate swaps, and mortgage securities*. Boston: Harvard Business School Press

Baz, J., & Strong, R. (1997). The bias in delta as an indicator of the actual likelihood of option exercise. *Finance Practice and Education*, 7.

Brach, M. Z. (2003). *Real Options in Practice*. Hoboken, New Jersey: John Wiley & Sons, Inc.

Brown, G. R. (1991). *Property Investment and the Capital Markets*. London: St. Edmundsbury Press

Bruce, B. R. (Ed.). (1991). *Real Estate Portfolio Management: Analysis & Evaluation for Fund Managers, Sponsors and Consultants*. Illinois, Chicago: Probus Publishing Company

Brueggeman, W. B., & Fisher, J. D. (2002). *Real Estate Finance and Investments* (11th ed.). McGraw-Hill/Irwin, NY.

Chan, R. (2010). *GIC loses in New York Project – Owners of Huge Housing Complex in Manhattan Default on Debt Payment, The Straits Times press newspaper article, 12 January 2010, Singapore*.

Claurette, T., & Sirmans, G. (2002). *Real Estate Finance: Theory and Practice* (3rd ed.). Cincinnati, Ohio: South-Western/Thomson Learning.

Cox, J., & Rubinstein, M. (1985). *Options Markets*. Prentice-Hall, Inc., NJ

Cox, J., Ross, S., & Rubinstein, M. (1979). Option pricing: A simplified approach. *Journal of Financial Economics*, 7, 229-263. https://doi.org/10.1016/0304-405X(79)90015-1

Donna Mitchell. (2002). *Borrowers Eye Mezzanine Loans*. Unpublished manuscript.

Geltner, D., & Miller, N. (2001). *Commercial Real Estate Analysis and Investments*. Upper Saddle River, NJ: Prentice Hall.

Ho Kim Hin/David, & Sing Tien Foo. (2003). Effects of Mezzanine Debt on Optimal Capital Structure: Risks & Returns. *Paper presented in AREUEA conference 2003*.

Ho, K.H.D. (2007). *International Real Estate – Asia's Potential from a Research Perspective Real Estate Perspective. NUS Press, National University of Singapore* (Chapters 20 and 21).

Ho, K.H.D., & Shun, C.K.L. (2014). *Direct & Indirect Investment Analysis – An Asian Real Estate Perspective. McGraw Hill Education (Asia)* (Chapter 9, pp. 397-409).

Howard Esaki. (2002). Commercial Mortgage Default: 1972-2000. *Real Estate Finance*, 18(4), 43-52.

Huang, J. Z., & Kong, W. (2003). *Explaining Credit Spread Changes: Some New Evidence from Option-Adjusted Spreads of Bond Indexes*. Smeal College of Business, Pennsylvania State University.

Hull, J. C. (1997). *Options, Futures and Other Derivatives*. USA: Prentice Hall Inc.

John F. McDonald. (2007). *Optimal Leverage in Real Estate Investment with Mezzanine Lending*. A Great Cities Institute Working Paper, Center for Urban Real Estate, University of Illinois at Chicago.

Joost Driessen. (2002). *Is Default Event Risk Priced in Corporate Bonds* (Published thesis). Faculty of Economics and Econornetrics, University of Amsterdam.

Kau, J. B., Keenan, D. C., Muller, W. J., & Epperson, J. F. (1990). Pricing commercial mortgages and their mortgage-backed securities. *Journal of Real Estate Finance and Economics*, *3*, 333-356. https://doi.org/10.1007/BF00178857

Louargand, M. (2007). *Real Estate in the Next Recession Revisited.* Pension Real Estate Quarterly, Winter.

Maris, B. A., & Yang, T. T. (1996). Mortgage prepayment with an uncertain holding period. *Journal of Real Estate Finance and Economics*, *12*, 179-194. https://doi.org/10.1007/BF00132266

Market Microstructure and Asset Pricing: On the Compensation for Market Illiuidity in Stock Returns. (n.d.). London Business School of Finance and Accounting Working Paper.

Maxam, C., & Fisher. (2001). Pricing commercial mortgage-backed securities. *Journal of Property Investment and Finance*, *19*(6), 498-518. https://doi.org/10.1108/14635780110406860

Michael LaCour-Little. (1999) Discrimination in Mortgage Lending: A Critical Review of the Literature. *Journal of Real Estate Literature*, *7*, 15-49. https://doi.org/10.1023/A:1008616203852

Mueller, G. (2000). *Equity Research, Real Estate Market Cycle Monitor, February.*

Nicole EL Karoui, & Lionel Martellini. (2002). *A Theoretical Inspection of the Market Price for Default Risk.* Published Research Article, Centres de Mathematiques Appliquees, Ecole Polythenique, France. Marshall Schoolof Business at the University of Southern California.

Ong, S. E., Ooi, J., & Sing, T. F. (2000). Asset securitization in Singapore: A tale of three vehicles. *Real Estate Finance, 17*(2), 47-56.

Patrick Corcoran. (2000). Stress and Defaults in CMBS deals: Theory and Evidence. *Real Estate Finance, 17*(3), 63-72.

Petch, J. (1997). *Somewhere Between Debt and Equity*. The Institutional Real Estate Letter, March.

Petros Sivitanides, Jon Southard, Raymond G Torto, & William C Wheaton. (2001). The Determinant of appraisal-based capitalization rates. *Real Estate Finance, 18*(2), 27-38.

Ralf Rodepeter, & Joachim K. Winter. (1999). *Savings decision under life-time and earning uncertainty*. University of Mannheim.

Randy Anderson., Philip Conner, & Youguo Liang. (2001). *Mezzanine Finance: Completing the Market*. Prudential Financial.

Rosen, K., & Anderson, M. (1999). The Coming Real Estate Cycle Peak—This Time It's Different. *Pension Real Estate Quarterly*, Fall.

Schwartz, E. S., & Torous, W. N. (1989). Prepayment and the valuation of mortgage-backed securities. *Journal of Finance, 44*(2), 375-392. https://doi.org/10.1111/j.1540-6261.1989.tb05062.x

Stanton, R. (1995). Rational prepayment and the valuation of mortgage-backed securities. *The Review of Financial Studies, 8*(3), 677-708. https://doi.org/10.1093/rfs/8.3.677

Thode, S. F. (2000). CMOs, Duration Risk and a New Mortgage. *Journal of Real Estate Research, 19*, 73-103.

Tim Ballard, & Scott Muldavin. (2000). Does Mezzanine Real Estate Investing make sense today. *Real Estate Finance, 17*(2), 37-45

Watkins David E., Hartzell David J., & Dean A. Egerter. (2003). Commercial REMI Finance: Market Opportunities. *Real Estate Issues*, *28*(3), 34-45.

William B. Brueggeman, & Jeffrey D. Fisher. (1997). *Real Estate Finance and Investment* (10th ed.). United States: McGraw-Hill.

William C. Wheaton, Raymond G. Torto, Jon A. Southard, & Robert E. Hopkins, JR. (2001). Evaluating Real Estate Risk: Debt Applications. *Real Estate Finance*, *18*(3), 29-41

William C. Wheaton, Raymond G. Torto, Petros S. Sivitanides, Jon A. Southard, Robert E. Hopkins, & James M. Costello (2001). Real Estate Risk: A Forward-Looking Approach. *Real Estate Finance*, *18*(3), 20-28

Willie Tan. (2001). *Practical Research Method*. Singapore: Prentice Hall

Wilson, S. H. (Ed.). (2000). *Modern Real Estate Portfolio Management*. New Hope, Pennsylvania: Frank J. Fabozzi Associates.

Yaniv Grinstein. (2003). *Discussion of Paper "The Risk and Return Effects of Mezzanine Debt" presented by David Ho Kim Hin and Sing Tien Foo in AREUEA conference 2003*.

ENDNOTES

1. See Crawford and Rosenblatt (1995).
2. See Economist (2005).
3. To our knowledge, only Glaeser and Gyourko (2006) have mathematically deduced the form of the autocorrelation and mean reversion for housing price dynamics. Their model fails to explain high-frequency positive autocorrelation.
4. See http://economictimes.indiatimes.com/Singapore_hottest_property_mkt/articleshow/2217394.cms
5. Wigren and Wilhelmsson (2007) provide a detailed review on this issue based on recently published articles, while DiPasquale (1999) offers a more complete review.
6. Cho (1996) extensively surveys the literature on housing market inefficiency.
7. An incunabular work modeling the demand functions of both disposition and momentum investors can be found in Tao Guan's unpublished Chapter.
8. The detailed explanations on solution of second-order difference equations can be found in most mathematical textbooks.
9. See page 380 in McQuinn and O'Reilly (2008) for the linear format and the detailed derivation.
10. This is calculated according to the relevant reports from Singstat. In this study, we set it 30%. In McQuinn and O'Reilly (2008), the value is also 30% for Irish.
11. More details can be found in Gregory and Hansen (1996).
12. Here, $\frac{\alpha}{\alpha - \beta_1} = \tilde{\beta} = 0.02$ is controversial, relating to our hypothesis stating that α, β_1 are positive. We explain this issue from two perspectives. Regarding the alternative hypothesis, the policy effect, which is excluded by our hypothesis, plays an important role in the Singapore housing market. Regarding the market clearing condition, it is theoretical. In reality, the real estate market is at a disequilibrium most of the time (see Riddel, 2004; Ho, 2006).

13. This implication can also be deduced from our disposition and momentum model: because all of the parameters, α, β_1, β_2 are assumed to be positive, the $\tilde{\alpha}, \tilde{\beta}$ must share the same sign. Hence, if one of $\tilde{\alpha}, \tilde{\beta}$ is positive, then the other is positive as well.
14. The changes in housing loan rates and earnings are also considered, but not reported. Their effect on the autocorrelation and mean reversion parameters is consistent with that from housing loans.
15. See the lushhomeonline comment entitled "Analysts see no property bubble" at http://lushhomemedia.com/category/property-bubble/
16. "The government will continue to monitor the residential property market in a bid to ensure that prices remain stable, according to National Development Minister Mah Bow Tan," Lushhome : Online news and information on Singapore property market (2008). http://lushhomemedia.com/category/property-bubble/
17. See Appendix 2 for the detailed trend.

www.ingramcontent.com/pod-product-compliance
Lightning Source LLC
Chambersburg PA
CBHW030923180526
45163CB00002B/446